Anna O.

Anna O.
Fourteen Contemporary Reinterpretations

Edited by
Max Rosenbaum
and
Melvin Muroff

THE FREE PRESS
A Division of Macmillan, Inc.
NEW YORK

Collier Macmillan Publishers
LONDON

The Free Press
A Division of Macmillan, Inc.
866 Third Avenue, New York, N. Y. 10022

Collier Macmillan Canada, Inc.

Printed in the United States of America

printing number

1 2 3 4 5 6 7 8 9 10

Library of Congress Cataloging in Publication Data
  Main entry under title:

  Anna O.: fourteen contemporary reinterpretations

    Includes index.
    1. Psychoanalysis—Methodology—Addresses, essays, lectures.   2. Psychotherapy—Addresses, essays, lectures. 3. Breuer, Josef, 1842-1925.   Studien über Hysterie— Addresses, essays, lectures.   4. Pappenheim, Bertha, 1859-1936—Addresses, essays, lectures.   I. Rosenbaum, Max   II. Muroff, Melvin.   [DNLM: 1. Psycho- analysis—History—Case studies.   2. Hysteria—Diagnosis —Case studies. WM 40 A613]
RC506.A56   1984   616.89′17   83-48147
ISBN 0-02-926940-7

Contents

About the Contributors   vii

Introduction   ix
   Max Rosenbaum

1.   Anna O. (Bertha Pappenheim): Her History   1
   Max Rosenbaum

2.   Anna O.: Insight, Hindsight, and Foresight   26
   George H. Pollock

3.   The Case of Anna O.: Then and Now   34
   Philip S. Holzman

4.   Reflections on Anna O.   42
   James F. Masterson

5.   Analytic Biography of Anna O.   47
   Walter A. Stewart

6.   The Case of Anna O.: Cultural Aspects   52
   John P. Spiegel

7.   Anna O. As Seen by a Child Psychiatrist   59
   Joseph D. Noshpitz

8.   Anna O.: Psychoanalysis and Group Process Theory   71
   Melvin Muroff

9.   The Psychopharmacological Treatment of Anna O.   85
   Joseph T. Martorano

10.   Anna O. and Bertha Pappenheim: An Historical Perspective   101
   Marion A. Kaplan

11.   Anna O.: Female, 1880–1882; Bertha Pappenheim: Female, 1980–1982   118
   Anne Steinmann

12. The Case of Anna O.: Aggression and the   132
     Narcissistic Countertransference
       Hyman Spotnitz

13. The Family Therapy of Anna O.: Other Times,   141
     Other Paradigms
       Donald A. Bloch

14. Anna O.: An English Object Relations Approach   149
       Gerald J. Gargiulo

     Conclusion   161
       Melvin Muroff

     Index   179

About the Contributors

MAX ROSENBAUM, Ph.D, is a psychologist and psychoanalyst. He is Co-Director of the American Short Term Therapy Center and Clinical Professor, Post Doctoral Program, Adelphi University.

MELVIN MUROFF, Ph.D, is a Diplomate in clinical psychology and a member of the Topeka Psychoanalytic Society. He is Associate Clinical Professor of child and adolescent psychiatry, New York Medical College.

DONALD A. BLOCH, M.D., is a psychiatrist and psychoanalyst. He is Director of the Ackerman Institute for Family Therapy and editor of the journal *Family Systems*.

GERALD J. GARGIULO, M.A., is a practicing psychoanalyst and past president of the Council of Psychoanalytic Psychotherapists.

PHILIP S. HOLZMAN, Ph.D, is a psychologist and psychoanalyst. He is Professor, Department of Psychology and Social Relations, Harvard University. He is a training and supervising analyst, Boston Psychoanalytic Society and Institute.

MARION A. KAPLAN, Ph.D, Associate to the Director of the Leo Baeck Institute, New York, is the author of *The Jewish Feminist Movement in Germany: The Campaigns of the Jüdischer Frauenbund, 1904–1938*.

JOSEPH T. MARTORANO, M.D., is a clinical psychopharmacologist and psychiatrist. He is medical director of PMS Medical Group.

JAMES F. MASTERSON, M.D., is a psychiatrist and psychoanalyst. He is Director of the Character Disorder Foundation for Teaching and Research and Adjunct Clinical Professor of Psychiatry, Cornell University Medical College.

JOSEPH D. NOSHPITZ, M.D., is Clinical Professor of psychiatry at George Washington University School of Medicine. He is the general editor of the *Basic Handbook of Child Psychiatry*.

GEORGE H. POLLOCK, M.D., Ph.D, is Director, the Institute for Psychoanalysis in Chicago, and Professor, Department of Psychiatry, Northwestern University. He is past president of the American Psychoanalytic Association.

John P. Spiegel, M.D., is a psychiatrist and psychoanalyst. He is Professor of Social Psychiatry, Brandeis University. He is president of the American Academy of Psychoanalysis and past president of the American Psychiatric Association.

Hyman Spotnitz, M.D., Med.Sc.D., is a psychiatrist and psychoanalyst and honorary president, Center for Modern Psychoanalytic Studies in New York City.

Anne Steinmann, Ph.D, is a clinical psychologist and psychoanalyst. She has conducted research on male and female roles since 1952.

Walter A. Stewart, M.D., is a psychiatrist, training analyst and long-time member of the New York Psychoanalytic Institute.

Introduction

Max Rosenbaum

What can we learn today about psychotherapy as we study anew the case of Anna O.? How did Bertha Pappenheim, or Anna O., a woman whom Joseph Breuer despaired of after she relapsed following his treatment of her, turn out to be such a vital human being—a pioneer social worker—and an important figure in the women's movement in the Germany of the 1920s? When Anna O. was originally seen by Breuer, he diagnosed her as a hysteric. Today the diagnosis hysteria is rarely used. Does this reflect the culture of the world today? Does this reflect the fact that the life we live today—the tensions we live under, the threat of the nuclear bomb—lend themselves to more acute disturbances so that hysteria is no longer seen as a significant or common disturbance?

In the new psychiatric diagnostic manual, DSM III, there is no such word as ''hysteria'' per se. Listed is ''conversion disorder,'' or ''hysterical neurosis, conversion type.'' Also listed is ''dissociative disorder,'' meaning ''psychogenic amnesia, disturbances in recall.'' There is listed a diagnosis named ''psychogenic fugue,'' which is unexpected travel away from a customary setting with the person adopting a new identity and being unable to recall the previous identity. There is the diagnosis ''factitious disorders,'' meaning disorders which are considered ''not real, not natural, not genuine.'' These disorders are believed to have psychological symptoms. So the diagnosis hysteria is a far more refined diagnosis in current psychiatric thinking.

One of the questions we ask today is ''Would we call these 'hysterics' borderline psychotics?'' At the time of Anna O. it was believed that anything that was repressed was the causative agent for what was called hysteria. Hysteria was related to repressed unconscious material. Today, especially concerning sexual problems, there is much more openness and no need to repress or hide sexual difficulties. As a result, the symptom conversion need not be primarily or secondarily attached to sexuality.

In the early twentieth century it may have been easier to diagnose patients as hysterics because of the belief that it would be easier to treat a hysteric. That would make hysteria a simpler diagnosis which could be used as a wastebasket diagnosis. It appeared to be an easy diagnosis for both a physician and a patient to accept. It became clear that handling of the simple cases of hysteria could be done by the internist or family practitioner, who could discuss with the person some of his or her hidden problems. A major question is whether Bertha Pappenheim was truly a hysteric. Was she rather a borderline psychotic—a diagnosis applied to more and more patients today? That is why two of our contributors are psychiatrists who have devoted much of their professional life to work with people who are diagnosed as borderline psychotics. Their reactions to Anna O. are very pertinent. When we use the diagnosis borderline psychotic, is it that we are more sophisticated about diagnosis, or is it that the degree of pathology was not recognized years ago? Or is it that years ago there were some hysterical aspects or symptoms which therapists were content to remove? Today we are often aware that when we remove surface symptoms, we see a much deeper pathology.

We are more aware of the different nuances. By removing certain symptoms, we may be in touch with a more serious underlying pathology which therapists were not aware of many years ago. Breuer and Freud, in his early cases, got in touch with the first level of emotional problems. Breuer, if he had been able to recognize his own emotional responses to Bertha Pappenheim, his countertransference, might have been able to resolve Anna O.'s problems. But the evidence also suggests that even if he had done that, there was deeper pathology on a different level which today we might call that of the borderline psychotic.

Another question to be asked is "Would a hysteric patient walk into one of our offices today?" The answer is probably no, since in modern society there is more openness to talk about things and there is not the need to repress the sexuality that was so common in the Victorian age and in the Viennese culture surrounding Bertha Pappenheim.

Today we might repress other things we are ashamed of and it would not come out as hysteria, but more profound disturbances. There are more and more patients who exhibit characterological defects. Is it that in a nuclear age people don't have the luxury of being hysteric? Hysteria is dismissed in our culture with the phrase "Don't be hysterical" or "You are just hysterical," whereas at the time of Anna O. it was seen as a more serious disorder or illness. Again, this may be related to the discovery of its newness in Breuer's time as a psychological disorder. Many of the phobic responses we see today may be·a type of hysteric response, a conversion symptom, which is acceptable in today's culture. Major authorities on the phobic response point out that underneath the symptom is enormous pathology and the phobic response is the patient's effort to cope with this pathology. Yet some phobias and phobics are treated effectively and rather quickly. The hysteric of one hundred years ago might be called the phobic of today. Certainly Anna O. exhibited what might be called phobic fears. In the chapters in this volume, our contributors discuss some of the broad issues surrounding Anna O. and where we are one hundred years later in the treatment of emotional disturbance from the viewpoint of psychodynamics, developmental group process, and psychopharmacology, as well as the impact of the cultural setting in the United States and the Third World.

When we asked our contributors to share with readers how they would treat Anna O. if she walked into their offices today, we encompassed a modern psychoanalytic view, an object relations approach, a family therapy approach, and a drug therapy approach. The reader will be asked to judge whether the contributors have addressed the larger theme underlying the case of Anna O. How did this woman, believed to be a hopeless case by Breuer, manage to come out of her deeply pathological condition and live a reasonably fulfilling life? There are those contemporary experts in psychodynamic theory who express the belief that all of her later life was not really a fulfilled life, but an over-compensation for what she had in fact never worked out in treatment. They say that she lived out the problems—her unresolved relationship with her father, her sexual difficulties, her fantasies—and her everyday work activity was merely a masking. She, according to these people, was acting out her problems but in such a way that she could be in contact with society.

Contemporary approaches to psychotherapy emphasize the here and now and the importance of adjusting to the reality of the society, rather than dealing with the unconscious. The current mode in much psychotherapy is not to be too concerned with uncovering. The earlier medical model which applied to Anna O. emphasized causation and a more microscopic approach. Today we seem to want to emphasize a more macroscopic approach—a global approach in the here and now—where we recognize the cultural aspects, the pressures on the individual living in a particular culture, and the situational reality. A question often asked in contemporary psychotherapy is, How much value is there to understanding of the unconscious dynamics? Some people say there is no value. How much value is there to helping people cope with the here-and-now reality? Some people say that this is only a temporary solution. The reader may want to decide whether getting an individual to adjust to the here-and-now reality lets loose whatever positive forces reside within the individual. In a sense patients can take over their own psychotherapy. The therapy may become homeopathic in nature. Whatever self-curative forces exist will come to the fore. But here is a note of caution. There are other factors at work. What genetic forces or physiological materials are available to the individual to make use of? Bertha Pappenheim was an exceptional woman. Apparently some parts of her allowed her to make use of her strengths and to compensate. How many people are able to do this? This implies a certain genetic inheritance and physiological assets, a family life and a rich cultural system as a support pattern which gave her more strength than would at first appear to the observer. Her life style, which may not have appeared acceptable to some people, apparently enabled her to have some purpose and meaning in her life. A puzzling thing about her case is that she defies the rules of diagnosis. According to most theoretical conceptions of the borderline personality, such a person is unable to sublimate or derive satisfactions from activities such as work activities that do not provide direct sensual pleasure. But Anna O. was clearly able to sublimate and derive gratification from her professional life, so she does not appear to be in the category of borderline.

In the 1980s, psychotherapists might pay more attention to the family structure surrounding Anna O. She came from an upper-middle-class Jewish milieu, was in intense sibling rivalry with a slightly older brother, did not get along with her mother, and was the favorite of her dying father. His illness was tuberculosis, and she presented as a first symptom a cough that was believed to be hysterical in nature. She exhibited a facial neuralgia. Most women today are educated with a view toward entering the workforce. She was highly educated with no end goal to her education. She was not expected to use her background in any work setting. Until the most recent studies by Hirschmüller (1978), who carefully went over Breuer's work and the clinical history of Anna O., there has been no mention made of the fact that Breuer, a highly respected internist, had also been treating Anna O.'s father for his tuberculosis.

Breuer was reluctant to describe his treatment of Anna O. It was only Freud's persistence that resulted in the writing and publication of the classic *Studies on Hysteria* (Breuer and Freud, 1893–1895). Freud had a very complex relationship with Breuer in which he moved from a father-son experience where Breuer was very much his sponsor and mentor to one where he was angry with Breuer.

It is clear that Breuer saw Anna O. from November 1880 until June 1882. Often he saw her every day and sometimes twice a day when she was in Vienna. He was the only one with whom she would cooperate, and at times he even fed her when she refused to take food from anyone else. He certainly fits the picture of the dedicated physician. The general conclusion is that Breuer became involved in transference-countertransference problems with his patient and that when she developed her hysterical pregnancy he "retired in dismay," to use Freud's words (Freud, 1925). Breuer handled the case poorly by today's standards. When Anna O. became actively suicidal, six months after Breuer began treating her, he did not hospitalize her, especially since he had limited psychiatric training. She now had neuralgia and had become a morphine addict from medication Breuer gave her. Instead of placing her in a sanatorium, he visited her at the family's summer home, according to Ernest Jones's (1953) report.

She was a demanding patient, and Breuer's wife is said to have resented the inordinate amount of attention that Breuer gave to Anna O. Breuer was never aware of his countertransference, but when Anna O. wanted to return to him for treatment after her hospital stay in October 1882, he refused to see her as a patient. Apparently he was unable to handle the fact that his patient had fallen in love with him—an event Freud later descrived as transference love. More important, Breuer apparently could not handle his own feelings toward Anna O. While he was aware of his demanding patient's enormous needs, he had little insight into his own need to respond. Years after his treatment of Anna O.

he wrote a letter to a Swiss psychiatrist, August Forel, where he stated that it was "impossible for a general practitioner to treat a case of that kind without bringing his activities and mode of life completely to an end . . . " (Cranefield, 1958, p. 319).

Breuer never used the cathartic method of treatment after his contact with Anna O., although he continued to treat hysteric patients. His friendship with Freud cooled noticeably after they had coauthored *Studies on Hysteria,* and he continued to remain uneasy about Freud's approach to patients. By around the turn of the twentieth century there was a very strained friendship between the two men. Freud apparently had a great need for Breuer's approval and endorsement. Breuer's treatment of Anna O. apparently evoked in him many unresolved problems around areas of his life which he did not care to deal with (Pollock, 1968, p. 725).

It is especially important to note that the dedication of the professional to the interests and well-being of the patient are not *the* solution to the patient's problem. The therapist-patient relationship has been a very complex one and continues to be so more than one hundred years after the treatment of Anna O.

It appears more important than ever, when psychotherapists are asked to justify their interventions and when third-party insurance companies and federal and state governments insist on cost effectiveness with specific treatment programs and defined goals, that we study the case of Anna O. for whatever clues we may gain as to the process and outcome of psychotherapy as well as innovative interventions. Would Anna O. have been helped more quickly if there had been less attention paid to the intrapsychic and more attention paid to altering the family system with clarification of the interpersonal etiology?

Over the last decade, psychotherapy has appeared to be a blend of technology and mysticism. We observe that patients are able to choose from a smorgasbord—human potential movements, confrontational therapies such as primal scream and gestalt, biofeedback, transcendental meditation—and many approaches seem to be potpourri of approaches that offer *relief* for the loneliness and anomie that seem so much a part of our society. The current "popular" diagnoses are narcissistic and borderline disorders, with patients complaining of a sense of inner emptiness and deep-seated anger toward the society we all live in. The insensitivity to the environment we live in, an earth that is polluted, drained, and ravaged, is almost comparable to the infant draining the mother's breast with no awareness of the person of whom the breast is a part. Is it that the restraints at work in Anna O.'s time were such that she had to find her type of symptom expression? Is it that her hysteria was related to an earlier state of capitalism, as some writers speculate, where "there was acquisitiveness, fanatical devotion to work, and a fierce repression of sexuality . . . ?" (Lasch, 1978, p. 41.) Is it that we have no choice today but to move away from Freud's concern with instincts and drives and accept cultural determinism as basic to the pathologies of our time? Should we be moving away from concern with the unconscious and the repressed to a more behavioristic stimulus-response model to explain emotional conflicts? Freud reported what he was trained to observe, but his genius consisted of his capacity to expand his vision. Is it that patients and diagnoses have changed, or that we are more willing to give up our preformed concepts? Restudies of Freud's patients have indicated far more complexity than was at first believed. Is it that there are more borderline personalities as well as narcissistic disorders, or do the technological explosions of our time, especially television, enable us to see them more easily and quickly?

Earlier, reference was made to cost effectiveness of psychotherapy and increasing pressure on mental health professionals to justify various types of therapeutic interventions. It is difficult to research the efficacy of psychotherapy, and outcome studies are infrequent. It is inhumane to cling to a treatment strategy when a patient is in real distress. The therapist's first priority, as it should be, is to relieve suffering (Smith, Glass, and Miller, 1980). Among the most recent studies, the evidence indicates that psychotherapy does help patients and leaves many of them with techniques for handling and coping with future crises. There appears to be narrowing of the theoretical differences between verbal and behavioral approaches to psychotherapy (Andrews and Harvey, 1981). The improvements that patients report appear to be stable over a period of time. While there is research on briefer therapy approaches, there is little research on long-term therapy approaches. The Andrews and Harvey report questions whether longer treatment time leads to more benefits. The answers are unclear. This means that mental health professionals are hard put to justify interventions that are time-consuming and expensive. All of the most comprehensive studies of psychotherapy finally direct themseves to the central question: What psychotherapy techniques or interventions are most appropriate for which patients and under what conditions? (Beutler and Mitchell, 1981; Bergin and Lambert, 1978; Strupp and Hadley, 1979).

This book, then, is an effort to get psychotherapists to reflect on their approach to patients in the light of Breuer's early work with Bertha Pappenheim and to rethink the influence of the intrapsychic and the interpersonal and the entire area of psychotherapy techniques and philosophy of therapy.

References

ANDREWS, G., and HARVEY, R. Does psychotherapy benefit neurotic patients? *Arch. Genl. Psychiat.* 38:1203–1208, 1981.

BERGIN, A. I., and LAMBERT, M. H., The evaluation of therapeutic outcomes. In S. J. Garfield and A. E. Bergin, (eds.), *Handbook of Psychotherapy and Behavior Change.* New York: Wiley, 1978.

BEUTLER, L. E., and MITCHELL, R. Differential psychotherapy outcome among depressed and impulsive patients as a function of analytic and experiential treatment procedures. *Psychiatry,* 44:297–306, 1981.

BREUER, J., and FREUD, S. (1893–1895). *Studies on Hysteria.* Standard Edition of the Complete Psychological Works of Sigmund Freud, vol. II.

CRANEFIELD, P. F. Josef Breuer's evaluation of his contribution to psychoanalysis. *Int. J. Psycho-Anal.,* 39:319–322, 1958.

FREEMAN, L. From Freud to Feminism: *New York Times Magazine,* 30, 74, 78, 80, 82, 84, 86, 88, 90, 92, Nov. 11, 1979.

FREUD, S. *An Autobiographyical Study.* Standard Edition, vol. XX.

HIRSCHMÜLLER, A. *Psychoanalyse und Physiologie im Leben und Werk Josef Breuers.* Bern: Huber, 1978.

JONES, E. *The Life and Work of Sigmund Freud.* Vol. I. New York: Basic Books, 1953.

LASCH, C. *The Culture of Narcissism.* New York: Norton, 1978.

POLLOCK, G. H. The possible significance of childhood object loss in the Josef Breuer–Bertha Pappenheim (Anna O.)–Sigmund Freud relationship: I. Joseph Breuer. *J. Amer. Psychoanal. Ass.,* 16:711–739, 1968.

SMITH, M. L., GLASS, G. V., and MILLER, T. I. *The Benefits of Psychotherapy.* Baltimore: John Hopkins Press, 1980.

STRUPP, H. H., and HADLEY, S. W. Specific vs. non-specific factors in psychotherapy. *Arch. Genl. Psychiat.,* 36:1125–1136, 1979.

Additional References

GLENN, J., and KANZER, M. (eds.). *Freud and His Patients.* New York: Aronson, 1979.

ROSS, M. The borderline diathesis. *Intl. Rev. Psychoanal.,* 3:305–321, 1976.

SPITZER, R. (ed.). *Diagnostic and Statistical Manual of Mental Disorders,* 3d ed. Washington: American Psychiatric Assn, 1980.

Anna O.

Anna O. (Bertha Pappenheim): Her History

1

Max Rosenbaum

Anna O. is believed to be *the* patient who stimulated the growth of psychodynamic therapy, which later came to be called psychoanalysis. Anna O. was the protective name given to the young woman whose real name was Bertha Pappenheim. The real name was revealed by the Sigmund Freud's biographer, Ernest Jones (1953).

Bertha Pappenheim was born in Vienna on February 27, 1859. She was born in a city which was considered cultivated and which attracted people who were connoisseurs of music, theater, and fine food and dining. Bertha's family was orthodox Jewish and was a rather confined and strictly structured family. Bertha's father, Sigmund Pappenheim, was a grain dealer and came from the city of Pressburg (the ghetto). He was born on June 10, 1824, and died April 5, 1881. Sigmund's father had inherited considerable wealth, and the Pappenheim family was considered rich.

Bertha's mother, Recha, was born in Frankfurt am Main, Germany, on June 13, 1830. She came from the Goldschmidt family, which contained many very cultured peoples including Heinrich Heine, the poet. Bertha's mother came from a higher social class than her father. Bertha's mother married Sigmund, an arranged marriage, and moved to Vienna. Her husband was six years older, and it is believed that Bertha's mother was never particularly happy in Vienna.

Bertha's mother and father had four children, all born in Vienna. Henriette was born September 2, 1849, and died at age 17 of consumption when Bertha was 7 years old. Flora was born on October 24, 1853, and died October 15, 1855, of cholera. A younger brother, Wilhelm, was born on August 15, 1860. The family lived in the Jewish section of Vienna, called Leopoldstadt. In 1880, the family moved to a neighborhood called Liechtensteinerstrasse, which was next to the street called Berggasse, where Sigmund Freud had both his home and office from the year 1891 to 1938.

On her father's side, Bertha was considered to be descended, economically, from an upper-class family. Although her grandfather, Wolf, had been from a lower social class, his unexpected and very large inheritance was accepted by him with relative ease, and he felt quite at ease living with his newfound wealth.

On her mother's side, Bertha and her brother Wilhelm were able to trace their ancestry back many generations to some of the most prominent Austro-German Jewish families. One of her ancestors was Gluckel von Hameln, a widow who wrote in her memoirs what it was like to raise a family of twelve children without a husband. Her memoirs are a very accurate portrayal of life in the Jewish community of the seventeenth century, and were later translated by Bertha Pappenheim into German. The memoirs were also known to Mary Wollstonecraft, the English woman who is considered the founder of feminism.

Bertha had a governess, as was usual in a wealthy home, and attended a Catholic school which offered better education than was offered in other schools. In the case history of Anna O., Bertha is described as hating her governess. Yet Bertha Pappenheim described her governess as a kind woman. It is difficult to ascertain whether this was the same person or two different governesses.

At the end of November 1880, Joseph Breuer, a physician, was called to diagnose Bertha, who was age 21. She had been ill for some months. She had a variety of ailments including a cough that led her mother, Recha, to fear that she had contracted tuberculosis, a disease her father, Sigmund, had been dying of for almost six months. The father was being cared for at home by his wife and daughter. Breuer, the physician called to treat Bertha, was considered one of Vienna's most gifted physicians. Also he was a mentor and friend of another Viennese physician, Sigmund Freud, who at that time was age 24. Breuer was age 38. (Freud was born in May 1856 in Freiburg, a town in Czechoslovakia, and his father moved the family to Vienna when Freud was 4 years old.)

When Breuer came to attend Bertha Pappenheim, he found more than the cough. She had paralysis of the right arm, both legs were paralyzed, and she could move only the fingers of her left hand. She was unable to feed herself, and she was barely able to turn her head because of what appeared to be a paralyzed neck muscle. She complained of visual difficulty, so that she could neither write nor read. Other specialists had been consulted before Joseph Breuer, and they could find no physical basis for Bertha's complaints. Breuer recognized at once the mental and emotional problems that were involved.

Bertha spoke in half or broken sentences and complained that "black snakes" and "death's heads" were present in her room. Bertha's mother reported to Breuer that most of the time Bertha did not appear to hear what was being said to her. She appeared very weak and sickly and refused to eat any food that was given to her. A few days before Breuer's visit she had eaten a few oranges that were fed to her by a nurse. Breuer concluded that Bertha Pappenheim was *not* suffering from tuberculosis, but rather hysteria, derived from the Greek word *hystera,* which means womb or uterus. Most physicians of the nineteenth century considered hysteria a disease of malingerers. Breuer did not.

At the time that Breuer was called to see Bertha Pappenheim, her father, already 57 years of age, was slowly dying in another room of the Pappenheim apartment. He had been ill for six months with an abscess of his lung. Bertha had taken an active part in her father's nursing care and often stayed throughout the night in the same room where her father lay dying. Breuer and Freud (1893–1895, pp. 22–23) state; "In July 1880, the patient's father, of whom she was passionately fond, fell ill of a peripleuritic abscess which failed to clear up and to which he succumbed in April 1881."

Bertha was described as a rather frail young woman, with delicate and petite features. Her hair was brunette. Although considered frail when Breuer attended her, she had been a very active person who enjoyed dancing and horseback riding. Here then was the patient, age 21, dark-haired, blue-eyed, and pretty, attended by the 38-year-old handsome and renowned physician.

In addition to Breuer's noted skills as a medical diagnostician, he was familiar with hypnotism, which he used with some patients. The use of hypnotism by Viennese physicians was common in the latter part of the nineteenth century. It was not considered quackery and appeared to be successful with many women patients, who during hypnosis fell into a trance and were then instructed to "give up" whatever illness or symptoms they complained about. Breuer decided that hypnosis was the indicated method of treatment and hypnotized Bertha Pappenheim. She fell into a hypnotic trance quite rapidly, but Breuer decided not to get her to give up her illness, but rather to get her to speak to him in any or all of the four languages she spoke—English, German, Italian, and French.

Bertha seemed to fall into a deep sleep during the hypnotic trance, but when she awoke, she appeared quite agitated and would verbally attack her nurse and mother. She still spoke of her hallucinations, her "death's heads" and "black snakes." Interestingly enough, during her agitated state she was able to throw pillows on the floor with her left arm—which thus was apparently not paralyzed.

Breuer observed her agitated state while she was in a hypnotic trance and began to repeat to Bertha some of what she had said while in a trance. She would tell him stories while in the trance. The stories, some of which were told in German and some in English, had as a central theme the girl seated next to a patient's bed. But shortly after Breuer began this use of hypnosis, Bertha became mute while in a hypnotic trance and refused to talk for about two weeks. Breuer decided that she was annoyed and would not speak and urged her to speak about her annoyance, which she did with a resultant improvement of her behavior. She even agreed to eat if Breuer fed her. He agreed and she began to eat, come out of her lethargy, and apparently look forward to his daily visits.

Breuer described Bertha as having "two states of consciousness," and Bertha noted that there was a "bad" side of her and "real" side. What Breuer was dealing with was a very intelligent young woman who had, according to him, "penetrating intuition . . . great poetic and imaginative gifts." Under hypnosis, Bertha spoke of what troubled her. Slowly her physical symptoms began to disappear, and her mind became much clearer. Breuer's approach appeared to be very successful, for on April 1, 1881, about four months after Breuer's first contact with Bertha, she got out of her invalid bed and walked across her bedroom. However, tragedy came four days later, when Bertha's father finally succumbed to his illness. His death had a profound impact on her and she became agitated, depressed, and finally very subdued. At this point she said she could not see except for the recognition of Breuer when he would come to visit. Even then, she confirmed Breuer's identity by feeling his hands. She began to improve slowly and within two months was apparently in good health. But when her mother arranged to take her to the family summer home, outside the city of Vienna, she became violently agitated. She became overtly hostile, refused food, and threatened suicide. All of this behavior was related to her anger at being separated from Breuer, but this was not recognized by Breuer.

Breuer began to visit Bertha at what has been described as the "summer home"* of her family (Jones, 1953). This meant a trip out of Vienna. Since he was a very busy physician, he could only arrive by evening, and sometimes after a three-day absence. When there was a three-day gap, Bertha was generally cooperative the day after his visit. By the second day she was irritable, and after three days, very unpleasant. He must have been discouraged, because he was back to dealing with a young woman with a paralyzed left arm, a constant cough, and visual difficulty, since she squinted and apparently could not or would not see. But there was one important difference. Breuer did not have to hypnotize her because she fell into a self-hypnotic trance and spoke very freely as he listened. Later, Bertha described this talking as "chimney sweeping." She stopped squinting and saw clearly, and her other symptoms began to disappear. She saw another physician while at the "summer home" but refused to accept him as a substitute for Breuer. (Breuer apparently did not or would not recognize the importance of his relationship with Bertha, who would not engage in the "talking over" with anyone but Breuer.)

Bertha and her mother returned to Vienna in the fall of 1881, and Breuer hypnotized Bertha every morning and every evening. While she was under hypnosis, he encouraged her to talk about her symptoms and when they appeared originally. She shared a great deal of historical information about her background while under hypnosis, and most of her symptoms disappeared, although her cough would come and go. Her hallucinations seemed to pass, and finally the only symptom which remained was her paralyzed right arm. Breuer later wrote in the book *Studies on Hysteria*, ". . . from the beginning to the end of the illness, all the stimuli arising from the secondary state, together with their consequences, were permanently removed by being given verbal ut-

---

* According to Karpe (1961) the country house was a "great distance from Vienna" (p. 4). According to Ellenberger (1972) it was a "country house near Vienna" (p. 268).

terance in hypnosis. . . . this was not an invention of mine which I imposed on the patient by suggestion. It took me completely by surprise, and not until symptoms had been got rid of in this way in a whole series of instances did I develop a therapeutic technique out of it'' (Breuer and Freud, 1893–1895, p. 46). It was Bertha who named the therapeutic intervention ''the talking cure.''

Breuer would not settle for an almost cured patient and began to work on the paralysis of Bertha's right arm. She began to talk about this symptom, and in June 1882 she began to speak under hypnosis of her experiences during the time she nursed her father. The paralysis appeared to date back to a time at the summer home when Bertha was in complete charge of her father's nursing since her mother had returned to Vienna for a few days. One night while she was sitting next to her father's bed, her right arm over the back of her chair, Bertha fell into an exhausted sleep. She began to dream, and in the dream she saw a large black snake moving toward her father and ready to bite him. She attempted to raise her right arm to drive the snake away, but the arm was paralyzed and her fingers had become little snakes. She was awakened by a train whistle—the train that would bring passengers from Vienna. After she described to Breuer in great detail her terror at what had happened that night, Bertha's right arm was no longer paralyzed.

Breuer was pleased with his treatment and told Bertha that she no longer needed his services, and they bade one another farewell. She was about to go to the family's country residence. So the case ostensibly had a happy ending. The patient had apparently benefited from cathartic treatment.

But it didn't turn out that way. That very evening Breuer was called to the Pappenheim home, and there he found Bertha in a hysterical state imagining that she was giving birth to a child, which she told Breuer was his. Although he was in a state of shock, he managed to hypnotize her and calm her. He left the Pappenheim apartment in what he later described as ''a cold sweat.'' He never returned to the Pappenheim family, and the next day he is reputed to have left with his wife for Venice on a second honeymoon.

According to stories that have developed around this case, Breuer's wife was pregnant while he was treating Bertha. Breuer's wife is supposed to have become jealous about the amount of time and attention he gave to Bertha. Many have speculated that in some way Bertha had found out about Mrs. Breuer's pregnancy and that her phantom pregnancy was based on her attraction to Joseph Breuer—a sexual attraction that Breuer could not cope with. Freud's biographer, Ernest Jones, maintains that Breuer's wife had become depressed and even suicidal about her husband's preoccupation with Bertha's case. However, there are researchers who state that this is a fabrication and that the actual dates of Breuer's trip to Venice and his wife's pregnancy do not jibe with Ernest Jones's report; Ellenberger questions Jones's entire report.

Ellenberger's (1972) research elicited the information that Bertha Pappenheim was a patient in the Sanatorium Bellevue, a psychiatric hospital in the little Swiss town of Kreuzlingen, from July 12 to October 29, 1882, after Breuer left the Pappenheim home in "a cold sweat." Breuer wrote a 21½-page summary of the Anna O. case for her patient file there, and a follow-up was written by one of the physicians at the hospital. Breuer's report for the hospital file paints a much more complete picture of the Pappenheim family constellation.

Bertha is described as having difficulties with a "very serious" mother. Although Breuer never mentioned Bertha's brother, Wilhelm, in the book *Studies on Hysteria,* he stated in his hospital report that the brother and Bertha were quarrelsome. She is described as having a "passionate love for her father who pampered her." Breuer, in the 1882 hospital report, states that Bertha's sexual life was "astonishingly underdeveloped." He also reported her stubborn, childish opposition to medical prescriptions,* as well as her antireligious feelings. Although she was part of an Orthodox Jewish family, Breuer stated that she followed the ritual practices to please her father and described her as "thoroughly unreligious."

Ellenberger's study of Breuer's hospital summary gives us valuable information about Bertha that was *not* reported in the classic book *Studies on Hysteria.* Bertha had been a devoted nurse to her father, but during the last two months of his life she had not been permitted to see him and had been told lies about the condition of his health. As noted earlier, by April 1, 1881, Bertha was out of bed and walking. Four days later, April 5, her father was in his last hours of life, but when Bertha asked her mother about her father's condition, she was lied to and reassured. When Bertha finally learned about her father's death, she became agitated, depressed, and withdrawn. However, what actually occurred dynamically was that she felt "robbed" of a last chance to see her father or hear him speak. Her agitation and visual disturbances masked the very negative feelings she had toward her mother and, to some degree, her younger brother. She must have been very angry.

Ten days after her father's death the family called in a psychiatrist as a consultant, since Breuer was considered an internist. Whether Breuer had suggested the consultation is unknown, but the consultant was the famous Richard von Krafft-Ebing (1840–1902), who is noted for his extensive writings about sexual disturbances and his detailed clinical descriptions. There is no record of Krafft-Ebing's diagnosis and suggested treatment.

What Ellenberger's research did elicit is that it was difficult to keep Bertha in the Pappenheim home after her father's death. She was depressed and suicidal. She was transferred to a cottage close to the Inzersdorf sanatorium near Vienna. This psychiatric hospital was founded in 1872 and built on the grounds of a former estate of a titled family. There was a castle which was the main building, and some patients were apparently kept in cottages close to the

---

* When Breuer first met Bertha, he considered the possibility of a chronic meningitis, but very soon after this he became aware of the emotional aspects of her physical symptoms.

grounds of the main hospital building. At this point, Bertha could receive daily treatment from the staff psychiatrists and Breuer could visit her every few days. So the history of Bertha Pappenheim's treatment becomes more complex, and there are many ramifications. According to Ellenberger, Breuer was not visiting Bertha at her summer home, but a cottage "close to the sanatorium" (p. 276). According to Breuer, she was taken to the sanatorium "without deceit, but by force" on June 7, 1881. This is *not* the record of another researcher, Karpe (1961), who states that she was "moved against her will, with a nurse, to a country house. She awaited the move with great horror, and after it she went for three days and nights without sleep or nourishment." Breuer was *the* one who could make contact with her. The codirector of the sanatorium, Dr. Breslauer (Ellenberger, 1972), had to give her chloral as a sedative on those days when Breuer did not visit her (Karpe, 1961).*

Breuer and his wife went on a five-week vacation (the story about his taking a second honeymoon may fit here) and returned in mid-August 1881 to find a Bertha who was "emotionally very bad . . . moody . . . nasty." It was about this time that the "talking cure" really began, since Breuer found that certain of Bertha's flights of imagination or distortion could disappear when he was able to elicit the psychic origins.

Bertha returned to Vienna in November 1881, to the home of her mother, and it was then that Breuer saw her every day. But her condition deteriorated so that by December 1881 she was again quite agitated and related to Breuer many of the stories she had told him a year earlier. It is interesting to note that her greatest agitation arose during the last days of December 1881, a period of holidays in both the Christian and Jewish religions. For a Jewish family it is Hanukkah, a period of gift-giving and much celebrating. It is conceivable that this was the time she was most desolate about the loss of her indulgent father. There is no recognition of this in the reports of any writer. From winter 1881 until June 1882, Bertha appeared to be improving.

After Bertha developed her hysterical pregnancy, she was hospitalized in the Sanatorium Bellevue, in Kreuzlinger, Switzerland, from July 12, 1882, to October 29, 1882. There was no "talking cure," and the case history as described in the hospital records lists a number of medications that she was given. Apparently she had developed a severe facial neuralgia, which had become quite painful from December 1881 to mid-June 1882. During this time she had been given large amounts of chloral and morphine. She was given as much as 10 centigrams of morphine while at the Sanatorium Bellevue, and when she returned to Vienna she was on morphine as a medication. Her dosage ranged from 7 to 10 centigrams a day.

The report of the sanatorium indicates that she continued to be irritated with her family, exhibited hysterical features, and continued to disparage medicine and science as modalities of treatment. She continued to be deeply in-

* These are two different versions of this phase of Anna O.'s illness.

volved with her father and his memory. She is described in the 1882 report as being in "childish opposition" to her physicians. By the time she had left the Swiss hosptial, she was a confirmed addict accustomed to high doses of morphine and chloral. The general feeling of her physicians at the hospital was that she was an unpleasant person who exhibited hysterical behavior and who had neurological symptoms. According to Carl Jung, the patient had not been cured by Breuer—at least that is what Breuer told Freud, who in turn reported this to Jung.

Some years passed before Breuer, encouraged by Freud, agreed to set forth the story of Anna O. On November 18, 1882, Breuer told his young friend Sigmund Freud, who had by then completed his medical training (March 31, 1881), the story of his treatment of Bertha Pappenheim–Anna O. Freud, only three years older than Bertha Pappenheim, was on the way to becoming a medical research scientist, but Breuer's story of his contact with Bertha stimulated Freud to the extent that he was later to write "that on this day I first became aware of the power of the unconscious." Freud realized as he listened to Breuer, that Breuer had made a significant discovery in treating hysteria—the disappearance of a mental or physical symptom and the recall of an unpleasant or buried memory are related. But Breuer refused to share his discovery with the medical community of Vienna. He was apparently tired of working with hysterics. Freud apparently knew who Bertha Pappenheim was. He had become engaged in June 1882 to Martha Bernays, an engagement that was to go on for four years, and in a letter sent to her dated July 13, 1883, he referred to "your friend Bertha Pappenheim." Freud never indicated that he personally knew or met Bertha Pappenheim, although after his marriage to Martha, Bertha would visit the Freud apartment to converse with Martha.

Sigmund Freud had to give up his original research interest in physiology, since he wanted to marry and needed more money. He decided to practice medicine and became an intern at the Allegemeine Krankenhaus, the famous medical teaching hospital of Vienna. He became interested in neurology, and in May 1883 he transferred to the psychiatric clinic of the hospital. At that time, indeed until recently, psychiatry and neurology were in the same department, so Freud was exposed to patients with psychiatric problems. This exposure, as well as his personal friendship with Breuer, who treated hysterics, led Freud to study in Paris with Jean Martin Charcot (1825–1893), who taught at the Salpêtrière Hospital—a huge mental hospital and poor house which had women patients originally. Charcot stated that hypnotic phenomena occurred only in hysteric patients and symptoms could be dissolved through the use of hypnosis. Freud studied with Charcot for four months and was conversant with the techniques of direct hypnotic suggestion. When he shared with Charcot the idea of the "talking cure" (Bertha's language as Breuer related it to Freud), Charcot didn't find any particular significance in the concept and was not especially interested.

It is important to note that up to and through the seventeenth century, patients who were diagnosed as hysterics were believed to be possessed by demons. The concept of hysteria was known to the ancients, and there were many explanations by those who did not accept a theory of demonology. One of the theories was the floating-uterus concept—a theory which probably reflected the scientific knowledge of antiquity. (Vieth [1965] has covered the history of hysteria in great detail.)

Up until the end of the Middle Ages, demons and witches were believed to be the causes of behavior that was perceived as other than normal. In ancient times ghosts and gods were seem by most people as the cause of hysteria.

In the nineteenth century the diagnosis of hysteria was assigned to women and a few men. The diagnosis hysteria became a wastebasket diagnosis, since physicians could not understand its origins. Charcot was interested in disorders of the central nervous system, and his interest in hypnotism was directly related to his research in neuropathology. It was not until he had studied hysteria for many years that he realized that answers from the field of neuropathology were not a sufficient explanation. It was Charcot who clarified the concept of hysteria and moved its study to the point where it could be called an illness rather than the behavior of malingerers.

When Freud returned to Vienna in April 1886, he began again to speak with Breuer and elicited more and more information about Bertha Pappenheim. At this point Freud was fresh from his exposure to Charcot's clinics at the Salpêtrière, where neuropathology and hysteria were perceived as acceptable fields of study for a research scientist and physician. Freud followed Charcot's mechanistic paradigm at this point—hysteria could be perceived as related to a disorder of energy transmission in and out of the nerve trunks of the nervous system. When Breuer and Freud worked together in studying hysteria, Breuer found a learned associate, Freud, who was deeply skilled in the field of neuropathology. In essence, Freud was at the turning point; he had to look for the causes of hysteria in the psyche rather than in the nervous system. This is how Freud came to the unconscious as the explanation for human behavior.

Freud encouraged Breuer, who was rather reluctant, to speak at greater length about the case of Bertha Pappenheim, and Breuer finally revealed to Freud why he had terminated his treatment of this young woman. He described the hysterical pregnancy, and Freud realized that Bertha had become sexually attracted to Breuer—an attraction which was masked by the phantom pregnancy and childbirth. It is doubtful that he ever shared with Breuer his other realization—that Breuer was probably sexually responsive to the attractive young woman, Bertha, who idealized him. Freud was in the first stages of discovering the concept of "transference," in which the patient in psychotherapy transfers all feelings—love as well as hate—to the psychoanalyst. The analyst, using the transference, enables the patient to study the early experiences which elicited the intense emotional responses. Bertha's response to Breuer masked her attraction to her own father. Today we are equally interested in the concept of "countertransference," where the reactions of the pa-

tient stimulate irrational responses on the part of the therapist, based on problems the latter has not worked out. Breuer, out of his anxiety about Bertha's
phantom childbirth, did not pause to study the underlying dynamics at work.

It was from Breuer that Freud learned to encourage patients to talk about
events related to the symptom. Until then, a physician using hypnotism would
suggest or direct a patient under hypnosis to give up the symptom. Freud used
hypnosis for a time but felt that it was more fruitful to ask patients to speak
about whatever came to the mind—a technique and later a concept which he
labeled "free associaton."

It was now over a decade since Breuer had fled from the Pappenheim home.
Freud encouraged Breuer to coauthor an article for a professional journal based
on the "talking cure," or what Bertha Pappenheim had called her "chimney
sweeping." The article originally appeared in a German medical journal
devoted to the field of neurology, *Neurologisches Centralblatt* (January 1893). It
was a two-part article, "On the Physical Mechanism of Hysterical
Phenomena, Preliminary Communication." The article was also printed in
the *Berlin Medical Journal* and, soon after, reprinted in the *Vienna Medical Journal.*
A more detailed discussion of the case of Anna O. appeared in the book *Studies
on Hysteria,* which was published in 1895.

The 1893 article stressed the fact that "the hysteric suffers mostly from
reminiscences" that relate to symptoms which surface when an impulse to
behave in any manner is "repressed." The symptom appears "in place of" the
action. The original emotion and/or trauma is buried in memories, but the
symptom continues as "partial gratification" of the wish to act. Until the "im-
prisoned" emotion is discharged, through the "cathartic method"—or what
Bertha Pappenheim called "chimney sweeping"—the symptom will continue.
This cathartic method was considered by Freud to be the beginning of
psychoanalysis, and he stated this on several occasions. When he lectured at
Clark University in September 1909, he stated his indebtedness to Breuer's
work with hysteria.

The concept of the unconscious existed before Breuer and Freud. Descartes
recorded that on November 10, 1619, he awoke having had three consecutive
dreams in the same night and thought that he had "discovered" the foundations of an entire science. The German terms *Unbewusstsein* and *Bewusstos* were
first used by Platner in 1776 (Whyte, 1960, p. 66). The words are to be found in
the writings of Goethe and Schiller, the great writers of the German Romantic
era. In 1751, the term "unconscious" appeared in the English language, and
the word is to be found in the writings of the great English poets Coleridge and
Wordsworth. The word *inconscient* appeared in French after 1850 and is to be
found in a French dictionary published in 1862. The French described it as "a
word used infrequently." The great philosopher Leibnitz (1646–1716) touched
upon the unconscious in his writings. He wrote, "It is not easy to conceive that
a thing can think and not be conscious when it thinks." Herbart (1776–1841)
wrote about "ideas" which he described as the discharge of mental energy. He

wrote about ideas that are inhibited by other ideas and that are below the "threshold of consciousness." Freud was familiar with Herbart's ideas, which included the term *Verdrangung* (repression) and the concept of repressed ideas. Herbart also noted that when repressed ideas reappear, they meet with resistance (*Wiederstand*).

C. von Wolff (1679–1752), who influenced Immanuel Kant and J. F. Herbart, did not distinguish, as did Descartes, between unconscious and conscious. Immanuel Kant wrote of the unconscious that "the dark ideas in Man (and also in animals) is immeasurable." Freud was aware of the writings of F. E. Benecke (1798–1854), who stated that the mental life of the neurotic is entirely unconscious. He also was familiar with the writings of Arthur Schopenhauer (1788–1860), the German philosopher. When Schopenhauer published his major work in 1819, *Die Welt als Wille and Vorstellung* (The World as Will and Representation), he wrote of two unconscious forces—the sex instinct and the instinct for self-preservation. Thomas Mann, the novelist, noted in 1936 that there were similarities between Freud and Schopenhauer—the stress upon sexuality and unconscious motivation. Freud was also aware of the work of Nietzsche (1844–1890), who stressed the unconscious and related the unconscious to the "collective hallucinations that seized whole communities of primitive men" (Ellenberger, 1970, p. 273).

Nietzsche influenced Jung more than Freud. Jung used the term "collective unconscious," which he borrowed from Nietzsche.

The important point is that Breuer and Freud did not discover the unconscious. What their work originated was the first systematic study of the unconscious. Freud applied his scientific training so that he could study the irrational and unconscious and make it rational and conscious.

Breuer and Freud concealed the identity of Bertha Pappenheim by calling her Anna O. It was not until Ernest Jones's biography of Freud was published in 1953 that Anna O.'s true identity was revealed. There are many mental health professionals, as well as others, who believe that Ernest Jones had no right to reveal the real identity of Anna O. There is evidence that her family resented the disclosure.

Breuer discovered two basic truths in his work, and Freud recognized this. First, when emotions cannot find a normal release, neurotic symptoms will occur. Second, the neurotic symptom will disappear when the unconscious cause or causes are permitted to come to awareness. These two basic findings, which are taken for granted today, served as the cornerstone upon which Freud elaborated his many highly theoretical statements, many of which were speculative and set forth by Freud as hypotheses to be tested. Because of personal dislike for the subject matter, Breuer, a very thoroughly trained scientist, while aware of the possible truth of Freud's hypothesis—hysteria is caused by sexual repression—simply did not care to explore the hypothesis any longer and drew away from Freud. This possibility was acknowledged by Freud—that people would be repelled by the subject matter of his explorations. He said,

". . . powerful human feelings are hurt by the subject matter of a theory. Darwin's theory of descent met the same fate, since it tore down the barrier that had been arrogantly set up between men and beasts. I drew attention to this analogy in an earlier paper [1917], in which I showed how the psycho-analytic view of the relation of the conscious ego to an over-powering unconscious was a severe blow to human self-love . . . " (Freud, 1925(b), p. 173).

Freud did not accept with equanimity those who rejected his concepts of sexual repression. Alfred Adler was elected president of the newly formed Vienna Psychoanalytic Society in 1910, and joined with Wilhelm Stekel to coedit a new journal of psychoanalysis. All of this was under Freud's aegis. In 1911, Adler delivered three lectures to the society at the request of Freud. In these three lectures he criticized Freud's sexual theory. This resulted in scathing attacks upon Adler by those who sided with Freud. By the summer of 1911, Adler could not abide the attacks and resigned both his coeditorship and membership in the Vienna Psychoanalytic Society. Those members of the society who agreed with Adler would meet with him at his favorite coffee house, Café Central. This did not sit well with those who believed themselves loyal to Freud. Shortly after Adler's departure from the society, Hanns Sachs reported to a society meeting that members could not belong to the society and be supportive of Adler's ideas. Sachs's motion was accepted, and that night the six followers of Adler walked out of the society and went to the Café Central to celebrate with Alfred Adler. This pattern of adherence to the doctrine, so much like rigid church policy, was to plague psychoanalysis for many years. Karen Horney and Clara Thompson "took a walk" from the New York Psychoanalytic Society just before World War II. And there were other similar circumstances.

Anna O. ended up in a psychiatric hospital and was reported in a classic series of case studies, but what happened to the real person—Bertha Pappenheim? Over the years there were debates about the diagnosis of Anna O. Many students of human behavior maintained that the patients described in *Studies in Hysteria* were actually schizophrenics who had simply not been diagnosed accurately. As for Anna O. herself, there were few details reported through the years that added anything to the original information Breuer and Freud had presented. Freud suggested in 1924 that Breuer had been the object of "transference love," which he was unaware of. Perhaps Freud was kind to his earlier co-worker. He might have noted that Breuer was uncomfortable with and did not welcome "transference love." In 1925 Carl Jung gave a seminar in Zurich and stated that Freud had told him that Anna O. had not been cured. According to Jung, "there was no cure at all in the sense of which it was originally presented." But Jung further states, ". . . the case was so interesting that there was no need to claim for it something that did not happen" (Jung, 1925).

It has been noted that Freud's biographer Ernest Jones revealed the true identity of Anna O. in 1953, when Freud's biography was published. Jones presented his version of what happened. How much of this is based upon what Jones deduced or speculated about or on unpublished materials and conversations that Jones had with Freud is difficult to ascertain. However, Jones stated that he had been told by Freud that Mrs. Breuer had become jealous of the attention Breuer gave to Bertha Pappenheim, and that Breuer had developed an intense "countertransference" toward Bertha. This apparently was the real reason for the termination of treatment, which coincided with Anna O.'s phantom pregnancy involving Breuer as the phantom father-to-be. Breuer then left with his wife for Venice on a second honeymoon, at which time she became pregnant with a daughter, Dora. All of this is according to Ernest Jones, who also described Anna O. as eliciting a romantic response from the psychiatrist in charge of her case at the sanatorium she was taken to after Breuer abandoned the case. But now the Jones report and what we find out in more recent published material become quite divergent.

Breuer's daughter, Dora, was born in March 1882 and would have to have been conceived in June 1881. The eruption of Anna O's phantom pregnancy and her transfer to a psychiatric sanatorium occurred in June 1882. The psychiatric sanatorium that Jones described did not exist in the town that Jones named. He may have been confused here. The "summer home" of 1881 was a cottage near a psychiatric sanatorium. There existed a very superior sanatorium, Bellevue, complete will all kinds of recreational facilities, which was closed very recently. The sanatorium was in the town of Kreuzlingen, Switzerland, and Bertha Pappenheim was there from July 12 to October 29, 1882. A book recently published in Germany contains the entire case history of Anna O.'s stay in Kreuzlingen, with the surprising fact that Breuer wrote a case summary that was included in the patient's file along with other clinical data. Breuer's case summary contains much of the same language that was later used in the book *Studies in Hysteria* (Hirschmüller, 1978).

As I have noted earlier, when Breuer's case study for the hospital file is carefully studied, there are a comprehensive picture of the family and descriptions of a "serious mother" (whom Ernest Jones described as "somewhat of a dragon"), a brother with whom there was intense sibling rivalry, and a father—and there Breuer states that Bertha had a "passionate love for her father who pampered her." Bertha was described as stubborn and antireligious in spite of—or possibly because of—the Orthodox Jewish family she was part of. Outwardly, Bertha followed her father's wishes and observed Orthodox Judaism. The many details that Breuer noted clarify the depth of Bertha's involvement with her father and the impact of her father's death, since she apparently felt that she had not been given an accurate picture of the seriousness of his illness, as well as the times she had been forbidden to disturb him by visiting him. What emerges is the picture of a very sensitive, highly intelligent young woman raised in an Orthodox Jewish home, where to be male was the most important thing. Indeed, one of the prayers that Orthodox men chant at their morning prayers thanks God for having created them as men and not women. Today, with the insights of a cultural approach to mental disorder, the case of Anna O. would be seen on a much larger scale, and the contributors to this volume will elaborate upon this.

Anna O. became very agitated after her father's death. Because of her upset she was taken to a cottage near a sanatorium. (Jones describes this as a "summer home" or "country house.") She was agitated because of Breuer's vacation in the summer of 1881. She was disturbed again in November 1881, and after some improvement she had to be hospitalized by July 1882. She became addicted to morphine, not too differently from current patients who are addicted to tranquilizers. But through this entire period there is no recognition of a very attractive, highly intelligent young woman who could find no outlet for her creativity and idealism. No attention was given to her relationship with Breuer, which was very important to her. When Bertha Pappenheim left Bellevue Sanatorium, she moved with her mother to Frankfurt am Main, Germany, the birthplace of her mother and a place where her mother had an extended family. There is very little information about the six years that followed her hospitalization in 1882. But she appeared again in the public eye by the time she was 29. She was now living with her mother in Frankfurt. She continued to enjoy music and her extended family and especially enjoyed horseback riding. She did not seem to have much to do with men, although she is described as very vivacious, attractive, and someone who had many male admirers. Since the two important men in her life had deserted her—her father through his death and Breuer through his countertransference and abandonment of her—her avoidance of any deep involvement with a man is quite understandable. Also, there was no effort made in the treatment of Anna O. to explore her ambivalence to her father—her repressed hostility which may appear symbolically in Bertha's references to the ugly dog which her governess permitted to drink out of a glass—the dog possibly representing the father or younger brother.

By 1890 she had published in German *In der Trodelbude,* a book of stories which were similar to children's fairy tales. Bertha Pappenheim called herself Paul Berthold, who is listed as the author (Berthold, 1890). Berthold is the masculine version of her first name. The stories were concerned with family tragedies. *Trodelbude* may be translated as "rummage store." The objects that were found in the store related to unhappiness in various family settings, and it may be fair to conclude that Bertha Pappenheim was writing in a lightly veiled fashion about the facts of her own unhappy earlier life.

Shortly after the publication of her *In der Trodelbude,* Bertha became an active worker in the feminist movement. She read *The Women,* a publication edited by Helene Lange, a leader of the feminist movement in Germany. She translated into German in 1899 the famous work *A Vindication of the Rights of Women,* written in 1792 by Mary Wollstonecraft, the founder of feminism (Wollstonecraft, 1792).* She financed the publication of this work as well as

---

* Mary Wollstonecraft was the mother of Mary Shelley, who wrote the masterpiece *Dr. Franken-stein.*

writing and publishing in 1899 a three-act play titled *Women's Rights*. Bertha had earlier become interested in her own family background, and with the cooperation of her younger brother Wilhelm and her cousin, Stefan Meyer, she was able to detail her family background. She found that she was related through her mother, Recha Goldschmidt, to Gluckel von Hameln, a widow of Jewish background who lived in Germany in the seventeenth and early eighteenth centuries (1646–1724). Gluckel wrote a series of memoirs to her children which are an accurate description of what it was like to be a woman, a mother, a widow, and Jewish and the problems of survival in that time. She was a devoted mother, devoutly religious, successful in the business community, and deeply concerned about her community responsibilities. Bertha Pappenheim translated into German and published Gluckel's memoirs, which had been written in medieval German Yiddish (*Judisch-Deutsch*). Interestingly enough, Mary Wollstonecraft, the fighter for the rights of oppressed women, was also aware of Gluckel von Hameln. It would appear that in both Mary Wollstonecraft and Gluckel von Hameln, Bertha Pappenheim was able to find models of feminine certainty that could help her work out her own identity problems. There is even conjecture that in her depressed states Bertha behaved as she imagined Gluckel would have, and that she may have known of Gluckel much earlier than researchers have been able to ascertain (Pollock, 1971).

In my opinion, Gluckel's impact upon Bertha's later life cannot be stressed too much. Gluckel was born in Hamburg just before the end of the Thirty Years' War. This war destroyed much of Germany and inflicted great hardship upon the Jews who lived there in that time. Gluckel lived through a time when the Cossack leader Bogdan Chmielnicki inspired and carried out savage programs against the Jews living in Russia and Poland. Thousands died of sickness or outright massacre. Those remnants of the Jewish community who managed to escape found their way to a few cities in Germany. Gluckel observed that her father, a leader of the Jewish community, cared for, fed, and housed these unfortunate refugees. Gluckel's grandmother cared for the sickly refugees and became ill as a result and died.

Gluckel was engaged at age 12, and when she was 14 she was married to Chaim Baruch, a marriage which lasted thirty years and resulted in thirteen children, twelve of whom survived. After Chaim's death, Gluckel was grief-stricken, and during that period she began to write her memoirs. (In later years Bertha Pappenheim, during the acute phases of her emotional stress, was to follow the model of abreaction as a way of coping with the death of her father.) What is remarkable about Gluckel is her level of literacy in a time when few women were given formal instruction. She was well informed about her religious faith, Orthodox Judaism, and, most important, she enjoyed a peer relationship with her husband, who valued her judgment and consulted with her about business, even to the degree that Gluckel formulated the business documents. The affection and respect that Gluckel received from her husband apparently enabled her to carry on successfully after his death. This, plus the unusual experience of an educational background which most women did not have, served as a model for Bertha Pappenheim's move toward women's liberation. Bertha was always deeply resentful that her brother had been encouraged to study at the University of Vienna and go on to study law while she had to settle for a Catholic secondary school.

The year 1899 marked Bertha's active advocacy of the rights of women. Her play, *Women's Rights,* portrayed the two male characters as hostile to women, and the women were portrayed as helpless and the victim of cynical exploitation by these two men.

Just before this time, in 1895, Bertha had been introduced to welfare work in the Frankfurt community, since the Jews of that community were deeply concerned about orphan children of Jewish background who had lost their parents in the pogroms of Eastern Europe. Bertha was upset that wealthy young women did not care to acknowledge the degree of poverty and crime that existed and that had to be dealt with rather than judged as a moral weakness of the poor. In 1895 she accepted the position of directress (housemother) of the Jewish Orphanage for Girls (sponsored by the Hebrew Women's Organization) in Frankfurt. The job was to be a temporary one, but she held the position for twelve years. Thus she may be seen as a pioneer feminist and social worker in Germany. The German government recognized her pioneering achievements in social work when it issued a stamp in her honor in 1954. Bertha set up a sewing school at the time of her appointment, since she believed that both poor and wealthy young women should learn practical skills; founded a kindergarten; and worked at the Frankfurt center that cared for the poor. She was apparently very gifted as an organizer and was able to relate easily to both Christian and Jewish organizations. She clearly had a vision of what a woman could be, although there are some researchers who maintain that her dedication to women's emancipation was related to unresolved hostility to her father, brother, and Joseph Breuer (Karpe, 1963).

The remarkable fact is that this young woman, of a wealthy background, accustomed to a life of leisure, a devoted operagoer, accepted this difficult life task and worked at it constantly. She had no training in manual skills and insisted on organizing in fact several sewing schools, which were called mending schools. She insisted on a spartan regime for her young charges and encouraged a simple setting, adequate food with no effort to provide luxuries, character development, and attention to Judaism. Here, then, in 1895 was the spoiled, rebellious, antireligious Anna O. at age 36, some thirteen years after her most agitated state.

Bertha Pappenheim realized that the young women who left the Jewish Orphanage as they grew older needed a continuing recreational center, which would offer them educational and cultural opportunities. She organized a Girls' Club. It had a library, a kosher dining room, and a room where lecturers could come to speak to the young women. The club was organized democratically, and the members participated actively in the direction of their activities. Soon after this ambitious undertaking, she organized a Federation of Jewish

Women, which numbered among its members the many volunteers of Jewish
faith in the social causes of the day. This step enabled Jewish women to belong
to the German Federation of Women's Organizations, to which other major
religious groups composed of women belonged. Thus there was for the first
time a unified group speaking for the Jewish women of Germany who were active in public causes and the feminist movement. Bertha became president of
the Federation of Jewish Women, and from this point on the scope of her life
grew broader and richer.

In 1900 Bertha published a pamphlet titled *The Jewish Problem in Galicia.*
Galicia, a province of the Austro-Hungarian Empire, was actually the
southwest portion of Poland. The pamphlet was based upon reports that Bertha
heard from the young Jewish women refugees who left the ghettos of Galicia
and found their way to Frankfurt and other towns in Germany. According to
these refugees, the plight of the ghetto dwellers and especially the women was
abominable. Bertha stated in this pamphlet that education was one major way
to break the pattern of poverty and degradation that these young Jewish
women experienced. After Bertha was elected president of the Federation of
Jewish Women, she decided to travel to Galicia and see first hand the conditions of the Jewish community and especially the young Jewish women. Bertha
made the trip in 1904 and discovered to her dismay that young Jewish women
were being sold into brothels and that there was an organized white-slave traffic, which Jews were part of. She was not naive about prostitution, since she
had lived in Vienna, a city where prostitution was rampant. She became deeply
concerned about the plight of the young Jewish women who were being taken
from the ghettos of Galicia to the houses of prostitution. There are researchers
who maintain that she was still carrying on her fight against Freud and his
theories because of her total commitment to fighting the white-slave traffic
(Karpe, 1963). According to one writer, she identified with the oppressed
women who became prostitutes. This may be so, but it may also do disservice
to an intelligent and thoughtful woman who was shocked by the plight of young
women with little or no education who had no place to turn to and became part
of a life in a brothel, which was total degradation. Bertha wrote to many of her
friends in Frankfurt about what she found in Galicia, and her letters tell the
story of a now life-affirming woman who wanted to be of aid to the oppressed.
Her letters were published in 1924 and 1929. The main theme is the protection
of the Jewish minority and especially the low-income group, who she believed
could expect no protection from the state and whose members were easily influenced by Christian missionaries looking for converts.

Bertha's mother died in 1905 at age 75, and her younger brother, Willie,
had finally married four years earlier at the age of 42. Now Bertha could consider herself free of any family responsibilities, and she took on the burden of a
much larger family—the young Jewish women who were prostitutes. In 1906
she traveled in many parts of Europe—Poland, Russia, Greece—as well as
Turkey, Jerusalem, and Egypt, and collected considerable information as to

how the recruitment of young Jewish women for prostitution was a highly organized business. She brought back to Frankfurt orphans of the pogroms.

She heard the pathetic stories of impoverished parents in Galicia who either willingly or through trickery had sold their daughters into prostitution. She also discovered how glib confidence men would visit small towns and describe themselves as successful businessmen of Jewish faith who had returned to their place of origin to find suitable wives of Jewish faith and marry. Once the young women were tricked into marriages of convenience, they ended up in cities far from home or in far-off lands in North or South America with no conceivable way of return or rescue. Much of this lucrative business was financed by wealthy Turkish Jews. Bertha was warned that anti-Semites would use this information against the Jewish community, and indeed the Nazis did many years later, but Bertha did not flinch from telling the truth. She was able to obtain financing from a wealthy relative and founded a home for young Jewish prostitutes, some of whom had illegitimate children. The home was established in the town of Neu-Isenburg, Germany, six miles from the city of Frankfurt, and the project grew so quickly that it filled four houses. She conceived of and ran the home as a substitute family setting and offered a warm and loving environment.

Bertha traveled to the United States to visit the Jewish communities of the "new world" and to find out why many of the more recent immigrants had abandoned their wives and families in Europe. In 1910 she spoke at the International Congress to Fight White Slave Traffic, held in London, and in 1911 her report to the German National Committee to Fight White Slave Traffic (organized in 1899 by German feminists) identified the wealthy Turkish Jews who were profiting from their sordid business. The Turkish Jews would hire underlings in Galicia, who would visit impoverished families and offer to obtain jobs for their daughters as servants to wealthy families in Germany. The girls would be smuggled across the border into Germany, and from that point on they became part of a larger network that incorporated them into brothels. While the Catholic and Jewish relief organizations attempted to trace and find young women of their religious faiths who had been tricked into this network, until Bertha Pappenheim appeared on the scene no real effort was made to recognize these unfortunate women, some of whom were now burdened by illegitimate children.

By this time Bertha had become a sophisticated social worker, wise to the intricacies of government regulations and fundraising. When she established her Home for Wayward Girls and Illegitimate Children in Neu-Isenburg, she did so because it was in the state of Hesse, where the government had a more liberal attitude toward stateless residents than Frankfurt, a city in the conservative state of Prussia. She arranged for the girls to go to school and enlisted a group of visiting medical specialists to aid in her work. She was an efficient adminstrator and showed very few of the emotional disturbances that she exhibited years earlier. There were times when her associates described her as being overly sensitive or subject to outbursts of anger, but for the most part these episodes were hidden from view. She never married, although she continued to be described as a charming and vivacious woman who was attractive to many men. She is described by some as being hostile to psychoanalysis, but this may be a distortion and based upon one incident when she opposed psychotherapy for one of her young charges. She continued to be a very kind and sympathetic person all her life, with all of the "markedly intelligent" and "penetrating intuition" that Breuer had described in *Studies on Hysteria*.

She kept her home running through the years of World War I, and it was a difficult task. As the Germans began to lose the war, there was less and less food available and Bertha had to feed not only young women but their small children. She helped with the care and lodging of young Jewish women who were displaced persons, brought to Germany as a workforce as the Germans invaded and destroyed parts of Poland. Through all the travails of a defeated Germany—the chaotic inflation of the 1920s, the political upheaval, the riots, the assassinations, the resurgence of anti-Semitism—she was indefatigible in her commitment to the people in her charge.

She continued to be active in the field of social work and became friendly with Martin Buber, the philosopher and educator, who apparently admired her work and the depth of her commitment to Judaism. Much of this period of her life has been described by Dora Edinger, an educator and historian, who married a distant cousin of Bertha Pappenheim, moved from Berlin to Frankfurt, and worked with Bertha from 1923 until Bertha's death (Edinger, 1963, 1968). Edinger's thorough compilation of Bertha Pappenheim's letters, publications, and activities consistently paints the picture of an active, resourceful, and very dynamic woman. When Martin Buber was director of Lehrhaus, an adult study center in Frankfurt, Bertha Pappenheim organized and taught study groups in the area of volunteer social work. She appears to have been rather prudish in her attitude toward dress and clothing. She criticized one new board member who appeared for her first meeting at the home Bertha directed. Her criticism was directed toward the color of the nail polish that this woman chose—bright red. Apparently Bertha felt that it was not "appropriate." The reprimanded board member never returned to any board meetings. This attitude may have reflected Bertha's deep commitment to feminism and her belief that women should not appear frivolous. It may also have been her concern that women who were in contact with her charges at the home should present appropriate role models for impressionable young women. Bertha always stressed that the married women she met were people in their own right and not appendages of a husband.

Her appetite for living was great. In 1930, at age 71, she began to study the Greek philosophers and obtained a private tutor. She was very thoughtful about social issues, and although a dedicated feminist, she was totally opposed to abortion. She believed in this very deeply, and although she never married and remained childless (she did not emulate Mary Wollstonecraft and have children out of wedlock), she stated in a conference held in Austria in 1930 that "it is a woman's privilege and duty to have children. She becomes blessed through having children. . . . Abortion is a crime against the human race. If a woman becomes pregnant, she was meant to be" (Freeman, 1972).

Since Bertha is considered to be the first case in psychoanalysis, it is of interest to find out that she appears to some to have been opposed to psychoanalytic treatment. Many of the young women who came to the home she directed were severely traumatized and obviously in need of psychological counseling of some type. At one meeting at her home she became quite agitated when the suggestion was made that one young resident at the home consult a psychoanalyst. According to the report, Bertha was quite vehement in her hostility to the idea and the matter was dropped. Certainly, among the many professionals whom she enlisted and who volunteered to consult at the home she directed, the absence of a consulting psychoanalyst is quite obvious. Yet her attitude may be understandable. It may be that the population she dealt with was unsuitable for psychodynamic treatment of any depth. Edinger (1968, p. 12) quotes Bertha as saying, "Psychoanalysis in the hands of the physician is what confession is in the hands of the Catholic priest. It depends on its user and its use, whether it becomes a beneficial tool or a two-edged sword." Many people would agree with that evaluation.

By 1933 Bertha was a very tired but still active woman. Her emphasis on volunteer participation was rejected in many settings where she had been previously active. The stress was upon professional participation. The tide was running against her ideas, but she seemed not to be unduly upset by the fact. She suffered from severe abdominal pains, which she bore stoically. They appear to have been the beginning of a malignancy from which she would slowly die. She kept active in the Jewish community, although she considered herself a patriotic German. Nazism was coming into full bloom, and the infamous Kristallnacht took place on April 1, 1933—the day when the Nazis destroyed Jewish businesses and synagogues and beat up any passing Jew. On May 1, 1934, Bertha composed five obituaries on her life. In her fantasy she wrote the obituaries for different publications to meet different reader populations. All of the obituaries ended with the phrase "What a pity." The phrase appears to be somewhat sardonic, since each publication would have wanted her to be different. For example, the Orthodox Jewish publication would have desired that she be less ardently feminist. The Zionist publication would have described her as proudly Jewish and yet an active enemy of Zionism. Bertha continued to be active in the home at Neu-Isenburg but withdrew from activities on a national scale. It was 1934 and the Nazis had just completed their bookburnings. Bertha was clear-headed about the "overall barbarism." She made her last trip to Vienna, where she visited the Museum of Arts and Crafts, to which she had contributed a lace collection. On her way home, after a short vacation in the Austrian Alps, she became so incapacitated by her abdominal pain that she was rushed to the Jewish hospital in Munich, where an operation was performed. At this time she probably became aware that she was slowly dying of cancer, although her physician told her that it was not serious and that she would live many more years. Two months later she was back on her feet, and this time she traveled to Amsterdam for a Youth Aliyah meeting.

What happened at this meeting probably tells a lot about many German Jews. Youth Aliyah was part of a movement to get Jewish adolescents out of Germany—to Palestine, the promised land. This meant separating the youngsters from their parents. The position of Henrietta Szold, a pioneer American Zionist who spoke at the conference, was that extermination faced the Jewish community. Bertha Pappenheim did not agree and opposed the idea of sending the children away from their parents, the majority of whom believed that anti-Semitic outrages would in time disappear. Events proved Bertha and others to be tragically wrong. Here were Henrietta Szold and Bertha Pappenheim, approximately the same age, both unmarried and childless, both totally dedicated to the welfare of the community and especially the Jewish community, who were completely opposed to each other's viewpoint.

Bertha continued to work at her home for Wayward Girls and Illegitimate Children into 1936. She was age 77 but appeared as resolute as ever. She was summoned to Gestapo headquarters one day because one of the girl residents at the home, who happened to be mentally retarded, was reported to have looked at a photograph of Hitler and said, ''He looks like a criminal.'' An employee at the home had reported this to the Gestapo, and they wanted to find out whether Bertha was teaching the residents at the home this kind of philosophy. Bertha did not deny the statement of the young girl, and in a calm but dignified manner she pointed out this young woman was mentally retarded. By this time the Gestapo was using as propaganda Bertha's early reports of wealthy Jews being part of the white-slave network—propaganda which she had been warned about many years earlier but had ignored. The Gestapo did not arrest Bertha, and she returned to her work. She died on May 28, 1936. It was now too late to save most of the young women at the home. A few escaped to Israel. Most of them were sent to concentration camps or to the brothels that the Nazis organized for their German military. The home was burned by the Nazis in the pogrom of November 9, 1938. Today there is one restored building—a shelter for mentally retarded children.

Bertha had wanted to travel to Cracow, Poland, in 1936 to visit a seminary for Jewish young women. This was just before the time when the Gestapo summoned her for questioning. Her physician told her that she was too ill to travel, and she never made her visit to the seminary, which was concerned with the education of young women. She died before she learned that her treasured home for young women was to be destroyed by the Nazis. She died and never knew that all of the young women in the Polish seminary—all ninety-three—committed suicide when the Nazis announced that they would turn the seminary into a brothel. This happened in Cracow—the liberal, bourgeois city of culture.

When one reads the tributes that poured out after Bertha Pappenheim's death, it is a far cry from the helpless, frightened young woman that Breuer and Freud described. In a message read at her funeral, Martin Buber stated, ''I not only admired her but loved her, and will love her until the day I die. There are people of spirit and there are people of passion, both less common than one might think. Rarer still are the people of spirit and passion. But rarest of all is a passionate spirit. Bertha Pappenheim was a woman with just such a spirit. . . . Pass on her memory. Be witnesses that it still exists. . . . '' A co-worker who observed her closely wrote, ''A volcano lived in this woman; it erupted when someone angered her. . . . She fought only about things that were involved directly with her ultimate aims. . . . If she had the feeling that she had slid off factual ground and hurt the other person in a personal sense, she would unhesitatingly apologize and turn back her assault. . . . She loved people and she needed them . . . '' (Cora Berliner, as reported in Freeman, 1972, pp. 174–175).

In 1954, at the urging of the Freiburg (Germany) Welfare Department and Dr. Leo Baeck (formerly president of the Organization of German Jews), who survived the concentration camps, the West German government issued a Bertha Pappenheim stamp honoring her as a pioneer German social worker. The stamp is part of a series called Helpers of Humanity.

This, then, is the story of Anna O. and Bertha Pappenheim—one and the same. Would Breuer and Freud have guessed what her future would be? The pages to follow will point to the many directions that behavioral scientists can work to and work from in an effort to understand the case of Anna O. What have we learned in the last hundred years to help us in our work with the emotionally troubled? What paths are worth pursuing? Would our diagnosis read differently? The new Diagnostic and Statistical Manual III (DSM III) of the American Psychiatric Association would give Anna O. a different diagnosis, but would it make any difference? The publication of the DSM III this past year has reemphasized the issues of diagnosis, and the new manual is a significant departure from the thinking of Kraeplin. But there are many criticisms of DSM III, the primary one being that it places the center of the majority of mental disturbances within the body of the patient as opposed to studying the patient in the psychosocial field. Is Anna O. illustrative of the patient who should have been studied in the psychosocial field, and would she have been so evaluated today? The reliability of clinical judgment about her was quite contradicted by her subsequent life. Some contemporary students of therapy describe Anna O. as a borderline schizophrenic who simply managed to compensate. Others feel that insufficient attention was paid to her family history and the pressures she was subjected to. From this viewpoint, Anna O. was the identifiable patient in a disturbed family. Others wonder about the genetic and hereditary factors at work. Others feel that Anna O. merely acted out her rebellion against a male-dominated world where alert and inquiring women were restricted from advancement and upward mobility. Some believe that the early deaths of Bertha's sisters impacted upon her very profoundly and that Bertha compensated as the survivor by rescuing Jewish girls and young women. One writer stresses the degree of her pathological mourning. Some attribute the pattern of her life's work to anger at the men who mistreated her—her father by dying and Breuer by abandoning her—and a desire to help other women who were abandoned by men. Some call Bertha's life a remarkable illustration of the human capacity to grow beyond early trauma and to set new goals in life. Consider that this was the very same person who Joseph Breuer had once wished "would die and be released from her suffering." Can we demonstrate with longitudinal life studies how people deal with disturbances that are very severe? An analogous situation may be the survivors of concentration camps or prisoner-of-war settings. What processes are at work after trauma that lead to integration or deterioration? Have we paid enough attention to early childhood trauma? Some feel that in the 1980s more attention would be paid to the aspirations and dreams of a bright young woman who feels restricted and oppressed in a male-dominated society.* The current preoccupation in psychotherapy with the "here and now" and "interaction" may obscure the importance of the intrapsychic. Do many current approaches to psychotherapy deny the importance of the unconscious with a consequent detriment to the patient? What is the process of change all about? This appears to be the crucial issue that all serious researchers in psychotherapy must be concerned about. How does the change come about, and what changes in the patient—overt behavior, affective behavior, cognitive behavior? Psychoanalysts have been accused of emphasizing intrapsychic behavior as the sine qua non of change so that there is no emphasis on observable change. Can reevaluation of cases such as Anna O. serve as the bridge between the inner state (intrapsychic) and the outer state (the overt social behavior)?

What Freud recognized in Breuer's description and treatment of Anna O. was the importance of the unconscious. This is basic to the entire theory and practice of psychoanalysis and any psychodynamic therapy. This is why the case of Anna O.–Bertha Pappenheim remains important one hundred years later.

---

* While the complaints about sexism among psychotherapists of all theoretical persuasions continue to be as strong as ever, a recent study shows little support for the charges about sexism. In a study of eighty-six psychotherapists, each of whom viewed one of eight videotapes and completed a series of questionnaires, it was found that "in general, in making treatment recommendations and prognoses, the therapists did not discriminate among clients. There were no differences in recommended frequency of therapy sessions or length of treatment. Therapists recommended similar treatment modalities for all clients, including psychotherapy, supportive therapy, group therapy and chemotherapy. . . . The present study found little evidence that practicing clinicians tend toward sexist treatment recommendations or sex role stereotyping" (Stearns, Penner, and Kimmel, 1980, p. 549).

References

BERTHOLD, P. *In der Trodelbude.* Lahr, Germany: Moritz Schauenber, 1890. Second ed., Gotha, Germany: F. A. Perthes, 1894.

BREUER, J., and FREUD, S. (1923-1925). *Studies on Hysteria.* Standard Edition of the Works of Sigmund Freud, vol. II.

EDINGER, D. *Bertha Pappenheim: Her Life and Letters.* Frankfurt: Ner Tamid Verlag, 1963. English translation, *Bertha Pappenheim: Freud's Anna O.* Highland Park, Ill.: Congregation Solel, 1968.

ELLENBERGER, H. *The Discovery of the Unconscious.* New York: Basic Books, 1970.

ELLENBERGER, H. *The story of Anna O.: A critical review with new data. J. Hist. Behav. Sciences,* 8:267-279, 1972.

FREEMAN, L. *The Story of Anna O.* New York: Walker & Company, 1972.

FREUD, S. (1925a). *Medizin in Selbstdarstellung,* IV, p. 15.

FREUD, S. (1925b). The resistances to psychoanalysis: In *Collected Papers,* ed. J. Strachey. New York: Basic Books, 1959.

HIRSCHMÜLLER, A. Physiologie und Psychoanalyse. In *Leben und Werk Jahrbuch der Psychoanalyse Josef Breuers,* Beiheft 4. Bern: Verlag Hans Huber, 1978.

JONES, E. *The Life and Work of Sigmund Freud.* Vol. I. New York: Basic Books, 1953, pp. 223-226.

JUNG, C. G. Notes on the seminar in analytical psychology conducted by C. G. Jung, Zurich, March 29-July 6, 1925. Notes arranged by members of the class, Zurich, 1926, unpublished ms.

KARPE, R. The rescue complex in Anna O's final identity. *Psychoanal. Quart.,* 30:1-27, 1962.

MANN, T. Freud and the future. In *Essays of Three Decades.* New York: Knopf, 1947.

PAPPENHEIM, B. *Sisyphus-Arbeit: Reisebriefe aud den Jahren 1911 und 1912.* Leipzig: Verlag Paul E. Linder, 1924. *Sisyphus-Arbeit 2: Folge.* Berlin: Druck und Verlag, Berthold Levey, 1929.

POLLOCK, G. H. Gluckel von Hameln: Bertha Pappenheim's idealized ancestor. *Amer. Imago,* 28:216-227, 1971.

STEARNS, B. C., PENNER, L. A. and KIMMELL, E. Sexism among psychotherapists: A case not yet proven. *J. Consult. Clin. Psychol.* 48(4):548-550, 1980.

VIETH, V. *Hysteria: The History of a Disease.* Chicago: University of Chicago Press, 1965.

WHYTE, L. L. *The Unconscious Before Freud.* New York: Basic Books, 1960.

WOLLSTONECRAFT, M. *A Vindication of the Rights of Women.* London: J. Johnson, 1792.

Additional References

ABRAHAMS, B. Z. (ed.). *Gluckel of Hameln: Life 1646-1724.* New York: Thomas Yoseloff, 1963.

JENSEN, E. M. Anna O.: A study of her later life. *Psychoanal. Quart.,* 39:269-293, 1970.

POLLOCK, G. H. The possible significance of childhood object loss in the Josef Breuer-Bertha Pappenheim (Anna O.)-Sigmund Freud relationship. *J. Amer. Psychoanal. Ass.,* 16:711-739, 1968.

POLLOCK, G. H. Bertha Pappenheim's pathological mourning: Possible effects of childhood sibling loss. *J. Amer. Psychoanal. Ass.,* 20:476–493, 1972.

POLLOCK, G. H. Bertha Pappenheim: Addenda to her case history. *J. Amer. Psychoanal. Ass.,* 21:328–332, 1973.

Anna O.: Insight, Hindsight, and Foresight

2

George H. Pollock

All great art emerges from a struggle, but not all struggles result in great art or in scientific discoveries. This book has been written to celebrate a most interesting life, a most courageous woman, and a pivotal figure who played a crucial role in the early history of psychoanalysis and in the discovery of the unconscious.

There are few people whose lives are barren or of little interest, and to whom nothing has happened. Yet most lives are not noted in our histories, and little if anything is communicated about them to succeeding generations. The *Studies on Hysteria* (Breuer and Freud, 1895) in which the Anna O. treatment was first published contain fascinating clinical reports. The Anna O. therapeutic narrative was written by Breuer; the other clinical communications were written by Freud himself. The drama of Anna O. *did* catch and continued to attract our attention and our interest. Was this because the *Studies on Hysteria* was the first report—perhaps the one many of us read at the beginning of our careers? Or was it because it provided Freud great technical and clinical insights and so started him on his pioneering investigations of the unconscious mind, and in our identification with Freud we were able to relive his creative journey vicariously? In all probability there is no one answer to my query. What we do know is that the encounter between Anna O. and Breuer caught Freud's attention from the very first time he heard about the case from Breuer. He urged Breuer to write about his experiences with this gifted woman. We know Breuer was reluctant to do so. Finally, Breuer's resistance having been overcome, the chapter was written and some suggestions were offered to explain Anna O.'s illness and its supposed resolution.

We have more data now, thanks to Hirschmüller's (1978) careful research, that may explain Breuer's reluctance to publish the Anna O. report. Perhaps Breuer knew that he could not tell the story as it actually unfolded. In any event, the Hirschmüller book is a fascinating follow-up on the Anna O.–Bertha Pappenheim life. The outcome could have been tragic; it was not. Follow-up and outcome studies are significant methodological means of checking on earlier conjectures as well as ways of finding out about the unexpected. I have attempted to do some of this in my earlier studies of Bertha Pappenheim and Josef Breuer (Pollock, 1966, 1968, 1971, 1972, 1973). Now we can learn even more about the predecessors of Bertha Pappenheim and of the many contributions she made in her later life.

Freud moved beyond Breuer, and some have offered reasons for this. These motivational explanations, however, are somewhat conjectural and may be inaccurate. Here we do not have enough data yet to be on firmer ground. For example, we do not have Breuer's comments and statements and so can only infer the reasons for his unwillingness to share additional details. And I would want to underline this at the outset: It is very, very important that we make a distinction between evidence and conjecture, between constructions, fantasies, and truth. It is too easy for us to treat some of our more abstract reconstructions as if they were absolute fact. When new facts come to the fore, we must revise our ideas because of the new data. This is very legitimate. It is the way of science. But I think the danger is for us not to recognize the difference between our conjectures and what may have actually occurred.

Freud, who did not treat Anna O., unlike Breuer, who was very much involved with his patient, was unencumbered and was eager to pursue his hypotheses. This is one of the advantages of being a researcher and not necessarily the primary data gatherer. You are able to be removed, perhaps see things more objectively, and perhaps make observations about patterns which you are studying, unlike the person who is very much involved in the therapy of his patient. And so Freud moved in directions that set him on a course that resulted in many insights and discoveries, some of which have changed our whole orientation to man. It was Freud who opened the door to the inner psychological world, and how the outside affects and is affected by these previously overlooked universal inner dimensions of psychological life.

For us, I wish to underline some cautions. I have very much enjoyed the exciting historical detective work in my own research on Anna O. In the beginning, we should not be inhibited in our conjectures, but we must be constantly aware of the limitations and risks of arriving at conclusions that are based on inferences that go beyond the data. Unlike the living analysand, much information about Anna O. in her later life is lacking and we cannot retrieve it, at least from existing sources. Some of these data lacunae are being filled in. Many were omitted purposely, and some unintentionally. We know that Breuer's account was written long after his contact with Anna O. Although Josef Breuer was a scientist of the highest order and a most sensitive and devoted clinician, retrospective accounts are selective and may be inaccurate in some crucial details. It is literally impossible to give all details from an ongoing treatment in any event, and in addition the selection of information to be presented is always present, especially when one wants to protect the confidence of one's patient and oneself. This methodological problem is one that confronts biographers all the time, and in a sense when we examine a case history we are examining a biography. The psychoanalytic or therapeutic account is a biographical narrative, and some of the methodological problems inherent in the writing of biography and autobiography apply to these forms of writing.

Here is an illustration of such a problem. Two writers recently examined over 200,000 pages of documents in order to give a new slant to a historical legal case. And yet, after their careful examination and report, critics have questioned their accuracy and their ability to paint the full picture of the case. Two hundred thousand pages! Even with this overwhelming array of documents the picture is incomplete, and deletions, withheld information, unreliable reports, and biased narrative distort the account. Having all of the files would not necessarily establish the guilt or innocence of the accused parties involved, and prosecution documents by themselves cannot provide a balanced picture of the situation. What emerges in a particular version of the case shaped by one side. It is not suggested that in the clinical account of Anna O. we are dealing with a similar situation, but I am raising the question of evidence and the restrictions imposed upon us by the one-sidedness of the data and their interpretation. We cannot ignore this problem, and yet we can still learn from a case report. What we learn, however, is more than what we learn from reading clinical data. We learn about the writer, the treater, the audience for whom the report is written, the patient, the history of this person in historical context, and on and on. We are nowadays paying more attention to the style, form, and purpose of clinical reports.

Freud was aware of this issue of self-revelation when he destroyed his diaries, letters, scientific notes, and manuscripts early in his career. He wrote, "Let the biographers chafe; we won't make it too easy for them. Let each one of them believe he is right in his 'Conception of the Development of the Hero': even now I enjoy the thought of how they will all go astray" (Freud, quoted in Jones, 1953, p. xiii). But even if we grant our ideal biographer complete freedom of access to his sources, intimacy with his subject, detachment in his accounting, independence of taboos, and moral, emotional, and political objectivity, it remains impossible to evade the ultimate question about the nature of the truth he tells. The biographer who aims at completeness will seek to find in his mass of fact, actions, and patterns of behavior that which will contribute to a consistent explanation of the overall life of his subject. But the biographer does not simply generate or present; he interprets as well. And there is a tendency to select in order to interpret, and at times to invent in clinical accounts written long after the events reported.

One must question and seriously consider the possibility of a serious methodological problem when one relies on recollections and memories, especially in the face of reluctance to publish the report. Given the fact that the patient was well known to the community—and we know that Bertha Pappenheim was, as was her therapist Josef Breuer—we have another restraint at work, confidentiality, but yet everyone knew what occurred. So more caution is needed. And the game of the name in this case was an interesting one because, I would remind you, at one time in her career B. P. presented herself as P. B., Paul Berthold (Edinger, 1968). This was when she was involved in what I will conjecturally call a masculine identification. And so very innovatively in the *Studies on Hysteria,* instead of B. P. or P. B., Breuer used A. O. We do not need extensive study and decoders to see that this thin veneer was designed for the maintenance of confidentiality. It does indicate a sensitivity to this issue, especially in a relatively small community where everybody knew everybody else. But inaccuracies in the report can also be detected, and these unfortunately can cast doubt on the more important scientific and clinical issues presented.

So when we have a patient who is well known in the community, and we have a therapist who is well known in the community, and we have a certain reluctance to go ahead and acknowledge certain facts, it may well be that there are certain kinds of omissions and certain kinds of distortions which should be handled in other ways. There may be truth in fiction, but I would urge that we not see fiction as untested truth.

Let me raise a few additional questions at this point. We know that a sensitive therapist may act differently than he reports in a written narrative. We all have the experience where the written report is very much at variance with what actually occurred. Again, there may be many, many reasons for this, and it is not my intention to discuss these now. But let me cite one quote from Breuer's account that can serve as an illustration—and I think that it is a rather important illustration. In writing of the successful termination of his treatment of Anna O., Breuer asserts, "In this way, too, the whole illness was brought to a close." He refers to the fact that each symptom disappeared after she had described its first occurrence. "The patient herself had formed a strong determination that the whole treatment should be finished by the anniversary of the day on which she was moved into the country [June 7]. At the beginning of June, accordingly, she entered into the 'talking cure' with the greatest energy. On the last day—by the help of re-arranging the room so as to resemble her father's sickroom—she reproduced the terrifying hallucination which I have described above and which constituted the root of her whole illness. During the original scene she had only been able to think and pray in English; but immediately after its reproduction she was able to speak in German" (Breuer and Freud, 1895, p. 40). This is a most dramatic account that raises a host of questions about language, content, purpose, and the verbal aspect of psychotherapy.

To go back to Breuer: "She was moreover free from the innumerable disturbances which she had previously exhibited. After this she left Vienna and travelled for a while; but it was a considerable time before she regained her mental balance entirely. Since then she has enjoyed complete health" (ibid., pp. 40–41). There is a footnote in the Standard Edition (ibid.) which mentions a discussion between Freud and James Strachey regarding a hiatus in the text that indicates the end of Anna O.'s treatment was not as Breuer reported it.

Later research by Ellenberger (1972) and others has supplied us with many new data about the "end of the successful treatment" with Breuer. We know that Bertha Pappenheim went to a sanatorium. Presumably she was addicted to morphine. She had to be "weaned" from morphine. She went through some very, very harrowing experiences. And so, to go back to the last sentence of the Breuer account, "Since then she has enjoyed complete health," I do not know what complete health means, but it sounds to me as though there may have been some wish fulfillment here without there being a dream.

My point here is to raise questions about Breuer's written account of the case and its subsequent course. Breuer was a pioneer who ventured into new areas that had the potential for stimulating distress in any therapist. But in our discussions of the case history we must be careful to recognize that partial data can give rise to many new interpretations of the patient's pathology. If the data are incomplete or inaccurate, whatever flows from them should be seen as limited, although new ideas can still emerge from partial data. Breuer discovered a new technique. He was helped by Anna O. This may be all we can say about clinical outcome from the case as recorded in the studies. Public legends about Breuer's concerns and "countertransference" came into being. There are no data to support these legends; e.g., in one of my studies (Pollock, 1968) I found that Breuer did not run off to Italy for a second honeymoon with his wife who became pregnant. Not true. That Breuer was distressed we can conjecture with a high degree of probability. But the reason may have been Breuer's lack of success in the treatment and the possibility that Anna O. became iatrogenically addicted as a result of the treatment. I do not condemn conjecture, even fanciful conjecture, as a source of hypotheses, but if we truly are interested in developing a science, a science that has a responsibility for its hypotheses and method of testing, we must be careful of the data that we use, and we must be aware of the fact that we ourselves as data collectors may introduce a particular kind of bias or a skewed orientation to what we interpret.

One can reach appropriate and correct conclusions from inaccurate data, but this is rare. Evidence and verification problems exist, but these issues may be clarified, especially through the use of techniques that we are beginning to now employ in our studies of psychoanalytic treatments, namely follow-up and outcome investigations. Perhaps if we could have an accurate outcome study of Anna O., we would still say how she was a gifted person, a pioneer, a courageous individual, a fighter for the rights of the downtrodden, not only of women but of children and men. This translator of Mary Wollstonecraft, this individual who did confront the Gestapo—we would learn that this particular woman, maybe a little obsessional, maybe not quite resolved in her own bisexuality, nonetheless was active and contributing in her later adult life. How could she have had such turbulence earlier? Why the change? We can only speculate and speculate and speculate, which again is legitimate—but let us label our speculation as speculation and learn what we can from this unique life.

Let me briefly touch upon another area of consideration, nosology. The diagnosis given to the case of Anna O. and the explanation given for her illness reflect the theoretical orientation of the researcher and the clinician. Suppose we were to give, with the methodological cautions that I have raised, the bare-bones clinical data to a classical psychoanalyst, an object relations therapist, a self psychologist, an ego psychologist, a Kleinian, an Adlerian, a Jungian, etc., and ask them to formulate the case according to their particualr orientations, hypotheses, and explanations. They variously will say, as with the proverbial ten blind men and the elephant, it is a trunk, it is a leg, it is a tail, it is something else. Who is right? What data are used for the formulations? Differences would emerge, and yet who is to say that one diagnosis or another, one explanation or another, is right or wrong until we get evidence and proof and carefully examine the underlying assumptions? Then we need follow-up outcome data to attempt to further test our hypotheses.

We can say that Anna O.'s treatment with Breuer was the beginning of the psychoanalytic era. Anna O. with her "talking cure" and "chimney sweeping" contributed to what later became psychoanalytic technique. Her relationship with Breuer was the first psychoanalytic therapeutic alliance. From the treatment of Anna O. we can see the precursors to later important psychoanalytic concepts, e.g., catharsis, free association, anniversary reaction, pathological mourning, the importance of dreams, transference and counter-transference, reconstruction, and even ego mechanisms of protection. Any case that can yield such insights is worthy of study. But let us perhaps keep in mind that the level of abstraction that we get from the data depends upon more than a single case study. Accepted basic concepts of our science can be viewed from the perspective of hindsight and precursors, but more was needed. Freud had the insights nearly a century ago, and some of these lay dormant for various periods of time until their later emergence in clearer conceptual form and based on more clinical data. Freud used Breuer's experience in order to find meaning. This occurred and may have released Freud's immeasurable creative potentials. Anna O. was a significant figure whose entrance on the scientific stage occurred at a most fortuitous time. She is, and should be, acknowledged for her contributions, but I would maintain that Freud's insight and foresight were crucial. He had the power of going from the clinical report to the penetrating idea even before it had been worked into any testing methodology. So, Anna O., Josef Breuer, Sigmund Freud, we salute you one hundred years later for your contributions to us.

Pletsch (1982), in a recent essay on "Freud's Case Studies," notes that Freud in his careful description of individual cases, reintroduces "literary style as a tool of investigation in psychology" (p. 105). Pletsch goes on further to state, "As Freud came to understand hysteria better, his case studies became increasingly complex and entangled narratives" (ibid.). Mahoney (1982) has recently also written about Freud's literary style. This increasing emphasis on style, intent, mode of communication, and linguistic and semiotic analysis of clinical examples and case reports is potentially a very useful research approach. Nonetheless, the facts of a case must be differentiated from the style and purpose of the clinical account.

In considering a speculative, retrospective diagnosis, I believe one cannot exclude the possibility of a toxic psychosis—perhaps based on morphine-opium addiction. With such an organic disintegration there could be the emergence of deeper psychological issues, hallucinations, and the release of memories in cathartic "chimney sweeping"; and one cannot exclude the possibility that there also was something germinal for psychoanalysis, namely the "talking cure," which may have been the result of drug intoxication. This is speculative and does not diminish the contribution of the "chimney sweeping" or "talking cure." However, it should not be excluded from our consideration. With new data we may have new dimensions to consider for later clinical, technical, and theoretical extensions, without losing the basic contributions that the early pioneers utilized.

Let us speculate; let us not be concerned about the opposition of those who feel that we do not have a sufficient amount of data. But let us also be aware of our limitations, lest our speculations be considered only fantasies and not the beginnings of scientific creative activity.

"For the creation of a theory the mere collection of recorded phenomena never suffices—there must always be added a free invention of the human mind that attacks the heart of the matter. And: the physicist must not be content with the purely phenomenological considerations that pertain to the phenomena. Instead, we should press on to the speculative method, which looks for the underlying pattern" (Einstein, quoted in Dukas and Hoffmann, 1979, pp. 29–30).

References

BREUER, J., and FREUD, S. (1893–1895). *Studies on Hysteria.* Standard Edition, vol. II. London: Hogarth Press, 1955.

DUKAS, H., and HOFFMANN, B., (eds.). *Albert Einstein: The Human Side.* Princeton, N.J.: Princeton University Press, 1979.

EDINGER, D. *Bertha Pappenheim: Freud's Anna O.* Highland Park, Ill.: Congregation Solel, 1968.

ELLENBERGER, H. F. The story of "Anna O.": A critical review with new data. *J. Hist. Behav. Sciences,* 8:267–279, 1972.

HIRSCHMÜLLER, A. *Physiologie und Psychoanalyse.* Bern: Verlag Hans Huber, 1978.

JONES, E. *The Life and Work of Sigmund Freud,* vol. 1. New York: Basic Books, 1953.

MAHONEY, P. *Freud as a Writer.* New York: International Universities Press, 1982.

PLETSCH, C. Freud's case studies. *Partisan Review,* 48(1):101–118, 1982.

POLLOCK, G. H. Mourning and childhood loss: Their possible significance in the Josef Breuer–Bertha Pappenheim relationship. *Bull. Ass. Psychoanal. Med.,* V(4):51–54, 1966.

POLLOCK, G. H. The possible significance of childhood object loss in the Josef Breuer–Bertha Pappenheim (Anna O.)–Sigmund Freud relationship. *J. Amer. Psychoanal. Ass.,* 16:711–739, 1968.

POLLOCK, G. H. Some historical notes on Bertha Pappenheim's idealized ancestor: Glückel von Hameln. *Amer. Imago,* 28(3):216–227, 1971.

POLLOCK, G. H. Bertha Pappenheim's pathological mourning: Possible effects of childhood sibling loss. *J. Amer. Psychoanal. Ass.,* 20(3):476–493, 1972.

POLLOCK, G. H. Bertha Pappenheim: Addenda to her case history. *J. Amer. Psychoanal. Ass.,* 21(2):328–332, 1973.

The Case
of Anna O.:
Then and Now

Philip S. Holzman

In this chapter I will focus on aspects of the history of the psychoanalytic move-ment that can be dated from the time of Bertha Pappenheim's treatment by Joseph Breuer, rather than on specific aspects of her treatment or her life, which you have read about in the preceding chapters.

Without doing very much violence to the facts, one could cite Charles Dickens on the France of the latter part of the eighteenth century to describe the state of psychotherapeutics, and psychological investigation in general, in the latter part of the nineteenth century: "It was the best of times; it was the worst of times. It was the age of wisdom, it was the age of foolishness, it was the epoch of belief, it was the epoch of incredulity . . . it was the spring of hope, it was the winter of despair."

The phenomenal successes of nineteenth-century medicine in breaking through the mysteries of such conditions as Addison's disease, Bright's disease, and tuberculosis were clearly unmatched by progress in any mental disorder, be it pellagra, paresis, or paranoia, or hysteria, obsessional neurosis, or phobic attacks. Yet the very absence of progress made it possible for practitioners like Charcot, Breuer, and Freud to innovate, invent, and improvise, and thus to enter a new phase fertile for discovery of new methods and delivery of new knowledge.

It is my belief that there are sets of contradictions that inhere in this dynamic psychological movement that was begun one hundred years ago.

The first contradiction one observes is that Breuer was open to Anna O.'s ideas, directions, her "chimney sweeping," the turnings and twistings of her thought that indicated hitherto unsuspected meanings of her behavior. Yet this very openness exposed Breuer to the merciless appetites of the intimate rela-tionship between doctor and patient that, in the absence of a theory to guide him, eventually destroyed the treatment. His open receptiveness to all of Anna O.'s personal thoughts both disclosed a view of the vastness of mental activity and stimulated fantasies of desire in his patient that could not be satisfied by mere listening. It requires no stretch of imagination to place a sexual motive at the core of her fantasy that she was pregnant with Breuer's child, and no stretch of understanding to comprehend Breuer's response of bewildered discomfort. Today we are faced with a related but opposite situation. The systematizing of analytic technique has made it possible to understand, observe, and control the transference, which has become the fulcrum of the entire psychoanalytic technique. But in this process some analysts seem less open to the words of their patients. The techniques of many practitioners have become routinized and formalized to the point where some analysts seem no longer to be led by the patient's quest for meaning. Rather, they lead the patients toward what may be their own preconceived ideas about the meanings of symptoms, dreams, or experiences.

A principal feature of this turn in the path of psychoanalytic development concerns the range of facts or data available to the analytic investigator then and now. The body of knowledge gained from the treatment of Anna O. and the other specimen patients—Elizabeth von R., Lucy, Emmy, and those treated even later—positively accelerated up to about the end of the fourth decade of the twentieth century. This phase encompassed the development of the several drive theories, ego psychology, the broad statements about analytic technique, the bold excursions into social, literary, and artistic realms, and the general developmental psychology that integrated biological, psychological, and social determinants. Then for a while we experienced a plateau, although a few advances in clinical analysis did occur, especially in the work of child analysts, as in the work of Melanie Klein (1932), Anna Freud (1955), and David Levy (1942), the clinical observations of Fenichel, the psychosocial theory of Erikson, the extensions of analysis into adaptative theory by Hartmann, and the systematizing attempts by Rapaport. And then, beginning perhaps in the 1950s, a negative acceleration began. Had analytic studies mined all there was to know about human behavior in conflict?

Concomitant with this decline in accrued psychoanaltyic knowledge, there was a clear increase in the complexity of the organizational aspects of psychoanalysis. On the local level the training curriculum began to increase the number of course requirements until many of the institute catalogues were weighed down by theoretical courses. Today it is not unusual for four or five courses to be devoted to metapsychology alone, for example. Clinical courses in which actual cases are discussed showed very little corresponding increase.

The lesson of Breuer taught us that total openness without constraints by theory as a guide makes one unwittingly vulnerable to the power of the key aspect of the analytic process, the transference. This is a feature of the first contradiction. Breuer was almost totally unsupported by any body of theory that could help him put in perspective the erotic nature of Anna O.'s fantasies and importuning, particularly since he had regarded her hysteria as a hypnoidal hysteria, one without a sexual etiology. But who, in that same situation of dramatic urgency, unbolstered by precedent, unsupported by any sense of familiarity with repeated and expected patterns, would not also experience bewilderment, coupled with excitement? The full data were not yet gathered from which one could induce principles about the erotic nature of the relationship and further about its etiology in past patterns of loving. The free and open exploration begun by Breuer yielded great amounts of information about the secret inner life of persons; but the absence of theory prevented a fuller, useful integration and control of that material. Today we understand much about the transference, and if there is in contemporary literature a lively debate about its essential manifestations and the nature of the optimal technical interventions (Gill, 1979; Lipton, 1977), it is surely no mystery or surprise that the transference, conceived of as styles of loving and hating, came to dominate the psychoanalytic exchange. Yet the curriculum in most institutes has become so laden with theory courses as to overshadow the essence of psychoanalysis: the clinical phenomena. Preoccupation in the psychoanalytic literature for some years now has shown a distinct imbalance in favor of abstract theoretical papers—the so-called metapsychology. What was once a guide to understanding clinical data has begun to dominate the data so that the latter can now barely speak for themselves about the din of metapsychology. We are protected against the tyranny of the transference by a wall of theory, increasingly abstract and removed from the behavior and words of the analysand. A contemporary task is to find our way back—not to the ingenuous gropings of a century ago, but to the optimal balance of theory and fact that permits further search and discovery rather than monuments of rigid abstractions that divert us from observation and innovation.

On the national level the organizational structure of the American Psychoanalytic Association has become increasingly labyrinthine with its dual functions of monitoring professional standards of training and practice and presenting scientific forums and discussions. It could even be concluded that the very proliferation of organizational and training standards and regulations has diverted attention from the Breuer model of openness to the primary data of the analytic process, and therefore from innovation.

These issues can be discussed from yet another historical perspective. Psychoanalysis began within the medical profession—specifically neurology—as a treatment for conditions that had no obvious organic component. Breuer undertook Anna O.'s treatment as a physician. The theoretical formulations that issued from the experience with Anna O. and the other patients discussed in the *Studies on Hysteria* clearly follow the disease model so popular in the nineteenth century: the Koch model of infections disease. Find the toxic agent that is alleged to produce the disease; inject that toxin into another animal; and if the disease develops, the causal agent has been found. Freud's first search for the causal agent of neurosis centered upon actual sexual seductions of childhood, incestuous liaisons. But the evidence required by the Koch model failed to confirm that theory. Such actual seductions were found to neither necessary nor sufficient for the development of a neurosis. Fantasies of such seductions, representing wishes, became the next hypothesized causal agent, but with a significant shift in emphasis. Since such fantasies seemed to occur so frequently, they could not be the sole noxious agent, and therefore not the sufficient condition. The Virchow model thus replaced the Koch model. It was a matter or relative strengths of the "tissue" of the personality and of the noxious fantasies. This model required probing into the problem of how the personality acquired its weaknesses or strengths. This investigation implicated historical and perhaps genetic factors and thus turned Freud's attention from solely pathological formations toward personality development, motivation, cognition, sociology, the historical context, the nature of conscience, the role of myths in mental life, and the role of mothering, to name but a few areas into which his data led him. He was, in fact, led from the medical beginnings into an arena that defied strict definition or even bounding. Surely the area was no longer only medical.

It is striking indeed that many patients seeking treatment present problems that do not reflect, centrally, conflict between basic motives of sex and aggression on the one hand and countermotives, perhaps born of conscience, on the other. Rather frequently we can understand patients' contemporary problems in the context of what Hartman (e.g., Hartmann and Loewenstein, 1962) called "intrasystemic conflicts": issues of choice, renunciation, ambition, loyalties, commitment, self-betrayals. This in no way denies the continued effects of sexual and aggressive motives and their role in symptom formation. In many instances there is a relative absence of clear-cut symptoms in the complaints of patients, and a presence of complaints such as "I can't decide whether to stay at this job or to branch out," or "I can't make up my mind whether to marry X or not," or "I get no satisfaction out of what I'm doing." To deny the role of sexual or aggressive motives in these complaints, as does Kohut (1977), is to miss much of the complexity of the problems. But to conceive of them as purely *intersystemic* conflicts also misses the complexity. And once one grants the widening ramifications of such *intrasystemic* conflicts, it seems to me that we have superseded the Koch and Virchow models of disease. The nature of the disorders, then, transcends boundaries of pathology and disease, and thus of the territory of the medical practitioner.

It was in *The Question of Lay Analysis* (1926) that Freud most vividly and decisively described his awareness of the vast reaches of psychoanalytic inquiry as it ceased to be merely a medical investigation. Clearly it could be employed not only for relief of neurotic suffering but for self-exploration even in the absence of psychopathology. Of course it continues to have therapeutic effect, although there are now quicker and less expensive treatments available for many but not all of the conditions helped by psychoanalysis. But Freud saw that psychoanalysis could accomplish more than to take away suffering; it could add to the analysand's experience of awareness of motives, actions, and counter actions; it could contribute to a changed view of oneself, responsive to the paradoxes of life. It was, above all, an *educational* experience.

Karl Menninger stated this view succinctly. "I trust this will not be taken to

indicate hardness of heart; I have spent a lifetime attempting to relieve suffering. But as I see it now, the greatest good for the greatest number depends upon
the application of the principles and knowledge gained from the science of
psychoanalysis rather than upon its therapeutic applications in particular instances. To the educational value of psychoanalysis we must add its value as a
research tool. No other therapeutic method has taught us so much about the
human mind'' (Menninger and Holzman, 1973, p. xii).

This *de facto* demedicalization of psychoanalysis, however, has been
matched by an ever-stricter *de jure* medical domination over psychoanalysis.
Nonmedical scientists and scholars seeking training in psychoanalysis find it
extremely difficult to gain admission to training institutes even if they can bear
the huge burden of the cost of such training. Thus the growth and influence of
psychoanalytic inquiries are threatened with being stunted by a concentration
on only one aspect of applied psychoanalysis, its therapeutic usefulness. Some
nonmedical scholars of great promise cannot obtain training in established institutes because of a judgment about the relevance of the research area that they
represent. Yet one hundred years ago, who would have predicted the areas that
psychoanalysis has touched or has been touched by? A judgment of relevance is
generally a very risky venture.

It surely is refreshing to recall Freud's admonitions about these issues.
''For we do no consider it at all desirable for psychoanalysis to be swallowed up
by medicine and to find its last resting place in a textbook of psychiatry under
the heading, 'Methods of Treatment,' alongside of procedures such as hypnotic suggestion, autosuggestion, and persuasion, which, born from our ignorance, have to thank the laziness and cowardice of mankind for their short-lived
effects. It deserves a better fate and, it may be hoped, will meet with one. As a
'depth psychology,' a theory of the mental unconscious, it can become in-
dispensable to all the sciences which are concerned with the evolution of human
civilization and its major institutions such as art, religion and the social order.
It has already, in my opinion, afforded these sciences considerable help in solv-
ing their problems. But these are only small contributions compared with what
might be achieved if historians of civilization, psychologists of religion,
philologists and so on would agree themselves to handle the new instrument of
research which is at their service. The use of analysis for the treatment of the
neuroses is only one of its applications; the future will perhaps show that it is
not the most important one. In any case it would be wrong to sacrifice all the
other applications to this single one, just because it touches on the circle of
medical interests'' (Freud, 1926, p. 248).

The task is to find a solution that considers these factors: first, the best interests of patients, for whom careful diagnostic work is required before specific
treatment by a highly competent and well-trained person is decided; second,
the interests of the medical community, who are concerned with both standards
of practice and with the economics of practice; and third, the discipline of
psychoanalysis. Today many disciplines confront and deal with psychoanalytic

issues, including, for example, the fields of psychology, sociology, the law, literature, the arts, and anthropology. Here, then, is a contemporary contradiction: as the intellectual content of psychoanalysis pushed beyond its medical origins, selection and training criteria for analysts become more, not less, medically oriented and entrenched within medicine.

Another observation about the medical origins of psychoanalysis deserves more than passing comment: one hundred years ago the setting for treatment was quite informal, even impromptu, with little attention paid to the meaning of the treatment environment. Today there is a systematic formalizing of the office contacts with perhaps an obsessive overextension of the realm of technique into the personal relationship. Let us look at this a bit more.

In Breuer's time treatment was undertaken for hysterias just as for any condition with clear organic factors, and the treatment meant that the physician visited the patients at their residences. House calls were the usual practice in medicine. It was only when medical treatments became more effective, with the introduction of new equipment and instrumentation, that doctors began to see increasing numbers of patients in clinics or in their own offices, fixing special office hours on specific days. But only the more advanced therapeutic disciplines could boast of such instrumental discoveries. The therapeutic tools available to Breuer and his younger colleague, Freud, were at best episodic in their success, and more often ineffective: rest and various electric-current infusions, for example (Freud, 1898, p. 267). So house calls were the general rule, and if the physician received patients at his own home, it was to see those who could not afford the house call, or to see the agents of the rich—their butlers, maids, and secretaries who relayed to the doctor the symptoms of their affluent employers (cf. de Swaan, 1980).

Even after Freud opened his own office in 1886, he saw most of his patients, perhaps with the exception of Lucy R. and a very few others, in their own homes and apparently thought that this was of no significance for the treatment. The specimen dream of Irma's injection, analyzed at length in Chapter II of *The Interpretation of Dreams* (Freud, 1900), reveals that Irma attended a birthday party for Mrs. Freud. Such socialization of doctor and patient was not uncommon. The Wolf-Man had to check into a sanatorium as a condition for starting his treatment in 1910, since Freud had no time to see him except when he was visiting another patient at that sanatorium.

In the very beginning hardly any attention was paid to the personal meanings such visits may have had for the patients. But as analytic practice became more popular, the office visit replaced the house call and certain situational arrangements became standardized—the couch, the duration and frequency of the interviews, for example. And this standardization allowed the analyst to have more controlled awareness over the patient's responses to the analytic arrangements. It appears, however, that with this standarization, too many analysts have also shut off their general spontaneity in listening and in reflecting and replaced it with cool, often cold detachment. This has even occurred to the point that silence, which should be employed as a technique of listening, became an intervention.

Lipton (1977) has argued convincingly that the technique invented by Freud and used by him for over forty years distinguished the personal relationship between the patient and the analyst from the actual psychoanaltyic technique itself. This distinction permitted Freud to speak of these aspects of transference: a positive transference derived from repressed sexual impulses; the negative transference derived from both sexual and aggressive impulses; and the positive transference of affectionate, friendly feelings which are admissible to consciousness. Only the last requires no interpretative work or technical interventions or maneuvering; rather, the ordinary interactions that can be expected to occur between people are encompassed by this "unobjectionable element of the positive transference" (Lipton, 1977, p. 261).

Freud's offhand comments, his lending of money to some patients, his offering food to others, were not considered by him to be mere technical interventions. Nor were his comments about events and issues that were not specifically interpretative; these comments include remarks involving courtesy and civility and arrangements about the treatment such as absences, schedules, fees, and payments. It is crucial, however, to emphasize that the so-called unobjectionable positive transference can take on special meanings for the analysand, in which case it becomes an issue for clarification and interpretation.

I earlier stated that as the analytic technique became codified, the casual nature of the therapeutic interchange became more systematized into regular office visits at specific times. The interchange, however, was always in the nature of a conversation, a conversation that should continually deepen, in Gerald Aronson's felicitous phrase (personal communication). The codification—or rule-making—was necessary to help maintain a structure within which the transference could be observed.

Today many analysts have extended the concept of technique to cover all of the interchange that takes place between analyst and analysand, and in this process the conversational nature of the interaction has been lost. In that effort, the analyst's neutrality, that is, his or her technical stance that abets neither drive nor defense, has been replaced with aloofness and stiffness—a listening attitude with silence. Thus a distinction between technique and the personal relationship that arose in order to maintain a helpful detachment from emotional overinvolvement with the patient has become a vehicle that prevents the unfolding of a genuine and individual relationship appropriate to the task with each patient.

These, then, are some of the contradictions that I have observed within the development of psychoanalysis: a shifting of openness and control over the transference; a responsible medical involvement with some disciplines that embrace psychoanalytic considerations; a model of dysfunction and of education. Both the then and the now contain contradictions, and it is no easy task to work toward resolving them. It is a challenge that the first one hundred years have presented to us, and meeting it is not only an intellectual, scientific task. It is laden with economic, political, and territorial issues that threaten to over-shadow the scientific ones.

References

FREUD, A. *The Psycho-analytical treatment of children.* New York: International Universities Press, 1955.

FREUD, S. (1898). *Sexuality in the Etiology of the Neuroses.* Standard Edition, vol. III, pp. 261–285.

FREUD, S. (1900). *The Interpretation of Dreams.* Standard Edition, vol. IV.

FREUD, S. (1926). *The Question of Lay Analysis,* Standard Edition, vol. XX, pp. 179–258.

GILL, M. M. The analysis of the transference. *J. Amer. Psychoanal. Ass.* 27 (supplement):263–288, 1979.

HARTMANN, H., and LOEWENSTEIN, R. (1962). Notes on the superego In H. Hartmann, E. Kris, and R. Loewenstein, Papers on psychoanalytic psychology. *Psychological Issues,* monograph 14:144–181, 1964.

KLEIN, M. *The Psychoanalysis of Children.* London: Hogarth, 1932.

KOHUT, H. *The Restoration of the Self.* New York: International Universities Press, 1977.

LEVY, D. Psychosomatic studies of some aspects of maternal behavior. *Psychosom. Med.,* 4:223–227, 1942.

LIPTON, S. Clinical observations on resistance to the transference. *Int. J. Psycho-Anal.,* 58:463–472, 1977.

MENNINGER, K. *Theory of Psychoanalytic Technique.* New York: Basic Books, 1958.

SWAAN, A. DE. On the sociogenesis of the psychoanalytic situation. *Psychoanalysis and Contemporary Thought,* 3:381–413, 1980.

Reflections on Anna O.

James F. Masterson

I would like to discuss some reflections on rereading Breuer's case of Anna O. after all these years from the perspective of having learned some more myself about treatment and particularly about the treatment of borderline and narcissistic conditions. My first reaction was that the article was published in 1893, eleven years after the work was finished. I would hate to have to write a paper on something I had done eleven years ago, particularly to have to do it in such excruciating microscopic clinical detail. That seemed to me to be a virtuoso performance itself.

I was struck by the sheer drama of the patient lying there in bed paralyzed, squinting and unable to talk. I have not seen a patient in that condition since I saw psychotic patients as a hosptial resident. It is easy to see how, at that time, the idea that this condition could be relieved by talk seemed inconceivable and revolutionary.

The phenomena which Breuer and then Freud investigated were, when identified, not ambiguous or unclear or obscure. They were very obvious motor and sensory impairments. Similarly, the objects of their investigations—painful memories associated with affect—were not difficult to follow, once they had identified them. I think this aspect of the problem helped them enormously in the path of their investigations, which led eventually to the concept of the unconscious, free associations, dreams, resistance, etc.

A few comments about diagnosis. I don't know whether it was Victorian reticence about including personal detail or some other motivation that resulted in so little background information on Anna O. Except for the history of psychosis in the family, there were no data either on the personalities of the mother and the father or on Anna's early development or her relationship with them. I puzzled over this material for some time to try to make a diagnosis and finally gave up, feeling that there just was not enough evidence, at least to my way of thinking. For example, the impending death of her father was obviously the precipitating stress, but it was difficult to tell what level of father she felt she was losing. Was it an oedipal father, as we have been taught, or could it have been a preoedipal caretaking father? It is almost impossible to say.

Certainly Anna O. showed intense separation reactions in the treatment. Whenever Dr. Breuer was away, her symptomatology flared up; then it decreased on his return, and she would talk to no one else. At one point he was the only person she would let feed her. Certainly this could be seen as a borderline phenomenon, but the presence of separation reaction alone in the transference is not enough to make the diagnosis. I think I would have to conclude that without more past history, without more idea of early developmental relationships, it would be almost impossible to say.

I was struck by the way the article stressed how tough-minded, bright, and able Anna O. was. I kept wondering why they were stressing this until I read the last part of the study of hysteria, Freud's article on psychotherapy, where he brings out that at the time Janet and Charcot believed that hysteria was due to "mental weakness." So Freud stressed that the apparent mental weakness was due to the dissociative phenomenon itself. Such patients are not mentally weak at all, and therefore weakness is not a predisposing factor.

I suppose the reason this caught my eye was that even today in medicine in general and psychiatry and psychoanalysis in particular, when we get into difficult alleys and can't find our way, it is very common to reach back to constitutional theories of explanation. This approach is common today with the borderline patient. If we can't establish a reason for what is wrong, we resort to theories about constitutional weakness such as hysterics were supposed to have had.

The treatment record prompted a number of thoughts. Hypnosis discharged the painful affect associated with recent memories and, according to Breuer, relieved the patient of this psychic burden. The content of this discharge, in other words what the patient expressed, was her painful feeling states related to more or less recent events. They certainly did not have to do with the past and with early developmental relationships with her parents. Therefore, the underlying early conflicts that produced the problem in her character structure were never reached. One wonders how much this failure must have contributed to Anna O.'s continuing problem with men. It might also explain why Freud's first case, Emmie von N., continued to have repetitive hysterical episodes after the treatment.

Freud, deciding to give up hypnosis, gave three reasons: (1) many patients could not be hypnotized; (2) it was not getting to the underlying causes; and (3) he had difficulty himself hypnotizing patients. You wonder upon reading him if Freud didn't also have a personal distaste for hypnosis.

Freud said that although the cathartic method was abandoned, the cathartic principle remained, and I think it still remains at the nucleus of psychoanalysis in the working-through process. In other words, the process of making available to the perceiving ego painful affect for discharge and working through is as important now as it was then.

Today, in working with borderline and narcissistic patients, the therapist has to be acutely aware of the patient's efforts to induce the therapist to take over or to serve as a target for transference acting out of the patient's rage. In other words, the therapist has to be on constant guard to protect his therapeutic neutrality and objectivity. This perspective, i.e., the paramount importance of therapeutic neutrality, impelled me to be struck by some of the actions taken by Breuer and Freud. For example, it seemed to me that Breuer, by feeding his patient, medicating her, and spending long hours alone with her at night, fostered what I would call the transference acting out of Anna O.'s intensive, dependent relationship with her father. Freud, in the case of Emmie von N., mentions casually that he personally gave her whole-body massage twice a week. I don't know what whole-body massage is, but I can't imagine combining psychotherapy with body massage. The harmful implications for both transference and countertransference are enormous.

I wonder how much Anna O.'s improvement really was due to the catharsis of painful affect about losing her father and how much it was due to replacing the father she was losing with a fantasy transference father in Dr. Breuer.

As I was reading the case, I was struck by the way Breuer described her. I had the feeling that he was talking as much about his feelings about her as about her objectively as a patient. His countertransference reactions to her fantasy pregnancy and to her attraction to him, causing him to drop the case and run, reinforced by impression about his countertransference: that what he was worried about was not her feelings toward him, but the feelings in him stirred up by her feelings toward him; in other words, countertransference, not transference. I was also curious to read that he had evidently talked with his wife about Anna O. so much that his wife was resentful about his working with this patient.

Freud, talking about Emmie von N., described how he got impatient with the extraordinarily tedious unraveling of detail required to plumb the painful aspects of her experiences. He expressed his impatience by suggestions which in essence told her to "get on with it." Here he evidently learned his most important lesson, because he was sharp enough to observe that she was very annoyed by his interventions and waved them away, as if to say, "Stop it and let me do the work by myself." He never forgot this lesson, which is just as true today working with borderline and narcissistic patients as it was with Anna O. The patients have to do the work. They have to do it in their own time, according to their own condition, and they cannot be hurried by the therapist.

A phenomenal event occurred when Freud, unlike Breuer, whose countertransference drove him off his case, stood fast when the patient reported sexual attraction to him. He analyzed the projection rather than react to it.

The study of hysteria was the vehicle for and led the way to the discovery of the unconscious and psychoanalysis along with the crucial contributions of the oedipal stage to personality development. The study of the borderline and narcissistic disorders is leading the way to increased understanding of the contributions of the preoedipal stage to development and, particularly, to the capacities for intimacy, creativity, and independence.

I'd like to conclude by drawing a contrast between the investigations of hysteria and those of the borderline. The phenomenology under investigation in hysteria was paralysis and various other kinds of often neurological impairments. With the borderline patient particularly, we are mostly dealing not with phenomena of that sort but with subjective symptoms like anxiety and depression and more often behaviors which are destructive to the person's best interest.

The vehicle for the study of hysteria was hypnosis. I think the vehicle for the study of borderline has to do with proper use of confrontation to establish a therapeutic alliance which then allows a working through of the problem.

The psychopathology that emerged from hypnosis of the hysteric was painful memories associated more or less with recent events. The psychopathology that emerged from confrontation of the borderline was an abandonment depression that went far beyond recent events to memories of childhood separation experiences.

The hysteric worked through the discharge of the painful affects, and the symptoms disappeared. The borderline patient in analytic treatment works through the abandonment depression associated with all the past separation experiences and the basic underlying conflict with the mother. The treatment of hysteria with the cathartic hypnotic method produced symptomatic improvement, but the character remained the same. Successful treatment of the borderline patient results in the discharge of the abandonment depression, the overcoming of developmental arrest, and profound change in character, as illustrated in the following case:

A young man in his early twenties presented with clinical symptomatology of a severe depression, passivity, and inhibition of aggression, particularly as it applied to learning, and more specifically as it applied to a strong talent he possessed: playing the piano. The same inhibition would occur when he tried to activate himself to understand his conflicts. He would become angry and depressed and inhibit the act of learning. In his self- and object representations, in the transference as derived from his early development, he seemed to have only two options, to play either the role of master or that of slave. In his early development he experienced his parents as concentration-camp guards, with himself as the victim of their persecution. He came to identify his victim status with persecution of the Jews in the Holocaust.

Early in treatment, as he began to become more aggressive and self-assertive and his true talent emerged, there seemed to be only one option for him. He either was the victim and his parents the guards, or he became the guard by trying to assert himself, which, however, made his parents the victims. As all of this unraveled, his inhibition while practicing the piano diminished, and be became quite proficient. He became a star student of a top instructor of the New York Philharmonic Orchestra and concomitantly developed an intense interest in the Jewish religion. He studied the religion and began to wear a yarmulke. As these two themes came together, he was ready to make his debut. He made a condensed statement about his debut that had a lot of meaning to him and to me. He looked me in the eye and said, "The Nazis had their day, and now we'll see." He went on to tell me that when he performed, he was going to wear his yarmulke. We didn't discuss it further, but it seemed to me that what he was demonstrating was that he had shifted his identity from being a Jewish victim to being of Jewish background in terms not of being a victim of persecution but of the rich Jewish religious, historical tradition.

Analytic Biography of Anna O.

5

Walter A. Stewart

On each reading of Breuer's case report of Fräulein Anna O., I am struck by how much she still remains a mystery. The diagnosis is unclear; Breuer's treatment was erratic and the results disappointing. The prognosis at one time was considered zero.

After the treatment with Breuer we know nothing of her life for some years. She virtually disappeared. Then began the long and fruitful work for which she is well known, recently documented in the book *The Story of Anna O.* by Lucy Freeman (1972). It is impossible to discuss the case without reference to Miss Freeman's valuable and scholarly work, and I have drawn on it freely. In spite of her documentation, and papers by George Pollock and others, we are still missing the essential information which would give us insight into the central conflicts of the psychoneurotic illness, undoubtedly because Breuer treated Bertha Pappenheim before the fundamental discoveries which led to psycho-analysis as we understand it today.

At that time scientific theory appropriate to the understanding of human behavior was not yet formulated. In the popular view the cause of psychoneu-rosis was a single traumatic experience whose recall to consciousness resulted in a cure. I think of Moss Hart's play *Lady in the Dark* and Hitchcock's film *Spellbound.*

Freud, even at this early date, had a more sophisticated view of the cause of neurosis. He wrote to Dr. Karl Müller-Braunschweig that the sight of the little boy urinating was not the cause of the little girl's penis envy, but the trigger. Thus he allowed in his concepts for the important role of disposition and the effect on development of earlier experiences.

Four other more immediately important discoveries were as yet also unknown. These were the discovery of infantile sexuality, that of the uncon-scious and the laws governing its functions, that of the development of the ego, and the recognition and analysis of the transference. Only now are we begin-ning to integrate these momentous discoveries into a coherent clinical theory.

Breuer was limited in his understanding of the origins of his patient's hysterical symptoms. Fortunately, his treatment led to the disappearance of her symptoms. He had no way of knowing that the memories uncovered from the analysis of the symptoms were screen memories. Like the manifest content of a dream, these memories should have been the beginning of analytic insight, not the end point.

Currently our investigation of the patient's experiences would of course go far beyond this form of treatment. As we study the life history of a patient, our goal is to construct an analytic biography. This biography focuses on childhood experiences which are likely to have a high probability for the creation of conflict—for example, sibling rivalry, primal scene experiences, operations on the body. What is implied is the central importance of a developmental view. This approach dictates the questions we ask and provides us with a knowledge of the childhood experiences that formed character and created the infantile neurosis.

Since we are ignorant of this essential information in the case of Anna O., it will forever be an unresolvable mystery. But in spite of our ignorance and in face of the dangers of speculation, I should like to risk a few comments about the possible dynamics of the case.

During the five months that she sat with her ill father in his sick room, the months Breuer termed the "incubation" period, experiences occurred which precipitated the adult neurosis. At the age of 21, she was exposed to events that were certain to arouse the conflicts of her childhood. Her father was dying. She was with him during the night while her mother was sleeping alone elsewhere.

Partly in response to the sexual nature of this arrangement, she resented these nightly duties. They meant she could not go out to parties and dances, and during the day she was too tired to go out. She was angry with her brother, who caught her eavesdropping at her father's door, scolded her, and shook her.

I should like to examine her adult life, which is well documented, and from this construct some of the infantile conflicts. This should then lead us to the understanding of her illness as reported by Breuer.

The most revealing comments on her character are contained in the polemical message expressed in her play, *Women's Rights*. The first act is set in an attic, the home of an impoverished woman and her 5-year-old child. An illegal meeting to organize the women workers is being held. The police have been informed, they break in, and the impoverished lady goes off to jail. In Act II a wife asks her lawyer husband whether she may give a small sum of money of her own to a needy woman she has met. He says no, and she leaves. A young man, who is a braggart, enters. He too wants to borrow money. He boasts of his conquests of women. He is told to leave.

In Act III the lawyer and his wife are on the way to visit the needy woman. The young man of Act II, who has just raped a young woman, passes them on the staircase. They enter an attic apartment, and, as one might guess, the needy woman is no other than the impoverished woman of the first act. Even more of a coincidence, she is the former mistress of the lawyer husband, who impregnated her and then abandoned her, presumably about six years earlier.

His wife is shocked, but decides not to leave him, because of the children. She announces she will refuse him sexual relations, which are her *Women's Rights.*

The meaning of the play is clear. Younger men are rapists; older men impregnate and abandon defenseless women. Being victimized allows the women to refuse sexual relations.

This is the dramatic statement of Bertha Pappenheim's lifelong resentment of the different ways in which men and women are treated. She felt, quite correctly, that women were discriminated against and not taken seriously. They were deprived of education, professional lives, and the respect they deserved.

Aside from the play, her other writings make it clear again and again that she feels being a woman means being victimized. She wrote, ''The girls are the ones who get hurt, the boys are the ones who derive pleasure.'' She also wrote, in 1922, ''If there will be justice in the world to come, women will be lawgivers, and men have to have babies'' (Freeman, 1972, p. 236). The implication is that women will be educated professionals and will also dictate to men—that is, they will ''lay down the law.''

This material drawn from her adult life helps in the reconstruction of the formative experiences of her childhood. It is not too great a leap of the imagination to see Bertha Pappenheim's resentment of the feminine role as originating in her relationship to her brother Wilhelm, with whom she fought constantly. The later conflict centered on the fact that he was provided with an education and a profession. In childhood he seemed constantly more favored than she. He got the mother's attention and care and, since he was the first and only boy, possibly the father's as well.

The metaphoric, primitive recording of early childhood would equate these experiences of his being favored with his getting the mother's breast and his having a penis. The important point is that Bertha was unable to come to terms with her feelings of envy and anger that her brother was favored—and with her anger at her mother and father for favoring him.

This is a typical constellation that often leads to a repudiation of feminity, expressed in the famous, or infamous, penis-envy complex. Bertha Pappenheim's illness and her later career, however, do not reflect a typical penis-envy solution to her repudiation of feminity. There was no behavior which was an imitation or caricature of the masculine role.

The focal conflict in her illness took a different form. She specifically resented the *sexual act,* seeing it as an aggressive act, a rape, and a humiliating surrender to the enemy. She felt that pregnancy would surely lead to desertion and the lonely and dangerous pains of childbirth. (The girls are the ones who get hurt.) Her resentment of the sexual act and the vulnerability she associated with pregnancy led to the asexual attitude, as described by Breuer.

Yet, paradoxically, Bertha Pappenheim wanted children. She wrote a prayer after visiting her mother's grave: "And I, childless, wish for myself, small memorial stones placed on the rim of the red stone. . . . " (Freeman, 1972, p. 256).

What is astounding about Bertha Pappenheim is her success in resolving the seemingly unresolvable conflicts of her life. In her care for orphans and prostitutes she achieved the longed-for role of motherhood. She became the educator and protector of countless young and needy women. Her strong and irrational resentment of the sexual act found the ideal outlet. She rescued prostitutes from the humiliation and degradation of paid-for sexual submission. We know she was poetic and imaginative; she was also energetic, and persistent to the point of obstinacy. Her anger was handled by reaction formation, producing a need to protect and to rescue. This is mentioned in Breuer's report and amply confirmed in her later years.

However, in her illness at age 21, the defense of reaction formation proved inadequate. As a next line of defense she developed a double personality. In the normal state, she was oriented but depressed and anxious. In the *condition seconde,* she was abusive, rebellious, moody, and naughty. The split in personality was an attempt to isolate the angry aspect of her character. Yet even in the normal state she felt angry at having to sit up at night with her father. She surely noticed that no one expected her brother to sacrifice himself in this way.

Most of her symptoms occurred when some incident aroused her anger or threatened to fulfill her destructive wishes: such incidents include her father's choking, her brother's shaking her, her anger when she felt unfairly accused, and her refusal to speak because she felt Breuer had in some way mistreated her. Many of the symptoms served to control or deny the anger.

I should like to comment briefly on the fantasies which she constructed during the day and which in the evening had to be verbalized to Breuer before she could rest. At first these fantasies had a Hans Christian Andersen quality and usually involved a little girl sitting at the bedside of her sick father. As the treatment progressed, the fantasies became less innocent; they were more tormenting, more frightening, and involved hallucinations of horrifying images.

The fantasies are derivatives of childhood masturbatory fantasies not unlike those described by Freud in the *International Journal of Psychoanalysis* (Vol. 4, p. 89; reprinted in Freud, 1936). The disturbing fantasies represented Bertha's bad, angry self with which, in her illness, she was trying to cope. This would explain why she could not be interrupted in her slow, painful retelling of the experiences which stimulated fantasies and symptoms. Further support for the fact that the fantasies were masturbatory in origin is that in later life she never kissed and seldom touched an adult, male or female. She felt that reading was a self-indulgence and a waste of time—in spite of the fact that at 21 she was a chronic daydreamer.

We are left with a great deal to discuss. Why did the patient relive the previous year in absolute detail? Was this part of a working through of her conflicts? Did it have an anniversary function, and if so, was it a mourning process, as suggested by George Pollock in his writings? How did the conversion symptom remove affect and content from consciousness? Why does the bringing to consciousness of the meaning of the symptom first intensify it and then lead to its disappearance?

Most intriguing is the question of the pseudocyesis with which the treatment ended. Did it signify a breakthrough in which the patient was finally able to accept the feminine role involving impregnation and childbirth? Or did it represent a virgin birth, with all its ramifications? Did it express the condition on which she could separate from Breuer—that is, only if she could keep what might be called a memento of the relationship? Finally, was it the enactment of what she most feared— that a man would seduce, impregnate, and abandon her, like the impoverished woman in her play?

These are the questions into which we would inquire if she were in treatment today. We now have a more sophisticated scientific view of the determinants which motivate behavior. Our clinical approach derives from a developmental view. The personal history therefore takes the form of an analytic biography. The focus is on the experiences in childhood that have led to a failure in the optimal resolution of the ubiquitous childhood conflicts.

This book invites us to look back one hundred years to the very beginning or even the preorigins of psychoanalysis. We find ourselves in the desirable and honorable predicament of still having more questions than we have answers.

References

FREEMAN, L. *The Story of Anna O.* New York: Walker & Co., 1972.

FREUD, A. *Writings of Anna Freud,* rev. ed., vol. II. New York: International Universities press, 1936.

FREUD, A. *Writings of Anna Freud,* vol. IV. New York: International Universities Press, 1945, 1949, 1954.

The Case
of Anna O.:
Cultural Aspects

John P. Spiegel

Although I have been a student of American subcultures for many years and have interested myself in Irish-Americans, Italian-Americans, Greek-Americans, and Spanish-Americans, among others, from the point of view of both research and training I had done no study of the Vienna of the 1880s and 1890s, and had not read the case of Anna O. for thirty years. Fortunately, there exists on the campus of Brandeis University the library of the American Jewish Historical Society—located just a few hundred yards from my office. From the materials there, I selected three books concerned with the culture of the time, upon which most of this material is based. These were:

Vienna, by Max Gruenwald (1936), which contains very good reviews of impressions of historians who lived in Vienna. It is, in addition, an excellent history of Viennese Jews from the eighteenth century to the present in Austria in general and in Vienna in particular.

The Adventures of a Bystander, by Paul Drucker (1979). Some readers may know that Paul Drucker is an economist and a consultant for business organizations but may not realize that he was born and brought up in Vienna. His book is a sort of autobiography, in the course of which he tells about his childhood in Vienna and his family's relationship with the Freud family, which was very close. There is some anecdotal material here which, although perhaps not entirely believable, is nevertheless interesting.

Third, a book by Frederic Grunfeld entitled *Prophets Without Honor* (1979), which discusses certain figures in Germany and in Austria like Freud, Mahler, and several literary figures. From the title one assumes these people were not considered prophets in their own countries and were not honored, but the author tends to present them in a new way. There is much interesting material about Freud and about the Vienna of his day in this book.

Much of what I have written here is factual, based on the material in Grunfeld's work, but I am going to go beyond his material and speculate on the reasons for the absence of family material and family and cultural data in all of

Freud's early case histories, particulary the studies of hysteria. My first question would be why isn't more family material included?

Second, what of the sociocultural, political, and economic factors in the Viennese Jewish society of the 1880s and 1890s that are pertinent both to the Anna O. case and to some of the other cases Freud discussed, and to the situation of psychoanalysis generally at that time?

Third, what was the impact of this particular Jewish culture on the Jewish daughters? As a part of my speculations I have invented something I am going to call the Viennese Jewish Princess syndrome.

Fourth, what were the general sources of anti-Semitism in Austria and Vienna in the nineteenth century? Because, as we all know, Freud articulated his thoughts about the anti-Semitic atmosphere of the city at that time.

Fifth, how does on go about comparing the manifestations of anti-Semitism in the societies of then and now, and what are the differences?

Now back to my first point about the absence of case history data. With respect to family data, there is a great deal of variation in Freud's case histories. In the case of Anna O. practially nothing was included that told us anything about the nuclear family. In the close-knit Jewish community of Vienna of that time it would have been impossible to avoid identifying the patient and her family if such data had been included. When one looks at the case histories, one tends to see more family data when Freud is dealing specifically with an infantile neurosis, because he has to discuss both the parents and the children in such instances.

In the case history of "the Rat Man" there is, as usual, very little family data. However, here Freud was dealing with an infantile neurosis and was therefore forced to talk some about the nurses, the mother, the father, and the way the family was involved. My impression, as far as family data are concerned, is that Freud included such material only when he had to in discussing infantile neuroses, or when the actual everyday incident which led up to the illness was such that the parents and the parents' friends had to be included.

One of the impressions I formed from my reading—and this is probably generally known—is that most of Freud's patients were Jewish. In fact, most of his patients came from a Jewish community in which almost everybody knew everybody else. Furthermore, he said at one point that (especially in his early period) he took only the toughest cases—the most severe cases—which meant that they had seen many other doctors before they came to him. Thus he was particularly careful about the publication of identifying material and went beyond the normal concern for preservation of confidentiality which all doctors follow. He had specific concerns that if he put too much information into his case histories, some of those other doctors might recognize their former patients. And since they were a very gossipy medical community, there was an extra reason for trying to protect the patients by leaving out data. Ernest Jones tells us, for example, that Anna O. was friendly with Freud's wife, Martha, and that they saw a lot of each other. To Freud it was almost like publishing case histories of members of his own family, or at least of his own social circle. This feeling was even more evident in the case of Dora, because Freud had originally see Dora's father and treated him for syphilis, and had then gone on to meet him socially at parties and within the community.

Next, concerning the absence of cultural data, it seems that Freud introduced and used cultural data in his case histories for only two reasons. One was that the information might prove helpful. This is what he did in the case of Katharina, one of the cases in *Studies on Hysteria.* The reader may recall that Katharina was a peasant girl whom Freud had met while on a summer vacation in the Swiss Alps. He had taken a walk in the mountains and happened across her. She acknowledged that she knew who he was—that she had seen his name on the guest list of th inn where he was staying. She began to tell him the story of her hysteria, her symptoms, and of the associated scenes of sexual seduction by her uncle. In a couple of hours' conversation Freud cured her—surely the briefest analysis in history. At any rate, in the course of writing up the case, he makes the following statement: "I owe a debt of gratitude for having had Katharina for a patient; for making it so much easier for me to talk to her than to the prudish ladies of my city practice who regard whatever is natural as shameful." The prudish nature of upper-class Viennese society is quite evident and is know to all of us. Freud is acknowledging that if there is a cultural difference that decreases resistance to discussing sexual material, it's a help to the progress of the treatment.

However, in some instances the cultural difference can prove to be an obstacle rather than a help. This was evidenced in *The Case of the Wolf Man,* originally published in Germany in 1918. In 1923 Freud added the following footnote, which is the only comment on culture of this nature that I know of. He said, "A national character which is foreign to one's own made the task of feeling one's way into the mind—into his mind—a laborious one." This was the first time the term "national character" was used in a psychological publication. But at the end of this footnote Freud made another little comment. He added, "It will have been easy to guess from my account that the patient was a Russian." Now that's a wry way of putting it from our contemporary point of view! Because he's not saying, "It's an important datum, you know, I should have told you about it in the first place." He's just saying, "Looking this case over, and after the war with Russia [this was after the First World War], it's become evident to me that I wasn't sufficiently able to conceal the national identity of the patient. It is not an important fact that he was Russian." It's in that incidental fashion that Freud includes what we would now report as an important datum in understanding the case. Thus, the second reason for including such data was when the exact cultural identity of the patient could no longer be concealed.

My second reason concerns the sociocultural, political, and economic factors in Viennese Jewish circles of the time. It is important to recognize the difference in the status of Jews in Austria-Hungary after the liberal constitution of 1867. Before 1867 Jews had no rights at all. They could not own property, which made them essentially tenants. Following the establishment of the liberal constitution of 1867, they were given the same civil rights as other citizens, including the right to own property. A very liberal democratic government was established, and under the new cultural and economic conditions the Jews flourished. They also developed a model—"Get rich." This liberal democratic state allowed the Jewish families, accustomed as they were to dealing with mercantile things, to become wealthy. They not only became wealthy but attained positions of great power. They attained positions in the government—they became ministers of state. They rapidly went into the professions—they became lawyers, doctors, teachers. There were Jewish members of the Supreme Court. All of this was encouraged by the Hapsburg monarchy, because the monarchy appreciated the tremendous contribution that the now rich Jews made to the cultural life of Vienna—to the arts, the sciences, and so forth—in the traditional Jewish fashion of participating and giving.

But, another development occurred in the social life of the Jews of that time: their identification with German culture. Remember, this was Vienna, not Germany. Although in Germany one would expect the Jews to identify with German culture, in the culturally diverse Austro-Hungarian Empire there were many choices. They could have identified with the Slavs, with the Poles, with the Czechs, or with the Croatians, but they identified with the Germans. They identified to such an extent that many of them converted to Christianity, and even many who didn't convert lost touch with their Jewishness. Many Gentile men married Jewish women. Some Jews accepted titles of nobility. The assimilation was tremendous.

It was, however, assimilation into German culture, and that meant loss of Jewishness, and to some extent it also meant loss of an appropriate realistic concern about anti-Semitism. So interested where these Viennese Jews in their identification with things German and so concerned were they not to be Jewish, that when anti-Semitism did begin to become evident, which was about 1875 (about five years before the commencement of the Dora case), their response to it was not quite surprising. Their attitude was as if to say, "We don't need to pay any attention to any anti-Semitism. It's contemptible. We'll just ignore it. We'll pretend it doesn't exist." Even beyond the denial of the growing anti-Semitism, Jews feared that if they protested too much, they would simply call attention to themselves as Jews and therefore they must keep silent. This avoidance of protest was quite damaging. On one occasion, for example, a rabbi, Dr. Bloch, who was a brilliant commentator of the 1880s, made a strong defense against anti-Semitism on behalf of the Jews and won a great law case which legally stopped some of the anti-Semitic activities that were going on. When Dr. Bloch achieved that kind of fame, the Jews would not support him. They renounced him. They adopted a similar attitude of hostility toward Theodore Herzl. One must remember that the concept of Jewish Zionism was first proposed in 1895, by Theodore Herzl, who was a Viennese Jew. When he published *Der Judenstat,* none of the Jewish community supported him.

Finally, from descriptions of Anna O.'s home one can tell that these Jews were extremely wealthy and that they displayed what we would now call "conspicuous consumption." They imported valuable art objects into their homes. They were obviously very interested in showing that they not only had money but were spending their money in a culturally approved fashion.

Let us now consider the impact of all this on the family life style, and the set of roles which tended to develop in Jewish families in this wealthy class. One of the things being wealthy meant was that the family had many servants. In fact, one of the witticisms of the day was that, according to the wealthy Jew, to be of the lower class meant to have only two servants. Otherwise one had many servants. The family women didn't enter the kitchen because the cook prevented them. If a housewife went into the kitchen, it was interpreted as meaning that the cook wasn't trusted. The men did no work in their homes. Sometimes they even had servants to follow them down the street carrying whatever needed to be carried. Such was the state of affluence and elegance in the Jewish home.

These conditions, combined with those inherent in the Jewish tradition, made the second-class status of the woman very severe. Women sat in the balcony in the synagogue; they were allowed no participation. If they were to be powerful, they had to rule from behind the throne. It was the man who was important, and women were permitted no careers. Paul Drucker makes a comment about his grandmother, who was a very gifted pianist. She had at one point played for Johannes Brahms, who was very impressed with her ability, but her family did not allow her to have a professional career. The most she could do was to give concerts for charity performances. That was considered permissible, since she wasn't being paid.

Thus women were oppressed and kept subservient. They were not allowed to have a university education. The separation of Anna O. from her mother would have been extremely difficult, because mothers supported their daughters in the service of their fathers, and this is how we come to the Viennese Jewish Princess syndrome. Gifted daughters like Dora and Anna were not allowed to express themselves. There was no such thing as individualism. They could not take advantage of the opportunities available to their brothers for an education and a career. They were, we could even say exploited by their fathers on behalf of conspicuous consumption, dressed in fancy clothes in order to show off the affluence of their fathers. A somewhat similar thing has occurred in modern American-Jewish life, with its own Jewish Princess syndrome, but in Vienna the exploitation had a deeper basis. The father was supported by the mother in a sort of sexual ambience—the mother could identify with the daughter's sexuality. In Anna O.'s household there were plenty of servants and plenty of nurses. The mother would not have needed to stay with the sick father all day, as she did, nor would Anna have needed to care for the father all night, as she did. This was the kind of exploitation to which many daughters of the Jewish families were exposed.

One must also consider the culture shock that young Jewish girls were exposed to when they got into the social world of Vienna. Remember that this was ''wicked Vienna''—the Vienna of the Strauss waltzes, the Vienna of the rather loose sexual arrangements that Arthur Schnitzler wrote about in his play *La Ronde*. Imagine the culture shock undergone by Jewish girls who had been kept in an inferior position and under the tight control of their parents, and who had no sexual education and permission even to talk about sex when they were introduced into the gay social life of Vienna. Exposed to this extremely permissive sexual atmosphere, how did they handle it? A wonderful scene occurs in the Anna O. case. She develops a nervous cough while she is sitting by her father's bedside listening to the sound of dance music next door, longing to be there. Certainly she would also have had a conflict about being with her father. But we may infer that the sexual suppression and anxiety of the women of that era had to do not only with closeness to the father (encouraged by the mother) and exploitation by the father, but also with the culture shock of being exposed to that carefree, romantic, sexually competitive life of the Vienna of the time.

Essentially Anna O. was a victim of the Viennese Jewish Princess syndrome. Without going into clinical detail, we can assume that such victimization would have generated anger and rage on the part of the daughters toward the fathers, and probably toward the mothers also, with no permission to express it. A well-brought-up (i.e., submissive) daughter was not allowed to express criticism and anger toward a parent directly. So what would have happened to that aggression? In Anna O.'s case, as we know, anger was associated with many of her hysterical syndromes. She made suicide attempts that Freud does not highlight in his clinical report. Only as a casual note in passing does Freud mention that Anna attempted suicide. Certainly that was the most florid indication of the amount of rage she had stored up.

Given the cultural victimization she had suffered, it should come as no surprise that when Anna O. finally managed to recover from her illness, she expressed her anger in terms of a social protest. She became one of the first examples of feminine protest that we have in the Western world. Here was a woman who expressed her anger through social action and institutionalized it, setting up an orphanage, taking care of children (she had no children of her own), acting the way good parents should act toward victimized children. Also, she rescued women who had been victimized by men and carried out an extensive campaign against the victimization of women by men. Where did she get the courage to do all this? She was not particularly gifted in intelligence or appearance. But in her adult years, and even old age, it appears that she had changed from a Viennese Jewish Princess into a Career Queen. She carried herself in a very queenly manner, with a commanding presence. She had managed to find the courage to institute this kind of novel feminist protest on the basis of the experiences she had had.

As a final point, let me discuss the anti-Semitism that Freud and psychoanalysis generally were exposed to. It is well known that this anti-Semitism did not come from the Gentiles, but rather from the Jewish community—particularly the doctors in the Jewish community. Because the criticism of Freud and psychoanalysis as a method came from the Jewish doctors, it is essential that we take note of several components of that criticism. One was that Freud charged for his services. The members of the Jewish medical community feared that this would foster the impression of Jews as avaricious. Their response to this charge was to engage in much charity work and see many patients free of charge. It was simply not done to charge for every patient, so Freud was perceived as violating the code of Jewish medical practice by making medicine a trade, commercializing it, while at the same time shaming the other doctors for all the money they were making.

A second component of the medical community's criticism was introduced from a scientific standpoint. Such criticism of psychoanalysis still takes place today. It began in Vienna, because the Viennese doctors were positive philosophers dedicated to scientific objectivity, and felt that Freud used the same explanation for every kind of neurotic illness. The unconscious was always there, there was always a castration complex or an Oedipus complex—whatever the illness the explanation was always the same. And since they were living in a scientific era in which every disease had its own explanation, how could this notion of Freud's be true? It was regarded as no more than an invention.

Third, they were very critical of Freud's mode of expression—of the romantic aspect of the case histories, which read like novels. This was not considered scientific. In addition, Freud was interested in literary people and wrote articles about Leonardo and others. The whole thing was terribly unscientific. Paul Drucker comments that Freud's complaint that psychoanalysis was neglected in the Vienna of his time was not true. It was not neglected. It was highly attended to—talked about, listened to—but in a critical fashion. He was a prophet not only without honor but with dishonor in his own time. Psychoanalysis was seen as something that dishonored the medical profession in Vienna, and because of that the Jewish doctors, in particular, were interested and active in opposing it. They felt it was discrediting them and adding to the anti-Semitism of which they were secretly so afraid. So it is to Freud's credit (and also to the credit of Schnitzler and a few others who handled anti-Semitism in a dignified fashion) that he recognized the need to combat anti-Semitism.

References

DRUCKER, PAUL. *The Aventures of a Bystander.* New York: Harper & Row, 1979.
GRUENWALD, MAX. *Vienna.* Philadelphia: Jewish Publication Society, 1936.
GRUNFELD, FREDERIC V. *Prophets Without Honor.* New York: Holt, Rinehart & Winston, 1979.

Anna O.
As Seen by a
Child Psychiatrist

7

Joseph D. Noshpitz

There are clearly some striking differences between the Viennese culture in which Anna O. was raised and our present culture. A very important difference is found in the nature and quality of relationships among and within families. Thus, in Anna O.'s family—despite their obvious wealth—both mother and daughter cared for the bedridden father. It is clear they could have afforded a live-in nurse to sit by his bedside. The father in turn was a genuinely philanthropic person who had done much for people in the community. Moreover, the doctor who cared for the father visited him twice a day. Indeed, one has the sense of an intense quality of giving and caring among these people; everyone was deeply concerned about everyone else, and they went to great lengths to help one another.

This caring attitude seemed to extend into the professional realm. It was from this matrix that psychoanalysis came forth with that most extraordinary habit of seeing patients—originally—six times a week.

There is a very different quality to the relationship patterns within which we live and work, a style which varies widely from those which apparently prevailed in nineteenth-century Vienna. For example, analysts rarely see their patients six times a week. More often they see them four or at most five times, and seldom for more than 45 minutes. In regard to family and community relationships, current statistics point to the disintegration of many of these connections: high divorce rate, broken families, suicide among the young, etc. As for those good Viennese burghers, with all their neuroses and their numerous problems, the quality of their involvement with one another, of caring for and giving to one another, is quite striking. It is not at all suprising that years later, as part of her recovery, Anna O. developed a life pattern of giving and caring.

Because of this contrast in cultures, it is difficult to be as accurate as one would like in exploring how one would treat Anna O. Within the obvious limitations, I will consider the case of Anna O. from the viewpoint of the child psychiatrist. In so doing, I will offer a sense of how this discipline operates and will describe how I imagine it would approach the management of the case of

Anna O. To be sure, as is true with all branches of medicine, there is a great deal of room for the vagaries of individual style and personal predilection; all in all, however, I believe there are certain overarching principles at work in the way any child psychiatrist would approach a given case. For the moment, let us consider the nature of child psychiatry itself.

Child psychiatry derives from a basic science which provides it with its fundamental theoretical infrastructure. From this foundation stem a number of applied sciences, which are in turn translated into a set of techniques, the actual empirical methodology of the field.

The basic science of child psychiatry is child development. This body of knowledge is extraordinarily complex and involves psychosexual development in the classic sense; separation-individuation theory according to Margaret Mahler; the stages of psychosocial elaboration as constructed by Erikson; ethological attachment concepts like those of Bowlby and Harlow; cognitive development in the sense of Piaget and other writers; neurological unfolding in terms of reflex, coordination, and response pattern as the developmental neurologists are beginning to report it; the studies of perception, motor patterns, lateralization issues, and sensory integration as the neuroscientists are starting to recount them; the interactive sequences between mother-infant pairs and within families that a host of infant researchers are busy describing; endocrine development; electroencephalographic development; and so on and on. In short, there are a great many different dimensions of growth which come under the category of child development. Together these constitute a canon of basic information about what a child is at any given moment during his/her personal sequence of growing up.

This foundation serves as the touchstone for the child psychiatrist. When asked a question concerning management of the child or family, he turns instinctively to his developmental map to check the information or the problem against the basic schema. From this primary science of development flow the several applied sciences of child psychiatry.

These include diagnosis, psychodynamics, therapeutics, prevention, and consultation. Thus when the child psychiatrist sets himself to the task of diagnostic assessment, he is really engaging in an evaluation of his patient's development. Given a child of such and such an age, sex, and socioeconomic status, what should he/she look like? Immediate reference to the coordinates on the scale provides a flood of data for comparison with what is known about the actual child. Without further ado one is aware of deviations in terms of lag, or precocity, that literally shout out at the observer. Thus diagnostic thinking really reduces to a record of disturbances of development; in fact, every syndrome can be translated into such terms—and indeed should be.

Again, the science of therapeutics is largely one of trying where possible to restore to a child the freedom to continue deveopment, to help him compensate for areas where he cannot develop because of organic impediment or insuperable fixations, and to change his environment or to create new environments, so that, especially in the face of the more serious deficits, he can function optimally and continue to grow as much as possible.

In one sense, the developmental framework gives rise to a pragmatic eclecticism within an overarching framework of dynamic theory. By and large the child psychiatrist looks to the child to tell him about the character structures, the strengths and talents, the areas of real or potential difficulty, the communication channels or modes of expression, and the primary symptoms that together will contribute to determining the character of the treatment plan. He looks to the family to discern some of the vectors that press on that child—the communication patterns, the cultural styles, the models, the superimposed roles, the parental relivings, all the many elements that flow from intrafamilial trends, the genetic history, the character of paranatal events, the nutritional history, growth patterns, the medical history, accidents, surgery, hospitalizations, seizures, learning difficulties, speech problems, coordination disturbances and the like. And he pays especially close attention to the development of personality, cognitively, affectively, interpersonally, through each of the stages of psychosexual development. In particular, he ponders possible traumatic elements, patterns of attachment and loss, hints and evidences of deprivation, or accounts that suggest overstimulation.

Given this framework, the therapist approaches the matter of treatment from the perspective of what blend of therapeutic and diagnostic modalities to employ. His treatment is almost invariably multileveled.

In Anna's case, he would give particular heed to her early interactions with her father in terms of strong affinities. Was she very much a "daddy's girl" as a child? Were there any early traumatic events which might have involved exposure to overstimulation—for example, bathing with father, spending a good deal of time in the parental bed, or seduction by some member of the household, such as a relative or a servant? Would the informants describe any early suggestions of neurotic tendencies, such as unusual fears, separation difficulties, compulsions, intense clinging behaviors, rituals of various sorts, or other evidences of great tension? Were there any health care issues in her early years in which she was involved, either as patient or caretaker or caretaker's helper? What was her subsequent development like? Did she have friends as a grade school child; did she develop any interest in boys as she grew older? What was her engagement with puberty like, and how well did she handle the assumption of feminine identity? Such issues would be explored carefully, tactfully, but in depth, in order to clarify the nature of the factors making for her vulnerability. These items are not intrinsically different from what the child psychiatrist explores in any case. No adequate therapeutic program can emerge unless it is based on a thorough exploration of the patient's history and current functioning.

Let us begin our study of Anna O. from such a perspective. First we must consider the level of development with which we are dealing, and then take the clinical data available and see how our patient fits into that schema.

At the onset of her illness, the patient was 21 years old, which would put her in the young adult developmental age range. As with every stage, there are general personality configurations which accompany each particular developmental level. We can assume that Anna O.'s endocrine level and her biological development were well past the pubertal and reasonably stable. A hundred years ago the onset of menarche would have occurred a good deal later on the average than it does today; nonetheless, by age 21 we could expect the endocrine perturbations of the time to have settled down. On a psychological level, puberty is usually accompanied by a recrudescence of oedipal fantasies; ordinarily, this would have initiated a process of distancing from the parents and the search for new love objects outside the family.

The biological changes of this pubertal epoch are basic and pervasive. There are obvious transformations associated with the appearance of the secondary sexual characteristics (the primary ones allow the doctor who delivers the baby to say "It's a boy" or "It's a girl"). They include the growth of breasts, the appearance of pubic and body hair, the onset of menstruation, growth in height, a redistribution of subcutaneous fat so that the girl's body becomes rounded and "feminine," widening of the pelvis, a sharpening and specifying of facial contours, and the achievement of the capacity for orgasm. Of equal importance are the accompanying emotional developments. There is a massive upwelling of instinct, a great upthrusting of yearnings from the biological matrix, a set of fantasies and needs, wishes and impulses, urges and desires, all of which come to hammer on the gates of consciousness and produce many forms of personality stress.

There are some less obvious characteristics such as the onset of ovulation with accompanying fertility, major changes in patterns of endocrine secretion, and, as important as any, some crucial advances in brain function.

Thus there are pronounced cognitive developments that come with puberty. The youngster enters the stage of what Piaget calls "formal operations," a capacity to think abstractly and to reason logically on a new level. There is an emergence of a new ability to generalize, to manage symbols and concepts in a novel fashion, to work with ideas and to love or hate ideas. Intellectually the youngster seems to take an immense step forward.

Socially an equally striking series of events begins to transpire. The welling up of instincts described above brings with it some of the childhood reaching for oedipal attachment-the youngster was drawn to mother and father as objects of sexual interest, and as rivals. With this, the superego is drawn into the fray—unlike the pretentious 4-year-old, a young teenager, especially a precocious one who is menstruating, feminine, and fertile, could be a realistic rival to her mother-and the superego will forbid and contain such impulse, and cry "Shame!" At the same time, social forces in the form of peer comments, the eyes of adult men, the admonitions of concerned adults about posture and body management, the discussion with mother when shopping for clothes all collectively speak to the youngster's new condition. In sheer self-defense, the teenager begins to distance herself from the parents, finds much about them to criticize, and complains that she can't talk to them, they don't understand her.

The peer group is often turned to at this time to give some of the help, the support, and the modeling formerly supplied by the parents. The erotic impulses seek new objects; the heterosexual component turns to other young people; the homosexual drives attach to ideas and form the nucleus of later idealism. At the same time, there is a reencounter with and a searching reexamination of the superego.

With the advance into mid-adolescence, a major transfiguration of values sometimes follows, new causes are sought out, new heroes or models turned to, and dramatic shifts and turns made in basic affinities. Conversion may take place to a new religion, new missions adopted as a life plan, or new leaders accepted as inspirational and fulfilling. This may occur in early adolescence, but it is more typical of the middle or late teens, and, more to the point, it not infrequently carries over into young adulthood. In a good many instances, of course, it works itself out by the end of the adolescent period and young adulthood becomes a time of post-idealism.

The young person appears almost to wake up from a dream, he begins to think of himself no longer as a youth, but now as a man or woman. The sense of play, of nothing being quite serious, everything still reversible, the sense that nothing bad can really happen—these feelings begin to attentuate and give way to a much more burdened feeling of being responsible now, for money, for pregnancy, for one's own choice of clothes, lodging, laundry, earnings, fines, taxes, insurance, companions, education, job, future—a host of variables intrude, each with a claim to responsibility, each demanding decision. Obviously these changes are accompanied by stress and, not infrequently, ambivalence. Many a youth avoids decision and refuses commitment; he either extends his education or drops out of school to escape the finality of choice. Many another takes a low-level job in order to evade the confinement of a true career pursuit. The tales of young adulthood are rife with such compromises, evasions, and tactics for avoiding responsibility. With quite a few young people, promiscuity, pregnancy, cohabitation, and marriage are part of the experimentation of late adolescence and become determining features of young adulthood; with others, asceticism, confinement in some ivory tower such as academia, or withdrawal into the parental home becomes a cardinal aspect of their adjustment. In 1890, social conditions might have ordained that a young woman did not leave home until she was "properly married," and that once married, she would set about having children as soon as possible. Neither of these factors prevails today, although as recently as 1960 they would not have been so unusual.

In more dynamic terms, we could say that under favorable conditions the identity experiments of the adolescent period now give way to a stable sense of who one is on a variety of fronts. Sexual identity consolidates: one is heterosexual or homosexual or some mixture of the two, one is more or less frigid or impotent, or more or less oversexed, or more or less average, and so on and on.

Social identity takes form: one has a ''good'' personality or lacks it, feels attractive or doesn't, is a popular person or a wallflower, knows how to get along with people or fears social encounter, and has, in general, a sense of social self. Career identity is at least on the drawing board: one is headed somewhere or nowhere, or should be on target but isn't, etc. Even in 1890 not all women thought only of marriage. There were teachers, governesses, nurses—a relatively small number of choices to be sure (I leave out actress, dancer, and other such vocations which might not have been considered respectable), but still, some alternatives.

Relationships with parents too should have been largely restructured by this time. The vicissitudes of dependence and independence might take the form of floundering lunges for ''freedom'' or of gradual, almost unremarked emotional emancipation, however it might happen to go in an individual life; in any case they would have found their level and some version of independence arrived at. The basic sense of not being someone's boy or girl but rather being one's own autonomously regulated man or woman is the proper status at which to have arrived. Alas, experience suggests that of all the accomplishments of adolescence, this is the one least calculated to achieve a fortunate consummation. Lingering oedipal and pregenital attachments to the parents all too often persist, and presently result in various combinations of regression, reaction formation, and acting out. This can vary in expression all the way from running away from home or from any home-approved role, to premature marriage or unmarried parenthood as an assertion of one's freedom from dependency and infantility, to refusing to leave home and finding good reasons to cling to direct (albeit embattled) involvement with father and mother.

In terms of object relations, the healthy outcome of this epoch is, of course, the postadolescent search for an appropriate object of attachment. The pubertal and teenage youth is experimenting, trying on new identities, and testing himself out in various social settings. Dating is the great crucible for the blending of id gratifications, ego defenses, and object-related experiences. One ascertains that one is or isn't attracted to this or that type of boy or girl, one learns about temptation and sensation and one's capacity to control oneself, or to control the other, or one's proneness to yield, one encounters at least some level of sexuality and copes. By the time of young adulthood, hopefully the earliest gropings are out of the way, and the idealization or the anxiety about the other gender, if it was present at all, is now less unrealistic if not entirely gone. In short, one knows at least something of one's competencies as well as one's vulnerabilities in the heterosexual arena.

Theoretically, oedipal issues in their more crudely sexual form should now be resolved. One of the tasks of adolescence was to do the working through, the final detaching of the libidinal and aggressive interests from the bodies of the parents and the transferring of these instinctual yearnings to appropriate objects in the outside world. If thing go well, the erotic attachments are connected to people and to ideas, and the aggressive drives to work. There follow the tempering and annealing of these new forms of attachment and coping, a process that goes on all during the adolescent years. Finally, the more mature young adults have made career choices and are ready for serious work, and they are looking for marriage partners; they are ready for intimacy, for tenderness, for sharing and caring.

With this as background let us take the data available to us in the case of Anna O. and see how well she fits into this framework. Developmentally speaking, how is she doing at 21? Well, the story is not an encouraging one. We do not hear about boyfriends or romantic ideas. There has been no love affair, apparently no dating, or whatever its nineteenth century Viennese equivalent would have been. (I must confess that I don't know precisely what it was. I assume young men would come calling. I assume young women might go to balls and picnics and soirées. But then, did one get escorted to the opera or theater? Did young people meet in groups for tea or gather in coffee houses? Surely there were social practices that even puritanical families accepted, or in any case some in which the children could indulge without the parents' knowledge.) There is one brief reference to her wish to be where the dance music was playing, which she paid for by developing a cough. For the rest, all we hear is of the patient's passionate fondness for her father—presumably a largely unsublimated oedipal wish.

In terms of work or career choice, she had certain minimal household chores which she carried through unexceptionally. Certainly a plus. But her primary commitment of constructive energy was to her daydreams—again not a very reassuring finding. In short, she functions like a latency child who has only partially resolved her transit through the oedipal experience and who still uses a great many early ego mechanisms in her pursuit of gratification and tension relief. Her capacity to keep this disposition concealed and to respond to reality in an intact fashion wherever necessary speaks for at least a basic level of ego strength, but at best she is vulnerable.

With the onset of her father's illness, her coping capacities are challenged. She takes over a major portion of the care-taking role and becomes his nurse, which both involves her with his body and arouses fears of his death. The one places her under enormous stress to ward off the clamorous incestuous wishes; the other poses her a most serious threat of object loss and thus rips at her sense of security and attachment and probably stirs up feelings of guilt (perhaps she feels that her unworthy daydreams about him have brought about this catastrophe).

One of the most common forms early childhood fantasy takes is that of acquiring highly prized and intensely desired objects by means of oral ingestion. The ultimate yearning is the wish for sucking and biting, for devouring and assimilating; the essence of possession is to incorporate the desired object into one's own substance. Where such oral taking in involves forbidden or ambivalently regarded objects, the result is often some sort of somatic symptom, or a syndrome such as bulimia and vomiting. In Anna O.'s case, one might well speculate that her snake imagery, anorexia, and coughing involve many fantasies about father's penis. Consider the black snakes that recur in the material; e.g. at one point her hand turns into a bunch of snakes. The phallic implications are obvious. However, there is more to this image than that. Black snakes are not necessarily phallic symbals. After all, things happen in a nursery. Sometimes mother comes in with the nurse and says ''Oh, my God'' because the child has been playing with feces—black snakes—and there is a terrible mess and a correspondingly intense parental reaction. For the child, each smeared finger becomes a wiggly black snake. This kind of memory can perhaps fit even more readily into the pregenital than into the phallic framework.

More than that, the young woman used her fantasies in a way that she called ''chimney sweeping.'' The manner of handling those fantasies was unusual; these peculiar stories had to be worked off. If you waited a day, she got irritable. If you waited two days, she got downright nasty. All in all this sounds like a constipated little girl. Wait a day and she's irritable; wait two days and she's nasty. And then mother and doctor come along with the enema (the chimney sweep), and she's all right until it happens again. Thus the data suggest that this kind of infrastructure is present beneath the surface of some of her troubles.

Hence she punishes herself by starvation and overwork, develops a nervous cough, and presently crumbles. At this point, the doctor is called in. He finds himself confronting a patient with contractures, daily cyclic mood swings, visual disturbances, language problems—a host of symptoms. Her head is filled with forbidden fantasies, many of which she is striving to repress. But her repression is not adequate; the thoughts threaten to break through. So she diverts them into her body: she need not think about forbidden movements because her musculature is in disarray; she will not have to struggle with forbidden words because her language has undergone a change; she cannot see guilt-evoking images for her eyes do not function; and so on and on.

To speculate a little further, what would a child psychiatrist have done with this case? To begin with, he would probably have hospitalized the patient, for diagnostic reasons if for no other. Her symptoms might arise from a wide variety of diverse causes, each of which would have to be checked out by a carefully orchestrated combined evaluation and therapeutic regime. The family would have been called in—or rather the mother, father was surely too sick—to give a careful developmental history of this girl and enable the psychiatrist to see if some hint of earlier trends could be discerned. If father's condition permitted, a caseworker might have gone to the home to get some data from him or to interview the whole family there. Meanwhile the young woman would have been referred for a variety of consultations—speech pathology, neurology, EEG, ophthalmology, endocrinology, internal medicine, etc.—all designed to check out the various conversion symptoms or other disorders. Psychological tests, especially the projectives, would have been employed as soon as possible to evaluate her reality testing, and an organic battery, possibly with neuro-psychological testing, would have been invoked to be sure there was not some unusual temporal lobe syndrome.

During all this, a series of behavioral observations would have been made by the ward personnel, and presently there would have been a case conference.

Since we are already specualting, let us assume that a number of problems have been diagnosed. To begin with, there is her own developmental lag; clearly she is operating like a much younger child, and she is fixated at a latency level—in a very real sense, she has not yet entered psychological puberty. Hence she needs a good deal of work in individual therapy to remove the psychological impediments which hold her back, and the therapist must seek a way to free her to move forward in her development. The goal of the therapy would be to work through those factors which keep her locked into this developmental impasse.

But, it is by no means so obvious how this should be done. When one got down to deciding on the psychotherapeutic approach, one issue that would have to addressed is this: should this girl be treated by expressive therapy with encouragement to communicate her fantasies and feelings in order to achieve insight, or would it be better to shade the technique toward the suppressive sup-portive mode and try to orient the young person toward displacement and sublimation? A case can be made for either stance.

On the one hand, it seems to me that any attempt at expressive therapy in such a case would have to go forward with fear and trembling. The very multiplicity of the symptoms and, in particular, her rather bizarre language patterns would be enough to give any clinician pause. Indeed, it is hard to im-agine anyone taking her into analysis today. Still, in 1890, when grand hysteria was more common, perhaps it was a less frightening condition. In any case, the therapist would probably not see the patient twice a day, every day in the week; one or two hours a week would be more typical. Moreover, in this work the therapist would pay a great deal of attention to the details of her ego defenses. (The existing record does not help much with that exploration; it is notable that the accounts of many of these early case studies do not lend themselves to sort-ing out defenses.) We know that Breuer chose the expressive mode for his treat-ment, but of course the whole approach to ego defense structure was not available to him, let alone any hints about working out the transference. He was able to ease a great many of her symptoms; nonetheless, her subsequent years were marked by considerable disability. When she finally did resolve the neurotic and addictive problems, she pursued a life course that raced along the great rainbow of idealism, giving herself to noble causes rather than to specific people. Her poetry tells us of the price she never ceased to pay.

On the other hand, supportive suppressive methods are no panacea either. The hypnotists who told patients to give up their symptoms had only limited success. Nonetheless, they may have been on the right track, in terms of defense theory they were surely reinforcing repression. The supportive therapist tends to avoid fantasy production or discussions of early experience; instead he shows interest in current activities and interactions. He plays an active role in the patient's life, gives advice, makes suggestions, sets limits, and takes charge of things, at least at first. In brief, he offers himself as an object of reality anchorage, attachment, and dependency gratification. If he does this skillfully, the patient wants to please him and to retain him, and can thus be led to try a variety of activities that could be gratifying and rewarding. Once engaged, some of these will be rich in sublimatory potential and, more important still, will offer many possibilities for appropriate object attachment. The supportive therapist watches these processes carefully and then, when he judges that the patient is ready, gradually begins to move her toward discharge. Anna O.'s therapist would wean the patient gently over enough time to allow for some working through of the sense of loss and privation. The hope would be that such a patient as Anna O. would begin to show some evidence of involvement with peers, possibly including some interest in men, to confirm the feeling of progress. It is hard to estimate how she would have responded; with the therapist actively stressing her healthy rather than her symptomatic side, she might well have done better.

Modern-day hospitalization and insurance practices being what they are, if she had gotten into the hospital in December or January, she would have emerged in ninety days at the most, and would thus have been home only a few weeks when her father died. Somewhere anterior to that her tic douloureux appeared. Her intense reaction would undoubtedly have led to a readmission. A longer period of care would now be necessary, with an initial goal of helping her mourn for father. Along with this, the supportive methods could continue.

Beyond the psychotherapy, there are still more details to her program that need to be discussed. There is, for example, the question of her role in the family. After all, it is not by chance that she was permitted to become father's nurse; while there might be a lot of good reasons, economic and otherwise, to have a daughter take on that duty, one might still wonder why in this wealthy family it was not delegated to a nurse. Surely in the affluent and sophisticated Viennese culture of that day, with the great medical center comprising a significant presence in the city, nurses were available for around-the-clock care in wealthy homes. With such a caretaker in place the family members would not be bathing or toileting the sick man, yet they would be free to devote a great deal of time to him and to offer many levels of companionship. They could converse with him, read to him, or just sit by companionably. Why, then, this intense involvement in physical care to the point where Anna wore herself out?

In such a situation this could arise because of the young person's own insistence and stem from an idealization of her role as nurse and minister to father's needs. In effect, it would be an unconscious acting out of oedipal wishes that gave her acces to and intimacy with father's body under the protective cloak of daughterly devotion. Or it could be a role tacitly assigned to her within the family.

Some sort of family evaluation might lead to work with mother, with or without the involvement of other concerned family members, in order to deal with this group of issues. If appropriate, the family meetings might well include Anna herself. This could be rather delicate. Thus, for example, it might turn out that Anna had been selected as the stay-at-home child whose duty it was to take care of parents forever and ever—indeed there are some children who are so designated. Should this be the case, then there would be much to address, alas, and no great promise that any amount of confrontation would change that state of affairs.

Next we come to some other sources of support for Anna's growth. Since we are assuming that her peer relations must be in considerable disorder, would some form of group therapy be of help? Yes, provided it was not in an overstimulated group where the overt obscenity and generally promiscuous style of some of its members would simply distress and alienate this girl. Possibly it might be best to begin with a young women's group, with later transfer to a co-ed group when she seemed more ready.

The ward physician would be asked to devise a milieu program for her. For one thing, he would have the anorexic symptom to address, and might very well initiate a behavioral program of some kind to try to deal with it. For another, there is the matter of her educational needs to consider. We hear that Anna never went as far in school as her good mind might have fit her to do, and an academic or tutorial program would have to be arranged. Then we know that one of her important sublimations was caring for people in need (in this sense, her attention to her father was only part of a more generalized personality tendency), so she would be assigned to help with some of the sicker patients in the hospital. More than that, some discussions of career choice might have been initiated via the family meetings or in individual sessions with the caseworker. If her parents' puritanical stance involved active synagogue attendance, then a rabbinical pastoral counselor might be called in to participate in some measure in the family work.

With all this, the question of medication has still to be considered. From this point of view Anna presents a complex picture. She is sad, she is anxious; she is clear, she is cloudy; she is cyclic with excited episodes; there is a pronounced disturbance in sleep-wake cycles—all in all an interesting and intricate problem. She would probably be given a dexamethasone suppression test. My own preference would be to try either nothing or a tricyclic; possibly one could justify a sortie into the realm of lithium—at best, there is room for a great deal of discussion.

To close, let me return to an earlier theme: the way child psychiatry goes about addressing the question of therapeutics. Fundamentally, it is a discipline which always uses multiple modalities in its therapeutic approach. With every initiation of child therapy there is at least some form of parent intervention, and usually some work with school. Not infrequently a child goes to activity group therapy along with individual therapy, and his parents may come into his hour occasionally for a family meeting. At home, a behavioral program may be established. The child may be on medication and be participating in some special education or tutorial work at the same time. There will be frequent phone calls back and forth among the several participants in his program, with the therapist acting as coordinator. This sense of integrating multiple modalities is characteristic of this field and is a direct expression of its interest in advancing development on a variety of fronts at the same time.

And so too would have been the mode of address to Anna O. She was a woman who suffered much before she achieved the level of recovery which was to be hers. Such a multimodal therapeutic approach early in life might well have eased her later burdens.

Anna O.: Psychoanalysis and Group Process Theory

Melvin Muroff

In 1880 a mother in panic called to her home a noted Viennese physician, Dr. Josef Breuer. Her daughter was strangely ill. Dr. Breuer's examination showed that the daughter not only had a cough—one of the original reasons for the call—but also was paralyzed in both legs and her right arm. He also noticed that she exhibited two entirely distinct states of consciousness. His clinical judgment suggested that he was confronted with a case of hysteria, a relatively common ailment of women at that time. As such, he resorted to one of the usual methods of treatment, hypnosis. His intent was to "cure" the patient of her debilitating symptoms. In hypnotizing her, he varied his method. This time—the reasons are unknown to us and it is not even clear whether it was due to purpose or accident—he *asked* the patient how she felt and what she was experiencing instead of *telling* her to "feel better." This seemingly simple alteration of procedure led to a remarkable result. It opened the door to a flood of disconnected thoughts, memories, and feelings from the patient. Gradually, Breuer came to realize that these apparent fragmentations of thoughts, memories, and feelings were parts of a process relating to Anna O.'s past and not just representations of her current reality. "When the existence of this amnesia was brought to light, there at once followed a realization that the patient's manifest mind was not the whole of it, that there lay behind it an *unconscious* mind . . . the problem was not merely the investigation of the conscious mental process . . . there were also unconscious mental processes, some specific instrument was clearly required . . . the instrument for this purpose was hypnotic suggestion . . . not for direct therapeutic purposes but to persuade the patient to produce material from the unconscious regions of the mind" (Breuer and Freud, 1957, p. xvii).

While he was working with this material in this way, it became increasingly evident to Breuer (and was then further developed and understood by Freud) that emotional conflict can be repressed and unconsciously become manifest in various, unrelated physical symptoms. As Breuer wrote so well, "Each individual symptom in this complicated case was taken separately in hand; all the

71

occasions on which it had happened were described in reverse order, starting before the time when the patient became bed-ridden and going back to the event which had led to its first appearance. When this had been described the symptom was permanently removed'' (Breuer and Freud, 1955, p. 35). Working in this way with Anna O., Breuer gathered information which, when analyzed further by Freud, led to the recognition that understanding and treating emotional disturbances required going beyond obvious symptomatic representations. The data effectively indicated that conflict existed in people on both an unconscious and a conscious level.

The variation in the usual hypnosis procedure in working with Anna O. demonstrated that her paralysis, the cough, and her other symptoms were not primary problems even in the hysteric. They were replacements, cover-ups, displacements, substitutions, or what have you, of more meaningful hidden emotional reactions which were being pushed away into the unconscious at the cost of the patient's developing her debilitating symptoms. As we all know, this simple discovery in the hands of Freud was molded into an extremely complex psychological theory of human behavior. Overt symptoms were no longer the issue, and analysts were trained, like detectives, to view symptoms as clues along the path to the underlying causes of emotional conflict. In this training, emphasis was placed on the development of intricate intrapsychic models to explain and understand the inner workings of the mind. Most often the development of these models depended on minute, microscopic—but introspective, anecdotal investigations. Although to a large degree these were not based on any acceptable experimental format, the first analytical case, the Anna O. case of one hundred years ago, did generate many theories and practical approaches which help us understand and work with the psychological conflicts in people. Thus what started out as a call for symptomatic relief eventually turned into a psychological system for understanding the nature of unconscious conflict. The conceptualization for understanding unconscious functioning as a way of treating people with emotional difficulties also uncovered the need to investigate past childhood experiences, to make conscious previous trauma, and to obtain an understanding of how the person experienced his growth process. To Breuer the root of Anna O's illness was related to her guilt coming from a repressed wish to leave the room of her dying father after hearing dance music ''coming from a neighbor's house'' (Breuer and Freud, 1955, p. 40). He worked to make conscious the repressed conflictual material, and especially that which was related to her father's illness, her taking care of him at that time, and his eventual death. ''If for any reason she was unable to tell me the story during her evening hypnosis she failed to calm down afterwards, and so on the following day she had to tell me *two* stories in order for this to happen'' (ibid., p. 29).

As we come to realize, the analytic treatment method is a long, time-consuming process and often not too suitable for, or desired by, all patients. Today, although most psychotherapists accept the need to understand unconscious functioning, there appears to be a trend developing to once again work with only symptoms. Thus, if Breuer was called today, it is very likely that he would seek immediate symptomatic relief for his patient through drugs and/or a psychological here-and-now therapy and never would make a house call. Also, it is quite possible that the mother would or could not tolerate the financial and emotional expense of long-term treatment. She too would possibly insist on a here-and-now symptomatic-relief type of treatment. This emphasis on the immediate relief of emotional pain, the quick fix, may be taking us back to 1880, when doctors were telling their patients to feel better rather than coping with and understanding what was behind the patients' symptoms. Today we are seeing a growing countermovement against the necessity for understanding unconscious functioning. Considerable opposition is developing in the psychotherapeutic field to the analytic method that was first described in the case of Anna O. and still remains the basis of psychoanalysis. "It will now be understood how it is that the psychotherapeutic procedure which we have described in these pages has a curative effect. It brings to an end the operative force of the idea which was not abreacted in the first instance, by allowing its strangulated affect to find a way out through speech; and it subjects it to associative correction by introducing it into normal consciousness . . . or by removing it through the physician's suggestion, as is done in somnambulism accompanied by amnesia" (ibid., p. 17). How is it, then, that this analytic method, an extremely promising and meaningful way to understand and work with human behavior, has become so unpopular?

Psychoanalysis, like any other type of treatment, has its defects, but to condemn it completely, as many do today, is unjust. Sometimes we forget that at its inception it was unquestionably unique and somewhat revolutionary. Certainly it has held up surprisingly well. But age does have its effects, among them rigidity and inflexibility, and it appears this 100-year-oldster psychoanalysis may be suffering from these conditions. Psychoanalysis has been cricicized for many reasons, but today perhaps its rigidity toward change is most important. There is no question that since the Anna O. case it has undergone considerable growth. However, its development has remained mostly one-dimensional in its dependency on its original discovery of intrapsychic functioning. It has advanced our knowledge in this area as well as our understanding of early childhood development, but it has had considerable difficulty in explaining interpersonal, social behavior. The usual, orthodox Freudian techniques most often study issues of ego functioning, transference and countertransference as related to the patient's internal problems, defense mechanisms, and in general the internal process of the individual. "It [psychoanalysis] does not attempt to explain the nature of external reality but rather deals with those factors which cause different individuals to apprehend this reality differently . . . its field lies in the exploration of the effect of inner reality on the ways in which individuals relate to external reality. In any given situation there is a mixture of internal and external reality factors . . . " (Pumpian-Mindlin, p. 133). Psychoanalysis has not been particularly successful in incorporating in its theories the interaction that exists between internal and external realities. Its difficulty lies in its isolation within its own system. It has accepted only a minimal amount of experimental psychological data, such as those found in group process dynamics theories. By not introducing into its methodology other experimental data for understanding behavior, psychoanalysis has become stagnant. The need for it to incorporate other dimensions of understanding behavior, including those reflective of the present time, as social psychology findings, is important if it is to survive.

Psychoanalysis approaches the understanding of human behavior on the basis of speculative constructions about the individual's intrapsychic life. However, it gives only minimal attention to interpersonal interaction and thereby fails to study the social, interpsychic phenomena that exist among individuals and affect human behavior. Its theory is most adequate when it discusses the first three years of child development, the major time for internal, intrapsychic interaction and development. It flounders when it tries to deal with child development past the three-year level, the time when the child is mainly concerned with social interaction. The analysts describe this period of life primarily in terms of oedipal, superego, and ego ideal conflicts, all parts of the individual's internal reality, and exclude the external reality of the socialization process itself. Thus, using the available data, even today most analysts will describe Anna O.'s case not too differently from Freud's earlier formulation. They reflect on the meaning of her symptoms as unconscious representations. They interpret the unconscious meanings of her symptoms—the ''black snakes,'' her difficulty with speech, her two levels of consciousness, and others—in seeking further understanding of what happened to Anna O. The more recent psychoanalytic formulations, although in fact extremely significant for the understanding of human development and behavior, are also considered to be one-dimensional. All still describe behavior in the language of intrapsychic developmental constructs. For example, if Anna O. is diagnosed as psychotic, her underlying disturbance may be described as a form of ego dysfunction related to difficulties (conflict) in her psychosexual development. In a general way, her symptoms may be seen as representing intrapsychic conflict between the structural elements of the mind, the ego and the id. Important as such a formulation may be, it disregards the fact that there exists a psychosocial developmental pattern alongside the psychosexual developmental pattern in the growth process.

This analytic approach emphasizes only the interactions between Anna O.'s instinctual drives and her adaptive ego functioning. As mentioned, this is most helpful in understanding the first three years of development but is inadequate to explain further child development. Methodologically, it is not appropriate to use intrapersonal dynamics to explain social interaction; they are two distinct and different processes, each with its own unique language and dynamics for explaining human behavior. This three-year-old level is the moment when, developmentally, the social, interpersonal interactions become as important as the internal, intrapsychic, narcissistic reactions, if not more so. In fact, the transition in emphasis from the intrapsychic growth to the interspychic growth is in itself a natural psychological conflict of major importance occurring on the three-year level.

Analytic theory has difficulty in integrating the dynamics of interpersonal functioning into its body of knowledge primarily, I suspect, because it has been unable to give up or to modify its basic model, which is strictly dependent on intrapsychic development. A prime position of this chpater is that it is not possible to explain interpersonal interactions by using the language and the dynamics of intrapsychic functioning. As mentioned, they are not from the same universe of data. Although it does help us to understand what goes on inside the individual, psychoanalysis does not yet offer a conceptualization for the understanding of individuals interacting with one another. It does not have a conceptual model that explains child development as part of a group process.

In reflecting back one hundred years to Anna O.'s time, we can understand it is no accident that psychoanalysis has had so much difficulty going beyond the individual internal dynamics. At that time and until recently, the model for all experimental methodology occupied itself primarily with studies of individual differences with their specific variations as causes of pathology. Most conceptual models in medicine and psychology have been verified by statistical measurement which used controlled variables to test uncontrolled variables. Physical science has also used this particular scientific method. It confines experimentation to the study of static systems and collects data on the basis of differentiation of variability. This method is dependent on and is derived from a statistical analysis based on the probability of an individual event reoccurring. It is only recently that, with the study of moving particles in a field, experimentation in the area of physical science, to some extent, also had to revise its scientific methodology in order to understand dynamic, interacting systems. The static model, the search for individual differences and their specific causes, could not include the possibility for understanding interacting units, whether they be moving particles in physics or human beings. So we see that Freud, as a product of his time, developed his ideas from a biological model essentially rooted in the Darwinian system, which concerned itself with individual differences. Thus Anna O.'s time was an era for men to be individuals, a time when individuals sought to emphasize their differences from one another. It was important to be unique. It was not a time for individuals to reach out and interact with one another, to have commonality. That was to come later.

In the early 1900s and perhaps up until the end of the Second World War, the focus was mainly on how individuals grew and how they were differentiated from others. The game of the day was King of the Hill. It was the time of the railroad barons and Theodore Roosevelt's rugged individualism. Because of this trend of separating out and studying the unique differences among individuals, it is not surprising to see, at least in this country, that considerable emphasis was placed on the individual finding his way against all adversity, becoming independent of others—the Horatio Alger syndrome. By 1916 this concern with individual differences led to the development of intelligence testing, which is also based on statistically and specifically separating out differences among individuals. Thus in Anna O.'s day the atmosphere of self-determination—being an individual separate from others, the group—dominated scientific investigation. It was no accident that individual differences were so important in the past since it was the underlying concern of culture at that time. If one would know the individual unit, first it was important to know it as a functioning identity before knowing how this specific unit interacted with other units. In this sense, it was necessary to understand intrapsychic functioning before being able to grasp the nature of interpsychic interactions.

Freud's thinking to a limited degree, indicated his awareness of the existence of interacting social forces. For example, he demonstrated his perception of group interaction in his 1914 paper *Some Reflections on Schoolboy Psychology,* where he discussed a boy's reaction to authority figures. There he showed an interest in the dynamics of the interaction between people and what takes place in a group situation. He also mentioned group interaction in *Totem and Taboo* (1912), *Narcissism* (1914), *Mourning and Melancholia* (1917), his paper *Group Psychology and the Analysis of the Ego* (1921), and *Ego and Id* (1923), and Freud apparently developed two different but related paths to his psychology: his theories on intrapsychic functioning, the core of present-day psychoanalytic theory; and his group, social psychology. However, Freud did not pursue the latter, most likely due to his lifetime opposition to group affiliation and group membership. He viewed social interaction, becoming a member of a group, as a regressive phenomenon. For him, the individual's differentiation and separation from the group were more important than maintaining group membership, which he regarded as equivalent to a psychological regression back to a state of greater infantile dependence. For Freud a primary group, one which has a leader, is composed of individuals who have substituted one and the same object for their ego ideal and have thereby identified themselves with one another in their ego. Again, without interpreting the meaning of this concept, we see an example of trying to understand group process, or interpersonal interaction, as though it were an internal process taking place only within the individual.

Freud devoted considerable time to comparing and relating the similarities of group membership with characteristics of the family group. For him, they were one and the same—he also described the oedipal period as a critical stage in the child's psychological growth. During this pivotal time the child's identification is with the father (the leader); inevitably this process involves much ambivalence. At first Freud thought that "social feelings" were based upon hostile feelings, which became, during the oedipal period, more positive in the course and the child's identification with the father. If one extends this line of reasoning and uses intrapsychic dynamics to explain social interaction, it follows that the adult who does something similar in a group gives up his ego ideal and is compelled to replace it with a group ideal. This, in turn, is fundamentally determined by the leader. In this way, group membership may be viewed as a regressive phenomenon. Freud established the position that there is much to lose by becoming a member of a group. He recognized that one must become identified with the leader and thereby with the inherent group the leader represents. Nonetheless, Freud stated that it is important to separate oneself from this relationship and thereby from the "primal horde." Thus, he would not consider the possibility or the need to work with groups in order to understand the functioning of the mind.

Freud's description of what a leader is leaves much to be desired. Whether it reflects Freud's own personal difficulties with fathers (authority figures) or the trend of the day, or a combination of the two, is open to question. Still, we do see his monistic, negative attitude toward the position of the leader in the group. He did not recognize that there are many different kinds of leaders. He refers to one type of leader who today would be best described as a tyrant. In 1921 Freud described the leader as a "dreaded primal father" and as one who is "the group ideal," which governs the ego in the place of the ego ideal (Freud, 1955a, p. 127). Therefore the leader is an individual who "only possess[es] the typical qualities of the individuals concerned in a particularly clearly marked and pure form, and need[s] only give an impression of greater force and of more freedom of libido . . . " (ibid., p. 129). In essence, Freud portrayed the leader as a person who needs to be loved by the group members but needs to love no one but himself. The leader is described as being "absolutely narcissistic." An identification with this leader (the father) requires much modification of the ego; it determines the development of the ego ideal and eventually the quality of the superego. The purpose is to dominate the child's ego with parental ideals. This tends to abolish the original oedipal situation by means of repression and presently results in the development of a conscience.

Returning to Anna O., could this conceptualization of the interaction of the child with father be a valid analytic explanation of her illness? Many analysts would accept the possibility that her ego disturbance was related to a fixation and conflict around her oedipal wishes for her father. Carrying this a bit further, can we say that her wish to rescue women from fearsome, slave-trading men was an acting out of this kind of conflict?

In any event, this was the way Freud structurally traced how part of the ego develops into the superego. The superego develops from the identification the child makes with both parents and the ego ideals he elaborates. The child's standards of conduct and self-control as well as the general structure of his conscience are determined by his emotional attachments to the parents. Social feelings rest on the foundation of these identifications with others and also on the ego ideals held in common with them.

Consistently, throughout his writings, Freud indicated that he considered most forms of social behavior to constitute a negative characteristic and, developmentally, one which preceded the culmination of the oedipal period; indeed he held that the formation of social behavior might be the result of a disturbance occurring during the oedipal period. His firm position was that the healthy individual strives continually to become independent of his early, primitive group attachments. If this notion were carried to its logical conclusion, then the result would be a society composed primarily of individuals so self-directed that they would have little or no concern for others. As Freud stated in his later writings, the interests of the individual clash with those of society; inevitably he is opposed to his fellow man (Freud, 1955b, pp. 94–97). Freud had little hope for civilization; according to him, every individual is in fact an enemy of his culture.

There is no question in anyone's mind that the growth process involves separating out from the primary family unit and becoming independent. The initial move toward separation occurs in the first years of the child's development. How this is done and its effect on the internal psychological structure of the individual are extremely important. Up to a point the analytic model does help us to understand what takes place. The formation of the superego at the end of the oedipal period makes for an individual who, in varying degrees, is ready to interact with others as a social being. It is at this time that socialization with people outside the immediate family begins. (Was this process Anna O.'s area of conflict?)

I wish to suggest that in this system, Freud's heritage and his era combined to prevent his developing a more systematic social psychology. In fact, present-day research and experimentation with group process and dynamics appear to be at considerable variance with basic Freudian doctrine. For example, studies on the individual in the group indicate that an individual can be separate and distinct only because he *is* a member of a particular group, that his identity is dependent on group membership as well as on his underlying character structure. As a member or leader of a group, one has a definite influence on what that group does or does not do. Further, it is now recognized that the leader does not function in isolation from his group members; in reality he is influenced and frequently directed by them.

Many attempts have been made to understand the transition from intrapsychic (instinctual) to interpsychic (social) functioning (Hartmann, Kris, and Lowenstein, 1946, pp. 11–38). For example, Mahler's insightful work with psychosis in children describes how the process of separation from the mother affects the child's growth process. Certainly this is an interpsychic process. In Mahler's work, the separation process is restricted to the mother-child relationship, where "... the infant and his mother are an omnipotent symbiotic dual unity" (Mahler, Furer, and Settlage, p. 822). In this formulation socialization has a biological maturational base and separation-individuation is seen as related to the interaction between the child and the mother and "stimulus and response between the two partners of the dual unity. The mother is both the external ego and the one who triggers separation" (ibid.).

Conceptualizing the mother as an "external ego" and as the one who "triggers separation" raises many methodological questions. Also, without using data from group dynamics research on the role of the leader in the group process (and two members make a group), it is highly possible to misinterpret the role of the caretaker in the child's growth process. However, Mahler's work is representative of today's analytic thinking. As such, how would it explain Anna O.'s case? Was her difficulty related to a disturbance in her interaction with her mother? Did her mother need to keep Anna O. dependent on her? We do not have adequate data to answer these questions, but we do know that Anna's father was dying and her illness related in some way to her psychological perception of him. How do we move from the symbiotic ties to mother to the social process of interacting with father? Again, this can be done only if we realize that this process is one which involves group dynamics and not just the process of the instinctual life. What is missing in the analytic formulation of child development is a conceptual model which would include the more current experimental data on group process dynamics.

Until recently the child has been viewed as though he grew up in a narcissistic vacuum. There was no recognition that in reality, from the start the child is a member of a group, wherein as an infant he experiences himself as the omnipotent leader. If we are further to develop analytic theory, we need to study and conceptualize the nature of the child's group, its members and the roles they play, and the dynamics of this process as perceived by the omnipotent child. Analysts need to recognize and employ the dynamics of interpersonal relations and to study its roots and development from early childhood. This would lead to a developmental model based on how the child experiences his world and would be a bridge connecting the *intrapsychic* with the *interpsychic* phenomena. The building of such a bridge might take the following form.

The newborn, a truly solipsistic individual, lives in a field, a life space, wherein he is totally in charge; from his vantage point, he is the leader. In effect he starts life as a group of one. Gradually there is a differentiating out of specific parts of the field. At the same time, however, as many investigators indicate, inanimate objects as well as people are experienced by the child primarily as extensions of himself. With further development, at around 6 months of age, the child responds as though people were there to serve him. They are the caretakers as well as the subjects of this omnipotent king. From this age on, the process is one of separation, with the further perceptual differentiation of this leader from the members and objects in his kingdom. This leader gradually becomes aware of the limits of his territorial space. Concurrently with this, we must incorporate the analytic descriptions of child development, although the focus here is on one end of the bridge, the developmental aspect of the socialization process. The child becomes more possessive as he experiences the concrete boundaries of his territory. He moves away from the caretakers, but for him they still remain members of his group.

Up to the age of two and a half to three or so, the child defines the boundaries of his field, his kingdom, and reinforces his position as an autocratic leader. At this time, this omnipotent leader is compelled to recognize more actively that there are forces outside of his domain, his life space, which are threatening his kingdom. Reality testing intrudes into the child's world. He thereupon makes strenuous efforts to keep his omnipotent position (which includes the symbiotic ties with his subjects, the caretakers) intact. Strangers, outsiders, and aliens all are the enemy. People who are not seen by the child as caretakers emerge for him as people who challenge his position as the leader of his group. Typically this alien force is represented by the father, who at this time comes to be perceived by the child as an outsider and not as a member of his group of caretakers. Here we might begin to revise our notions of the oedipal phase. In keeping with this formulation, it becomes something much more involved and significant than merely a sexual struggle. It is the highly critical time when the child feels that his leadership and his control over his group are being directly threatened. From his standpoint, the oedipal period is an attempt to hold and keep control over his group—in particular over mother, as member, as well as other caretaker members. It is not just a struggle for mother between child and father. It is a more deadly battle for possession of territorial space. This struggle holds true for the female as well as the male child. Should the father lose, then the child remains in possession of the territory, and, we would predict, with little hope for further psychological growth. In the eyes of the child, the father needs to win and become the leader. In giving up the leadership of his imaginary group, through the group process, the child is helped to separate from mother and other caretakers. With this, the child moves from his condition of infantile dependency, his primary narcissistic state, to secondary narcissism. Then the child is free and in a position to interact with other people who were not in his original group, the aliens from the outside.

Struggling with and then identifying with the successful aggressor, the father, brings the child into contact with the external world. In the interaction that follows, the child tries to be omnipotent; usually he is not too successful in this endeavor. From 4 to 6 years of age or so, the child tests his group membership with the others. He tests the leadership of the father, as well as the other outsiders, as one of the ways of testing reality. The final resolution, if successful, is the child's realization that the original group which he thought of or experienced as his own was never his territory to start with; it belonged strictly to his parents. It is a shock for all of us to discover, if we do, that in reality we were the outsiders and not the others. It is especially painful to become aware that we were never the leader of the group, but merely another member. This, then, leads to the realization that if one is to become a leader, it is necessary to start one's own group.

The application of this sparse, introductory group dynamics addition to the current analytic thinking of child development provides an interesting formulation of the Anna O. case. The few data we have do not say too much about her

early years, especially as to her relationship with her mother. There are no in-
dications that her emotional disturbance was evidenced before the presenting
illness and the eventual death of her father. Therefore we may assume that her
early development followed a relatively normal course—that she had experienced herself as the leader during the first two years of childhood. The
available data do not suggest any difficulties with her control over the
caretakers. In fact, Breuer's report strongly suggests that she responded to
him, and his treatment of her, as though he was a member of her group, as
though he was a caretaker, a mother. When she controlled the sessions, when
she was in control of her territory, much of her disturbance abated. When she
was compelled to accept reality (the third-year level), she rebelled and regressed
further into her private world. Perhaps this behavior reflects her unwillingness
to relinquish her omnipotent child position—to let go of the caretakers, to accept the existence of the outsiders. Interestingly, during her father's illness, she
herself acted as a caretaker. In her nursing of him, we might say that she was
acting out a conflict situation, the struggle between being a leader and being a
member of a group. Apparently she was not too able to move forward or
backward until eventually she did regress into her world of omnipotence, her
illness. The theoretical formulation presented here would suggest, then, that in
all likelihood Anna O., a dutiful, concerned daughter, had not adequately
worked through her difficulties in the transition from being a leader to becoming a member of a group. It is suggested that she had not resolved her early
struggles with her father. Her illness recreated and brought them to the surface.
To a large degree her omnipotency remained, and she was not able to appropriately separate from the infantile possession of her territorial space.

In examining the treatment situation itself, you may remember that Breuer
withdrew from the case when the patient began to exhibit fantasies toward him.
Her behavior has been interpreted as a transference reaction. Since then, we
have come to understand this to be a natural and necessary response in the
analytic treatment of patients. At the time, if Breuer had understood the nature
of this transference reaction, he might have continued with her and helped her
work through her conflicts. If we view her transference reaction from the viewpoint of this chapter, as the interaction of two group members, we must
recognize that most of her behavior toward Breuer was indeed related to this
transference phenomenon. Perhaps her sexual fantasies were ploys to capture,
control, and incorporate an outside threatening force which was coercing her to
move on to reality. There certainly was considerable resistance to change.

Thus, using a group process orientation, we obtain another view of the
transference reaction. From this standpoint the transference issue becomes a
conflict between Anna O. and an alien authority. A group process approach
would suggest that her conflict was developmentally on the three-year level and
she was having difficulty going beyond this period. Her struggles reflect a basic
conflict: whether to remain the leader (rooted in primary narcissism) or to
become a member of the group (moving on to reality testing). This conflict

represents the transition from the infantile omnipotent autocratic leadership position to that of being a social individual. The relinquishing of control over her infantile fantasy group required struggling with an authority figure, her father. As the data would indicate, he was not particularly involved with her, although she apparently devoted much attention to him. It is not surprising, therefore, to see that eventually the transference reaction took the form of sexuality. Sexuality can be used to fuse with or capture the alien authority: to minimize his power and to displace her control over the group. We can say, that when Breuer was perceived as an authority, he threatened to take over the leadership of her territorial space. However, he panicked and withdrew. By doing so, by not helping Anna O. to work through her position of omnipotence, he allowed her to remain fixated at the third-to-fourth-year level of development.

We see, then, that in the growth process the child's separation from mother is not just between mother and child. It is a process of separation from an entire system of experiencing oneself in a solipsistic world. Further, if this process of separation is to be accomplished, there needs to be an external authority force and one different from that of the caretaker, the mother. The degree to which the child is successful in this endeavor, letting go of his infantile leadership role, may determine his ability to relate to others and cope with reality. The position taken here is that in the child's developmental process, the essential role of the authority (the father) is to separate the child from his infantile dependency, his omnipotence, and his symbiotic ties with the mother. In understanding all this it is essential to remember that we are using a phenomenological approach and viewing information as a child might experience it. It is not he who is dependent, but all the others, the members of his group.

In this way, since Anna O. was not able to progress beyond her infantile leadership role, someone taking a group process approach to child development would predict that she would encounter considerable difficulty in relating to others. Also, he would predict that she would be especially distant toward men and other authority figures. It could further be postulated that she would remain isolated from all groups, since she was not too able to leave her own (imaginary) group. It is neither surprising nor considered accidental that eventually she devoted herself to work with deprived "white-slave" women who needed to be rescued from the domination of "cruel men". In essence, she committed herself to forming a group of her own where she was in fact the leader. This collecting "fallen" women was a sublimation which allowed her to live appropriately in consensually shared reality. At the same time, however, being the leader of the group enabled her to remain in an omnipotent, controlling position similar to one in her prime, infantile group where she initially struggled continually with alien authorities. In reality she continued to "act out" her unresolved infantile conflict where she was the benign authority, the leader, the father. Although she was rarely involved in direct power struggles with other authority figures, she continually encountered them with the purpose of defeating them.

Psychoanalysis started one hundred years ago with an anxious mother's call for help. Dr. Breuer's intuitive sensitivity to Anna O.'s symptoms was like a ray of sunlight piercing the dawn. In the artful hands of Freud this singularly simple crack of light was gradually expanded into a lightening of the sky that allowed us to see more clearly the dynamics of the mind. In their time, Freud's vital psychological theories revolutionized the thinking and treatment of emotional conflict. But as we age, we become more rigid and conservative; so too does psychoanalysis. We tend to protect what we have worked so hard to attain. We defend against new ideas and change. Psychoanalysis, the centenarian, has had and is having considerable qualms over incorporating new developments. It has no reservations in including new data related to individual (intrapsychic) differences and specific internal functioning of the mind. However, it does not appear to be comfortable in including the new data coming from research on group dynamics. It shows the most resistance to accepting the fact that group process not only affects behavior but also can motivate individuals to perform almost without regard to their underlying character structure. The thesis presented here is that it is necessary and essential to study the two variables (the intrapsychic and the interpsychic) which are operative at the same time in affecting the behavior of the individual. They affect one another and both directly influence the course of child development. Until now, psychoanalysis has studied the child as though he lived in a vacuum and had only an internal life. This void can be corrected by carefully examining the effects of the external group process on individual growth and behavior especially as this process is phenomenologically seen. Most of us tend to forget, or to deny, that from the start of life the individual develops in a solipsistic group process dynamics; the child sees himself as the center of the world, of the group, where other people are extensions of himself. If psychoanalysis is to continue to light up the sky in the next one hundred years, it will have to overcome its resistance to change.

References

BREUER, J., and FREUD, S., *Studies on Hysteria.* Standard Edition of the Complete Psychological Works of Sigmund Freud, vol. II. London: Hogarth Press, 1955.

BREUER, J., and FREUD, S. *Studies on Hysteria,* ed. J. Strachey and A. Freud. New York: Basic Books, 1957.

FREUD, S. *Beyond the Pleasure Principle, Group Psychology and Other Works.* Standard Edition of the Complete Psychological Works of Sigmund Freud, vol. XVIII. London: Hogarth Press, 1955a.

FREUD, S. *The Future of an Illusion, Civilization and Its Discontents and Other Works.* Standard Edition of the Complete Psychological Works of Sigmund Freud, vol. XXI. London: Hogarth Press, 1955b.

HARTMANN, H. KRIS, E., and LOWENSTEIN, R. M. Comments on the formation of psychic structure. *The Psychoanalytic Study of the Child,* vol. II. New York: International Universities Press, 1946.

MAHLER, M. S., FURER, M., and SETTLAGE, C. F. Emotional disturbances in childhood psychosis. In S. Arieti (ed.), *American Handbook of Psychiatry,* vol. I. New York: Basic Books, 1959.

PUMPIAN-MINDLIN, E. The position of psychoanalysis in relation to the biological and social sciences. In E. Pumpian-Mindlin (ed.), *Psychoanalysis as Science.* Stanford, Calif.: Stanford University Press, 1952.

The Psychopharmacological Treatment of Anna O.

Joseph T. Martorano

The scene is a small alcove in a large laboratory. Two young laboratory technicians, wearing white jackets over dungarees, are overheard talking to each other. In the background, a mammoth computer is functioning silently, producing massive mounds of printouts.

"How's that young paralyzed girl they just brought in doing?"

"Fine. Here's a copy of the computer printout."

"Interesting array of symptoms. Rather bizarre combination, the multiple paralyses, the difficulties with speech and sight plus some weird delusions. Death heads and black snakes."

"What does the computer say?"

"It recommended the initial use of an injectable bilevel third-generation fast-acting anxiolytic agent in the 5-mg dose range. This would have an 80 percent remission rate in an hour. If that isn't satisfactory, we can proceed with a second injection of a fourth-generation fast-acting tricyclic antidepressant which should be effective for any remaining symptoms up to a probability factor of 99 percent."

"Other 0.4 percent?"

"No need to worry. I already instituted treatment, and she is well enough to go home."

"Is she having any difficulty walking?"

"No, the paralysis wasn't of enough duration to have caused significant muscular atrophy."

"Good. I was afraid we were going to have to call a doctor in for consultation."

Is this a brave new world? Not really. We are standing on the threshold of a new frontier beyond the early primitive days of psychopharmacology, aided by a rapidly developing computerized technology. Except for a slight exaggeration in the amount of time needed for the drugs to be effective, the above scenario is capable of being produced today.

Treatment breakthroughs are emerging at an accelerating rate. Drug treatment is becoming increasingly specific and biological tests are being developed tailored to the exact needs of the individual patient, based on computerized symptom evaluation. An entire new generation of more effective drugs is going to be available in the immediate future to produce treatment results faster, more safely, and with fewer side effects.

The question of exactly how Anna O. might be treated today given the present state of chemotherapy is complex and intriguing. Most likely the initial treatment of Anna O. would be entirely psychopharmacological. The harried, overscheduled physician of today has little time to devote to the careful, time-consuming methodologies employed by Breuer in his investigations, which were carried on against the backdrop of a much slower world.

Further complicating the issue is the question of exactly how a woman of the sophistication and background of Ms. Pappenheim would present herself today. Certainly the symptomatology would be modified by exposure to a culture where hysterical paralysis and pseudocyesis are rapidly disappearing entities as the degree of psychological awareness of the population increases.

In the past century there was little real progress in psychopharmacological treatment approaches until thirty years ago, when the serendipitous discovery of chlorpromazine (Thorazine) led to a major revolution in the treatment of the psychiatric patient. So much has happened in these three short decades that the entire overall approach to the patient has been reassessed and modified dramatically. Not only have treatment strategies and expectations been radically changed by the direct effects of the new medications, but the medications have also influenced the development and style of present psychotherapeutic treatment modes as well as the evolution of a new, more effective and complete diagnostic system, which is described by DSM III.

There is no doubt, given the initially bewildering variety of symptomatology, that today Anna O. would be initially treated primarily with psychopharmacological agents. However, the wise clinician would use these agents to alleviate the distressing symptomatology to the point where the patient could effectively function in psychotherapy. This is a very important consideration, because if the treatment was too brief or completely drug-oriented, it is quite possible that our fast-moving medical time machine might well destroy all the valuable work that lay ahead of this ailing 21-year-old woman.

The psychopharmacological approach to Anna O. would differ from a primarily psychotherapeutic approach in a number of highly significant ways. First, the approach is more *operationally oriented*.

The psychopharmacologist has more highly structured criteria to evaluate the patient's symptoms. Further, the criteria are developed so as to monitor the ongoing condition of the patient. There are definitive structural guidelines as to exactly how long a medication regime should be maintained to decide whether the patient is going to improve. For example, on an antianxiety medication, the knowing psychopharmacologist is aware that 90 percent of the patients improve to maximum levels within a one-week period. This can be contrasted with the much longer onset of possible action in using common antidepressants, where improvement may not be visible for as long as one month after the onset of treatment.

In an operationally defined modality, the primary test of value is whether the drug produces improvement. Needless to say, this is a complex vector, and improvement may often be a balance weighed between overlapping positive and negative effects of the drug. For instance, sometimes the excessive sedation caused by a tranquilizer will negate the positive effects of the tranquilization.

In implementing operational strategies, the treating doctor is constantly using a "flow chart" approach to evaluation. The symptoms are first grouped into clusters that have been shown to be responsive to specific drug approaches. Then the treatment is instituted and evaluated after an appropriate period of time. If the treatment is ineffective, then the next line of treatment is considered. This approach offers the best means to consider retrospectively the psychopharmacological treatment of Anna O.

Psychopharmacological treatment also differs from pure psychotherapy in that *there is less lag between initiation of treatment and patient response;* some drug treatment may be almost miraculously immediate in terms of affecting a positive response.

Naturally, the use of psychopharmaceuticals presents a shorter, generally more effective approach to the vast majority of patients. In fact, they often produce such a dramatic improvement that the patient may withdraw from treatment, and unwittingly be deprived of further necessary treatment.

In the case of Anna O., if medication had produced a prompt and dramatic response, then the patient-doctor interface would have been greatly reduced, and this most likely would have radically changed not only the nature of her treatment course, but also her subsequent life. Almost certainly the abbreviated contact with the doctor would have eliminated many aspects of the transference (as well as the countertransference) relationship, decreased the patient's secondary gain, and abbreviated her need to remain ill. Almost certainly there would have been a substantial reduction in the initial suffering and discomfort experienced by the patient. The weakening of Anna's transference would probably also have prevented the pseudocyesis, and probably the subsequent hospitalizations would have been averted.

This chapter is organized to approach the symptoms in layers, starting with the superficial manifestations and then considering the underlying possibilities when the earlier symptoms are removed. I shall begin with the treatment of the overt presenting symptoms.

Breuer was originally consulted by the wealthy Pappenheim family to treat their 21-year-old daughter, who lay incapacitated by a bewildering variety of symptoms. Upon examination, Anna O. had a persistent nervous cough, had a complete paralysis of her right arm, had a bilateral paralysis of both lower limbs, and could only move the fingers of her left hand. In addition, there was severe impairment of her sight and speech, and a rigidity due to the paralysis of her neck muscles, which prevented her from turning her neck.

When Breuer was asked to examine her, he was not able to ascertain a physical cause for the symptoms. He then resorted to a series of hypnotic inductions, which eventually led the patient to transfer her dependency needs from her dying father to Breuer. Undoubtedly, the young Bertha was a manipulative, seductive young woman who succeeded in developing the first recorded countertransference in the good doctor, Breuer.

At times, she also complained of "black snakes" and "death heads" in her room. These visual hallucinations occurred with great intensity following a trance state. However, while visual hallucinations in a young female lead one to suspect organicity, secondary to toxic ingestion, there is no history of drug ingestion other than some morphine that was given her when she was a patient at a sanatorium.

To do justice to the intricacy of the case, it is necessary to consider the steps of drug treatment as they would have been rendered in the overall longitudinal unfolding of the case. Psychopharmacology is divided by therapeutic action into several major classes of drugs. Most drugs are used primarily for symptomatic relief. However, there are also a number of drugs which act on deeper cortical levels to actually cure the disease by working on the underlying physiological brain abnormalities.

What could drugs do in regard to the symptoms of Anna O.? Change could probably be affected on several different levels:

1. The stepwise use of drugs could be used to help in diagnosis. If a certain drug eliminated a certain symptom, then a working diagnosis could be established. Further, the incremental use of drugs could lead to a refining of the diagnosis by the progressive elimination of different symptoms. In other words, the diagnosis could be made retrospectively.

2. There could be alleviation of anxiety and tension by minor tranquilizers.

3. If there were underlying psychotic components of the disease state, these could be controlled by the use of a major tranquilizer.

4. If there was a demonstrable depressive component which produced significant neurovegetative symptoms, antidepressant drugs could effectively alleviate that segment of the disease state. The improved mood could lead to improved ability to direct and control certain behavioral manifestations.

5. The drugs could be used to control any underlying agoraphobia and other symptoms which needed to be differentiated, such as pseudo-neurotic schizophrenia.

The clinician would work closely with the patient, first getting a complete listing of all the patient's symptoms, then moving on to obtain a complete medical history, particularly with regard to past treatment, allergies, and any coexisting medical diseases that might interfere with drug treatment. Onset, duration, and any situations which might alter the severity of symptoms would be taken into account.

After the physician had evaluated the symptoms, he would carefully consider whether to try and treat only the presenting symptoms or to start by directly attacking the underlying condition. This is not always an easy decision. With Anna O., there would be some conflict even initially as to what to treat her with to get significant improvement. Since the severity of symptoms (hallucinations, paralysis) indicates the distinct possibility that the patient might be unable to report accurately, consultation with appropriate family members would be necessary. A family history, including detailed mental health profiles on parents and siblings, would also be indicated.

The presenting symptomatology in this case is compatible with the redefined diagnosis of conversion disorder. According to the recently released DSM III, the diagnosis of "Hysteria Neurosis Conversion Type" is based on the predominant disturbance being a loss or alteration of physical functioning in such a manner that it suggests a physical disorder.

In addition, the disorder involves psychological factors in three significant ways:

1. There has to be a temporal relationship between the environmental stimulus and the symptom.
2. The symptom enables the individual to avoid some psychological difficulty.
3. The symptom enables the individual to get additional emotional support.

The diagnosis should be made only if the symptom is determined not to be under voluntary control and cannot be explained by a known physical disorder.

Anna O. would seem to fit these criteria for the diagnosis of a hysterical conversion disorder very closely. Therefore the doctor could proceed directly with instituting the appropriate treatment. Since the physician would probably surmise that the severe decompensation was due to being overwhelmed by anxiety and that the patient had oversomatized her anxiety to such a significant degree that she was unable to function, he would want to institute treatment immediately.

The most probable initial choice of drug would be an antianxiety agent. These are the drugs most frequently used worldwide, and about 70 million prescriptions a year are written in the United States alone for a total of 10 million people. They are the drugs of choice in most psychological cases because they are very effective and overwhelmingly safe.

The common antianxiety agents are well known and are in widespread use through the world. Diazepam (Valium) is the largest-selling prescription drug in history. It is a drug of enormous effectiveness which generally relieves almost all forms of anxiety in a very short time. However, it provides *symptomatic, not curative treatment.*

All the minor tranquilizers act in a rather similar fashion to relieve anxiety and tension without producing sleep. As a group, they are very similar in total effect and differ mainly in their pharmacokinetics in regard to blood distribution and body elimination periods. Therefore Anna O. could also be treated by any number of drugs with familiar names like Librium, Tranxene, Centrax, Xanax, and Ativan.

The major difficulties associated with the use of minor tranquilizers are excessive sedation and a decrease of the capacity to maintain high levels of cognitive organization. But unless they are used together with other CNS sedative drugs such as alcohol or the barbiturates, minor tranquilizers are not likely to be abused, provided the physician gives the patient appropriate guidelines for using them and does not issue excessive unmonitored amounts of tranquilizers to the patient.

What would have happened had Anna O. been treated with effective doses of a minor tranquilizer? Certainly, it is likely that the hysterical aspects of her symptoms would have been greatly ameliorated within a very short time, ranging from a couple of hours to several days. However, modern psychopharmacology has used the symptom as a *functional* point of reference. Therefore, once the hysterical symptoms were removed by the judicious use of a minor tranquilizer, acting much as a scalpel providing an incision to allow further investigation, the patient's underlying symptoms could be examined more clearly. Also, as the arresting manifestations of anxiety and tension were diminished, the patient would be more accessible to verbal psychotherapy.

Thus the keen therapist would seize the opportunity of using the drugs judiciously to provide a breakthrough phenomenon, which would allow therapeutic access to a patient whose severe hysterical manifestations had interfered with speech and sight. In the case of Anna O., the therapist would then be able to talk with her about her feelings and investigate the psychological causes of the hysteria.

When Breuer was called in, he proceeded to use hypnotic induction techniques. The patient ventilated her symptoms, and each symptom progressively disappeared. Eventually, rather importantly, the symptoms were linked with the patient's inability to handle the imminent death of her father, who lay dying in the house. Unfortunately, instead of experiencing total relief, Anna transferred her dependency to Breuer so completely that she mentally conceived his child to preclude total separation from him.

The best response to anxiolytic treatment usually occurs in those patients having the highest initial levels of anxiety. The greatest, most dramatic improvements take place in the sickest patient. Furthermore, in such patients the high degree of sedation frequently associated with the benzodiazepines is often found to be desirable.

High response rates are also seen in those patients who present high levels of anxiety combined with somatic complaints. The presence of obsessive-compulsive and interpersonal complaints is associated with a low expected response to the anxiolytic agents, and patients with a high degree of depressive symptomatology usually improve less than patients without any depressive symptoms. If Anna O. was indeed inflicted with an underlying depressive disorder, it should be expected that her initial response to the anxiolytic agents would be minimal.

How long should Anna O. be treated with antianxiety medication?

This is not necessarily a simple consideration. Efficacy, the gradual build-up of tolerance, and the blurring of underlying symptoms are all important factors. One important predictor of response to benzodiazepine treatment is the degree of improvement obtained after one week of treatment. Rickels (1978) has found that nearly 90 percent of the patients who respond within one week will show improvement after six weeks. Therefore, the psychopharmacologist is almost continually monitoring therapeutic response and reevaluating it in refining the course of treatment. If no improvement is observed during the first week of treatment, another treatment plan should be devised and implemented.

New information about the way in which anxiolytics work is coming to light every day. In 1977 Squires discovered that there are *specific receptors in the brain* for benzodiazepines (Squires and Braestrup, 1977).

Benzodiazepines fall into different classes depending upon their individual pharmacokinetics. The most important of the parameters is the duration of action, which is a function of both the length of elimination half-lives and the formation of active metabolites. Drugs like diazepam and calordiazedoxidepozide, which produce active metabolites, have relatively longer spans of action. The duration of the prolonged half-life is important in preventing rapid onset or withdrawal reactions. Hence there may be some advantage in using drugs with slightly longer half-lives in potentially addictive personalities.

With a drug like diazepam, there is a *three- to tenfold accumulation* when taken on a multiple-dose basis. However, there is no *direct* correlation between blood levels and sedative effect. Rather the central nervous sedative effects of this drug tend to decline as the duration of exposure increases. This property is properly referred to as *adaptation*.

As for efficacy, data have been accumulated which suggest the dose efficacy against anxiety of the benzodiazepines is in the 70 to 75 percent improvement range as contrasted to an average of 35 percent for placebos.

If Anna O. was aided initially by anxiolytic agents, she would most likely fit into one of the patterns suggested by Dr. Frank Ayd as either a *short-term drug user* (one who stops taking the drug in less than three months) or a *long-term drug user* (who takes the drug three or more months). *Long-term drug users* are further subdivided into *single-drug users* and *polydrug users*. The single-drug user is usually self-regulated and doesn't abuse the drug (Ayd, 1980). The difficult patients are the polydrug users who take whatever drug they can for the sedative and, occasionally, euphoric effect. These patients almost inevitably misuse and abuse both licit and illicit drugs. However, Anna's prolonged treatment with morphine during hospitalization in Switzerland would alert the astute physician to the possibility of her becoming a drug abuser.

In recent years a radically different type of treatment has been rapidly gaining favor—the use of *beta-adrenergic blocking agents* like propranolol (Inderal). These drugs are dramatically effective in those cases where the peripheral manifestations of the anxiety predominate. These peripheral manifestations are due to overreactivity of the sympathetic division of the autonomic nervous system and consist of stress-related symptoms like a rapid pulse, perspiration, rapid bowel function, and increased urination. These symptoms are relieved by the drug's acting directly on the peripheral autonomic nervous system and actually blocking the sympathetic effects.

Certainly initiating treatment with antianxiety drugs would be one favorable and desirable course. However, Anna O. might represent a more difficult diagnostic entity which might not so easily be *completely* treated by the relatively simple intervention with a minor tranquilizer. It is possible that underneath the hysterical façade lay an extension of a premature grief—pathological mourning.

As the anxiety levels decreased, the patient might be better able to focus on her pathological mourning for her father and work through the symptoms. She would then experience great relief and some of the symptoms would disappear immediately, thus eliminating much of the secondary gain from having to stay ill. Furthermore, unfortunately for history, less time on the part of the treating physician would be required. Hence the famous duel between transference and countertransference would never develop.

However, the immediate relief of the more striking presenting symptoms is just the beginning! Once the top layer of symptoms is unwrapped, the experienced treating psychopharmacologist has a number of important considerations. The major question is whether the presenting symptoms are masking an underlying depression disorder. What of the Anna O. case?

A major operational change has occurred in that modern psychopharmacology has leaned toward a stepwise consideration, using the flow sheet model to make decisions at each critical juncture. Each processed piece of information is evaluated, and it is then decided how to proceed along the flow sheet until a definitive treatment plan is finally established.

What does this mean exactly in regard to the case of Anna O.? The initial cluster of symptoms—the bizarre paralysis of limbs and neck muscles coupled with the difficulties in speech and sight—suggests a *hysterical* reaction. Indeed Freud's monograph was entitled *Anna O.: A Case of Hysteria.* However, the alert clinician today would also make further detailed queries to establish whether or not the patient was suffering from an *underlying depressive disorder.*

The past three decades have enriched our knowledge enough to alert us to precisely when psychopharmacological intervention in treating depression is necessary. The first major step in this process was the differentiation of reactive and endogenous depression.

Was the depression reactive or endogenous? Was it a result of a normal loss or an extension of mourning into a deeper process with accompanying abnormal physiological changes?

If Anna O. had a reactive depression, the wise psychopharmacologist might √ well *undertreat* it, using small-measure doses of a mild tranquilizer to relieve tension and allow the patient to gain needed peaceful sleep. However, if there were underlying neurovegetative symptoms establishing the diagnosis of an *endogenous depression,* the use of antidepressant medications would be indicated.

The major symptoms to be considered in establishing a diagnosis of endogenous depression are insomnia with early morning awakening, a weight loss of over 7 pounds in a three-week period, severe anorexia, and complete inability to experience pleasure (anhedonia psychomotor retardation).

It is precisely this distinction which makes the retrospective study of Anna O. so very fascinating. As Breuer proceeded with the investigative work, the actual notion of catharsis rather amazingly originated from the patient herself. It was the patient who so wisely suggested that the relief of her symptoms was due to the cathartic ventilation, the "chimney sweeping." A major therapeutic breakthrough came in relating the paralysis of her limbs to the difficulty the patient had experienced in encountering her dying father. In terms of depression, these symptoms might be seen as an extension of the mourning process into a pathological area. However, today the astute clinician armed with almost two decades of computer-gathered information would also question the patient more specifically in the neurovegatative sphere.

Thus we come to the now familiar inquiries of the modern psychopharmacologist—

Are you experiencing any difficulty sleeping?
Do you wake up early?
How is your appetite?
Have you lost any weight?
Do you feel slowed down?
Are you constipated?

The neurovegetative symptoms these questions inquire about *fit into a cluster.* Usually the combination of early morning awakening, a weight loss of greater than 7 pounds in three weeks, anorexia, psychomotor retardation that is most pronounced in the morning, constipation, and persistent mood dejection suggest an endogenous type of depression that is amenable to intervention by modern drugs. The two major classes of drugs that have proved effective in endogenous depression are the tricyclic antidepressant and the mono-amino-oxidase inhibitors.

What would be the predicted response of Anna O. to antidepressant treatment? Antidepressant medications are currently not easy drugs to use. There is a long lag before the effective onset of action; the lag may be as much as three to four weeks. Seldom does the patient experience any relief, except for sedative side effects, before a two-week period has passed. In addition, the anticholinergic sedative effects of the medication are frequently incapacitating, and numerous patients either discontinue or decrease the medication before a desired result is obtained.

Therefore the treatment course would necessitate a four-to-six-week trial on antidepressants. The medication would gradually be increased over a two-week period. If the medication was too sedative, a single nighttime dose might prove a feasible alternative to the spacing out of daily doses.

The usual first signs of improvement are in the neurovegetative sphere. The appetite returns, the sleep improves, and the patient starts to put on weight. As the symptoms abate in these ways, there begins an improvement in mood, which continues as the patient is maintained on the medications. A tricky point which has unfortunately been demonstrated over and over again is that the premature discontinuation or decrease of the medication may result in the return of symptoms.

More specifically for Anna O., we would see a gradual remission of her paralysis, an increased ability to communicate, and the disappearance of her bizarre "black snakes" and "death heads" which might be attributed to a somatic delusion secondary to an underlying depressive disorder. As the depression improved, the patient would be maintained on the antidepressant drug for an extended period of time. As close monitoring suggested the disappearance of the symptoms entirely, the drugs would be gradually tapered off. In most patients, this period of treatment ranges from several months to a year. In addition, patients with recurring unipolar depressions may be maintained on tricyclics or other antidepressants to prevent the recurrence of the disease.

The major difficulties associated with such treatment are the long lag of the onset of action and the presence of many undesired adverse side effects, such as unwarranted sedation, hypotension, weakness, and cardiotoxic effects. Fortunately, there are several major new drugs currently awaiting FDA approval that promise significant improvements in producing speedier results with minimal anticholinergic or cardiotoxic side effects.

Another consideration is whether any of the symptoms were due to an underlying agoraphobia. While discussing antidepressant agents, it might be judicious to consider whether the symptoms could be attributed to an agoraphobic-type pattern as small, limited amounts of tricyclic agents have been demonstrated to be startlingly effective in the treatment of agoraphobia. Certainly, the striking withdrawal of this patient, her confinement to the house, and her self-limiting paralyses suggest the possibility of at least a partial agoraphobic symptom pattern.

If this was an important aspect of this case, it seems most likely that the initial broad treatment with anxiolytic agents would be partially effective in removing the symptoms and allowing the perception of the external environment with less fear and apprehension. However, if the clinician wished to further advance this process, a *trial* with small doses of imipramine (10 mg three times a day) would be suggested. This dose level is so small that there is little possibility of imposing a significant antidepressant action. Also, the treatment result can usually be evaluated immediately instead of having to wait the six weeks with the normal course of antidepressants. Like so many psychopharmacological approaches, this therapy is empirically based. If the patient improved on the low doses of antidepressants, it would suggest that there was a strong possibility of an underlying agoraphobic component to her disorder.

While there is little direct evidence, considering the overall symptom constellation and the eventual recovery of the patient, to indicate that Anna O. was in a pure *borderline psychotic state* without any hysterical and/or depressive overlay, the knowing psychopharmacologist would have a great treatment advantage in being able to use a trial of antipsychotic agents (major tranquilizers) to rule out the presence of an underlying psychotic disorder.

In this particular case it might be wise to refer back to the schizophrenic disorder originally described by Hoch and Polatin (1949), as there are many related aspects which are important to considering treatment. Their original description was of a patient who presented neurotic symptoms of every conceivable nature combined with latent paranoia and micropsychotic episodes. Between episodes, the patient reconstituted with a healthier façade.

Certainly, the global manifestations of the symptoms of Anna O. suggest that there may have been an underlying psychotic disorder closely resembling the clinical state originally described by Hoch and Polatin. This is especially true of the repeated occurrence of the psychotic-type material represented by the presence of the "black snakes" and "death heads."

The psychopharmacologist could best test for this possibility by using a trial of antipsychotic agents (such as chlorpromazine haldoperidol), which would greatly help in the eventual differential diagnoses as their effectiveness would directly suggest the presence of an underlying psychotic component to the disorder and indicate that the patient should be placed on a closely monitored antipsychotic drug regime.

There exists, of course, the possibility that Anna O. may have been suffering from *a combination of any of the above disorders,* and treatment of any one of these states might result in only a partial remission. For instance, it is quite likely that treatment with an antianxiety agent alone would have only a partial effect; then the therapist would have to decide whether to proceed with another drug or to combine the antianxiety agent and another drug.

Fortunately, psychopharmacology can be used along such parallel treatment lines (see flow chart on p. 96). If a decision is made to institute another treatment, such as a course of antidepressant agents, the first treatment can be maintained even if its efficacy was not complete. In actual fact, there are several types of drugs that combine antianxiety or antipsychotic agents with antidepressant medications to decrease the lag imposed by having to choose between treatment states and to improve patient compliance while saving time.

Since the combined agents have different onsets of action (with the antide-

Flow Sheet for Consideration of Psychopharmacological Treatment of Anna O.

Step 1

Treatment with anxiolytic agents
Decrease of paralyses, perceptual impairments, and hallucinations
    complete improvement
    partial improvement
    no improvement

Step 2

Treatment with antidepressants
Direct evaluation of neurovegetative symptoms (anorexia, insomnia, psychomotor retardation, etc.)
    complete improvement
    partial improvement
    no improvement

Step 3

Treatment with antipsychotic agents
Decrease paralyses, perceptual impairments, and hallucinatory material
    complete improvement
    partial improvement
    no improvement

Step 4

Consideration of combined treatment approach—of using various combinations of antianxiety, antipsychotic, and antidepressant drugs
    complete improvement
    partial improvement
    no improvement

Step 5

Consideration of addition of Inderal (Propranolol). If there is the continued presence of sympathetic symptoms such as increased pulse, increased bowel movement, increased urination.

pressant usually having the longer lag), it is possible to evaluate the efficacy of each of the components simply by noting the time of the onset of improvement. For instance, if a combined antipsychotic and antidepressant was given (the most common ones are Triavil and Etrafon), immediate decrease in the hallucinatory states of envisioning the "death heads" and "black snakes" would be properly attributed to a therapeutic effect of the antipsychotic agent. However, if there was no noticeable improvement until two or three weeks after the drug was instituted, improvement then more likely would be due to the antidepressant, especially if the improvement was best noted in a neuro-vegetative sphere. This pattern of prescribing is quite common to decrease expense and improve compliance, although many clinicians prefer to use two separate drugs to better monitor the blood levels of each of the drugs.

In any case, the psychopharmacologist has to be alert for the possibility of two or more disorders coexisting and prepared to treat either and/or both of them simultaneously.

The recent emergence of DSM III has provided several other possibilities for diagnostic entities. Although hysterical psychosis does not appear in DSM III, there are two categories that are roughly equivalent to this diagnostic category: (1) "Brief Reactive Psychosis," a brief florid psychosis in reaction to an overwhelming stress, and (2) "Factitious Disorder with Psychological Symptoms," in which the physical symptoms are not real. The term "hysterical" was avoided because of its multiple, often confusing meanings. While the former diagnosis could be considered in terms of using psychopharmacological intervention and diagnostic differentiation (e.g. a trial of limited amounts of antipsychotic drugs would ameliorate some of the major symptoms), the use of drugs would be of only limited, if not marginal, use in establishing or eliminating the diagnosis of "Factitious Disorder," which was originated to do away with the murky boundary between the act of malingering to achieve an easily understandable goal and the genuine psychotic experience over which the individual lacks any control.

What about negative aspects of a psychopharmacological approach?

The use of drugs is not without substantial drawbacks. While not all of these factors need be a concern in every situation, the patient Anna O. might have been significantly impaired by any of several different factors:

1. *Excessive sedation.* Most psychiatric medications are either central nervous system depressants (minor and major tranquilizers) or have anticholinergic sedative effects. This sedation impairs the ability of the patient to think clearly and to be able to organize cognitions satisfactorily. The drowsiness can be decreased by lowering the medication level or by the capacity of the nervous system to eventually adapt and moderate the sedative effect. Nevertheless, it is a serious difficulty for the person who has the potential to become a drug abuser or who has to function in a job that requires fine motor coordination. Fortunately, except for the brief therapeutic application of morphine in Switzerland, Anna O. does not appear to fall into this category.

2. *Side effects and toxic reactions.* Side effects are the unfortunate accompaniments which occur when a drug affects more than one particular system. The most striking side effect is usually the sedation referred to in the preceding paragraph; however, there are a number of serious side effects, particularly with the antidepressant drugs, which often limit their usage in the dose necessary to obtain the maximum therapeutic effect. In this case it is difficult to predict which, if any, of the side effects Anna O. might have developed. Toxic reactions are even more unpredictable. They can be most severe and even life-threatening under certain circumstances; the occurrence of a toxic reaction will necessitate the discontinuing of the medication and the loss of the therapeutic gain.

3. *Addictive considerations.* These are a problem only in relation to the minor tranquilizers. Unfortunately, there has been a great deal of media attention to and overemphasis on the addictive potential of the anxiolytic drugs. However, the actual difficulty usually appears only in relation to *the potentiation of other sedative drugs* (barbiturates, alcohol, etc.) rather than the abuse of the tranquilizer alone.

It is quite possible that there might have been some minor abuse by Anna O. even if she had been treated by only antianxiety agents. The best defense against this possibility is an alert clinician who prescribes carefully limited amounts of a drug on nonrenewable prescription blanks and then monitors the use of the drug.

4. *Decrease in the interpersonal contact with the treating physician.* This can be a very real loss. Certainly being deprived of the privilege of personal contact with a man as warm and as caring as Breuer could represent a real loss for a patient. This loss might be intensified if the patient had been first treated in intensive interpersonal therapy. Psychopharmacology, when it is misused, tends to be somewhat impersonal, and the individual patient can be lost in a crowd unless the doctor takes special care to demonstrate an attitude of concern. Without this attitude of caring, the patient can experience a potentially major loss of necessary support.

The idea of psychopharmacological treatment for Anna O. presents an intriguing question. Fraulein Pappenheim recovered and went on to become one of the leading figures in the German social work movement. Later in life, she became associated with distinguished, important people, including Martin Buber, and spent a very productive old age. Given this return to full functioning, it seems unlikely that she had suffered earlier from a severe psychosis. The more likely correct diagnoses was of a less damaging nature. Therefore it is important to question exactly what effect psychopharmacological intervention might have had in the long run.

There are numerous very practical advantages to a basically pharmaceutically oriented approach. First, there is an *economic* advantage. While this might not necessarily have been a significant factor in regard to the very wealthy Pappenheim family, it is a major consideration for most patients. But the economic base should be applied not solely to money, but also to the physician's time. Few could afford the absolute luxury of the time that Breuer was able to devote to this young lady. In this respect, psychopharmacology offers the very substantial advantage of allowing the physician to decrease the amount of time devoted to treatment.

Second, *more people would have been able to treat this patient.* The doctor need not have been an authentic genius such as Freud or Breuer. A relatively ordinary emergency room doctor could have given the patient immediate significant symptomatic relief to allow her to return home. And, returning to our initial example, the day is not far off when the treatment will be done quite effectively by a computer with the minimal use of backup personnel.

Third, *treatment would have been faster.* Using appropriate medications, the treatment of Anna O. would have been more rapid. There would have been little, if any, need for the extended treatment and the subsequent institutionalizations that occurred. It is quite possible that the patient would have rapidly returned to a normal functioning life in a very short while.

Drugs that are more specific biologically and have a speedier onset of action with fewer side effects are being developed, especially in the area of treating depression. For example, tetracyclics, a new generation of antidepressants, are becoming available. They are more potent and yet less toxic with fewer anticholinergic side effects. Biologicals will soon be developed to act against specific chemicals in the body, for example, to exclusively block dopamine or norepinephrine. As these biologicals develop and become even more specific, their efficacy and their capabilities will increase greatly. Treatment with such drugs would have been both faster and more effective, returning Anna O. to her normative baseline, and perhaps allowing her to be even more productive than she eventually became.

In the words of Count Vittorio Alfieri (1749-1803), the philosopher, "Often the test of courage is not to die but to live." The life of Anna O. clearly demonstrates courage and other fine qualities. Psychopharmacological intervention, if it had been available, would have freed her earlier from the impairment of unwanted illness and allowed her to start living.

References

AYD, FRANK J., JR. Benzodiazepines: Social issues misuse and abuse. *Psychosomatics,* 21–25, October 1980.

HOCH, P. H., and POLATIN, P. Pseudoneurotic forms of schizophrenia. *Psychiat. Quart.* 23:248–276, 1949.

RICKELS, K. Use of antianxiety agents in anxious outpatients. *Psychopharmacology,* 58:1–17, 1978.

SQUIRES, R. F., and BRAESTRUP, C. Benzodiazepine receptors in rat brains. *Nature,* 266:732–734, 1977.

Additional References

BALTER, M. B., LEVINE, J., and MANHEIMER, A. Antianxiety/sedative drug use. *New England J. Med.*, 290:769–774, 1974.

Diagnostic and Statistical Manual of Mental Disorders, 3rd ed. American Psychiatric Association, 1980.

GREENBLATT, D. J., ALLEN, M. D., LOCNISKAR, A., et al. Lorazepam kinetics in the elderly. *Clin. Pharmacol, Therapeutics,* 26:103–113, 1979.

GREENBLATT, D. J., ALLEN, M. D., MACLAUGHLIN, D. S., et al. Single and multiple-dose kinetics of oral lorazepam in humans: *J. Pharmacokinet. Biopharm.,* 7:159–179, 1979.

GREENBLATT, D. J., and SHADER, R. I. *Benzodiazepines in Clinical Practice.* New York: Raven Press, 1974.

HOLLISTER, L. F. Psychosomatics. *Benzodiazepines,* October 1980. Current update.

JONES, E. *The Life and Work of Sigmund Freud,* vol. I, pp. 223–226. New York: Basic Books, 1953.

MARTORANO, J. T., and TESTA, N. The use of tranquilizers in surgical patients: Anxiolytic agents. Part I—An overview. *J. Surg. Pract.,* vol. 7, no. 1, February 1978.

MELLINGER, G. D., BALTER, M. B., MANHEIMER, D. I., et al. Psychic distress, life crisis and use of psychotherapeutic medications. *Arch. Gen. Psychiat.,* 35:1045–1052, 1978.

SHADER, R. I., M. D. *Manual of Psychiatric Therapeutics,* p. 35. Boston: Little, Brown, 1975.

Treating the depressed patient. *Roche Report—Frontiers of Psychiatry,* vol. 10, no. 11, November 1980.

Anna O. and Bertha Pappenheim: An Historical Perspective

10

Marion A. Kaplan

If Anna O. were alive today, how would we treat her? I am not sure we would have the opportunity to treat her at all. This chapter posits the idea that if Bertha Pappenheim lived today she would probably not have become Anna O., the Patient. I will argue that the suffocating lot of nineteenth-century bourgeois women produced the case of Anna O. Her illness was a cultural construct, integrally related to the position of women of her day. The socially confining, intellectually stifling, politically and legally constricting conditions faced by women of her class and era and the particular intellectual vitality, social commitment and sense of justice of Bertha Pappenheim interacted to produce Anna O.

This chapter examines Bertha Pappenheim's early years and describes her career after the episode of her illness. Her life can be compared to those of other leading women reformers, many of whom suffered through crises similar to hers in kind, although not in extent. A study of the life of Bertha Pappenheim casts light on the place of women in late-nineteenth-century society and on the origins and nature of German-Jewish and, indeed, all feminism. Pappenheim's outrage at the injustices faced by women made her an indomitable fighter for equality. The enthusiastic response she evoked in German-Jewish women was the result of her ability to use her distinctive attributes to tap feelings based upon the solitary, but common, experiences of these women. Her anger against male dominance increased over the course of her career. At first she attempted to improve the status of women in the traditional organizations of the German-Jewish community and to draw the attention of these organizations to issues that concerned women's rights and welfare. Despairing of rapid progress with this approach, she forged new channels—women's channels—through which her followers could shape their world.

Pappenheim embraced the ideas of German bourgeois feminists who accepted the dominant image of women as dutiful and self-sacrificing wives and mothers. Like them, she used the language of traditional ''feminine'' qualities to enlarge women's public sphere, suggesting that ''social motherhood''—

women's contribution of their motherly talents to society at large—was as much women's domain as their homes and families. She demanded equal educational, career, and political opportunities for women so that they might better serve their families and nation. Pappenheim urged German-Jewish women to mobilize their womanly virtues in the service of the Jewish community.

Pappenheim applied German feminism to Jewish circumstances. Her convictions as a religious Jew were as intense as her feminist beliefs. While her feminism was often incompatible with Jewish tradition, bringing her into conflict with the Jewish establishment, she insisted that only greater participation by women in their community would prevent Judaism's decline. Further she hoped to preserve the communal and religious distinctiveness of her people while fostering tolerance and coexistence among Germans and Jews. Pappenheim regarded herself as a German, but she was sensitive to anti-Semitism. Hoping to defuse such prejudices, and stirred by compassion for victimized Jewish women in Eastern Europe, she engaged in a crusade against Jewish involvement in white slavery. Her collaboration with non-Jewish feminists was, in part, a means of combating anti-Semitism, but it was also proof to Pappenheim that there was a possibility for cooperation and friendship among German Christians and German Jews. In all of her adult life she seems to have been engaged in an effort to reconcile her feminist, Jewish, and German identities.

Bertha Pappenheim was born the daughter of wealthy, religious Jews. As "just another daughter" (the third) in a strictly traditional Jewish household, Bertha was conscious that her parents would have preferred a male child. The Pappenheims finally had a son, Wilhelm (1860–1937), their fourth child. Bertha and Wilhelm, the only two children who lived to adulthood, did not get along very well. Bertha may have been jealous of the special treatment accorded her brother, particularly the education that she was denied. Although this was an era in which most universities did not allow women to matriculate, she always felt that her lack of education was due to the Jewish prejudice which expected girls to marry and boys to achieve scholarly sucess. When her father became ill, Wilhelm was a university student, too busy to take on family responsibilities. Thus his sister, like many young women of her generation, was forced to share nursing duties with her mother. It is likely that she deeply resented this sexual division of labor between her brother and herself. Nonetheless she certainly would have hidden these feelings possibly even from herself, given the strong taboos against the expression of anger by women. (Wilhelm later owned one of the greatest libraries of social work in Central Europe, but his sister, a renowned social worker, rarely visited him).

Upon finishing high school, where she learned fluent French, Italian, and English, this attractive, imaginative young woman was expected to settle down and await marriage. Bertha's life, in her own words, was "typical of a *höhere Tochter* (a middle-class daughter of marriageable age) of the religious Jewish middle class." An intelligent woman, her intellectual gifts were stifled. She was expected to fill up the period between school and marriage with occasional social diversions and a great deal of embroidering. Referring to the life of the *höhere Tochter,* Helene Lange, the founder of German feminism, wrote, "one can still feel a belated horror at the thought of the countless numbers of wasted possibilities and unused energies."[1]

At twenty-one, after having nursed her dying father, Pappenheim experienced the symptoms that are described in the "case of Anna O." Breuer noted that while Anna engaged in her needlework (a hobby which she, unlike other feminists, enjoyed her entire life), she "embellished her life in a manner which probably influenced her decisively in the direction of her illness, by indulging in systematic daydreaming."[2] Freud suggested that women who did needlework, a popular pastime, were particularly prone to such daydreams.[3] Little is known about Pappenheim's life for the seven years after Breuer's treatment.[4] She had relapses, spent some time in sanatoriums, traveled, and eventually regained her health. She moved to Germany with her mother in 1889 and lived near Frankfurt am Main for the rest of her life.

The psychoanalytic and therapeutic professions have turned with particular interest to the case of the hysterical woman who later became a well-known feminist.[5] They have suggested that Bertha Pappenheim in her later life was sublimating the neuroses she had experienced during her illness. Some have suggested that her feminism was essentially her earlier problems in another form. These interpretations are typical of those of many mental health professionals and antisuffragists who have automatically associated feminism with mental illness. In 1918, for example, one Freudian wrote of feminists in general: "A certain proportion . . . are neurotics who . . . are compensating for masculine trends . . . others are more or less successfully sublimating sadistic and homosexual ones."[6] Some psychoanalysts, particularly Karen Horney, were sensitive to the cultural factors that impinged on women, shaping their personalities, but most have tended to minimize or ignore the social, economic, cultural, and political reasons why women retreated from the Victorian norm. Mary Ryan, in *Womanhood in America,* notes: "By the mid-twentieth century any questioning of woman's place was readily equated with neurosis by the Freudian psychologists and their popularizers."[7] She cites one Freudian who declared that the biography of Wollstonecraft (whose *Vindications of the Rights of Women* was published in 1792) read like a case study of hysteria and others who cavalierly dismissed suffragists as hopeless neurotics. Any argument against the sexual status quo was declared a perversion of psychic normality. When analysts focus on the psychological causes of feminism to the exclusion of the social, economic, popitical, and cultural reasons for it, they seriously misunderstand Pappenheim and the women of her generation.

In the Victorian era a constricting culture shaped the lives of middle-class women.[8] They could respond in several ways to the socially assigned roles of wife and mother. There were certainly women who were happy with their lot.

Brought up to serve and entertain men, some women accepted their roles with ease and grace. If their husbands and sons achieved professional fame or fortune and their daughters married well, they too felt successful. Most did not recognize or acknowledge their limited horizons. Overt rebellion was a second possible response to "woman's destiny," but it was likely to cause great pain and hardship. It often left the rebel destitute and deprived of her children. Since most women did not have the economic or legal means to escape the confines of their lives, many embarked on a third route. They became depressed or developed hysterical maladies. The "misunderstood" or "unhappy" woman was a common phenomenon. In fact, one historian of the German women's movement claimed that such women were "practically the norm in many circles."[9] German novelists described disorders like nervous tension, hysteria, backaches, and migraines as standard for women.[10] The author Fanny Lewald blamed the nervousness, indolence, coquetry, and extravagance of fashionable German women on their aimless and barren existence.[11]

These traits were not confinced to German women.[12] Historians have recently suggested that hysterical maladies were not only a socially recognized behavior pattern for middle-class American women, but, as such, provided legitimate behavior option for some.[13] Among these were women for whom hysteria or mental illness may have been desperate attempts to overcome obstacles that hindered their human development. England's leading abolitionist, Josephine Butler, suffered recurring breakdowns from nervous exhaustion.[14] In America, Jane Addams, the pioneer settlement house organizer, had "nervous depressions and a sense of maladjustment" as a young woman. She recognized that her distress was related to "a sense of futility, a misdirected energy."[15] Her solace and relief came only after she involved herself in social work and shunned the typical life of young middle-class women of her era. Elizabeth Cady Stanton, the American feminist leader, also struggled with her limited role: "I suffered with mental hunger, which, like an empty stomach, is very depressing."[16] The German suffrage leader Hedwig Dohm (born in 1833) described the pains of womanhood as she experienced them:

> When they robbed me of the right to develop my own individuality because of the circumstance that I was born with a female body; when . . . they put into my hand the really over-estimated cooking spoon,—they drove a human soul . . . into a desert of *wild fantasies* and sterile dreams.[17]

Finally, in the last decades of the nineteenth century, there was a breakthrough that opened a fourth path to small but growing numbers of enterprising women. They could opt for certain newly emerging careers, such as teaching, the civil service, and (by the turn of the century) social work. These new professions provided single women with an alternative, one which allowed some to reject traditional roles without social punishment or mental anguish. Hedwig Wachenheim was one of this younger generation. Born in 1892 and later a representative of the Social Democratic party, she grew up in a "rich, but not very rich'' German-Jewish family. Her mother's migraines belong to her "most vivid childhood recollections," and she spent her own years as a *höhere Tochter* embroidering, visiting, and daydreaming.[18] However, she was able to rescue herself from the life she hated by enrolling in the first school of social work. Her mentor at that school was Alice Salomon, who had also narrowly escaped marriage and domesticity. Born in 1872, Salomon had suffered through similar teen years, considering her youth typical of a daughter of well-to-do German Jews: "The unhappiest years of my life were between the ages of fifteen and twenty . . . I danced a lot . . . we were among the first . . . to play tennis . . . but . . . there were twenty-four hours in a day. . . . The life of a *höhere Tochter* was unbearable." [19] Salomon evaded the life prescribed for her by founding not only the first school of social work, but the entire field of modern social work in Germany.

Given the strictures of Victorian societies, it was certainly the woman of unusual temperament, perspicacity, and sensitivity who fought injustice where most succumbed to tradition. Indeed, one might even hypothesize that women who could *not* cope with the obvious injustices of their lot were psychologically "healthier" (that is, intent upon developing what Abraham Maslow has called "full humaness" instead of accepting "historically-arbitrary, culturally-local value-models"), than those who reconciled themselves to second-class citizenship and inferior status.

Although psychological explanations may be of only limited use in understanding the sources of Pappenheim's feminism, Breuer's description of Anna O.'s character traits are valuable to the historian. Some of the young woman's feelings and personal characteristics remained strikingly similar in the adult personality of Bertha Pappenheim.

Breuer recorded that during her illness she exhibited a sensitivity to injustice and a strong social consciousness.[20] Upon her recovery these character traits were reawakened by her female relatives in Frankfurt who were active in Jewish charities and, more importantly, by German feminism. Pappenheim read *The Woman,* a popular feminist periodical begun in 1894.[21] She admired its founder, Helene Lange, the president of the National Association of Women Teachers and the main theoretician of the German women's movement.[22] The German movement's demand for equal educational opportunities for women appealed to Pappenheim, who also appreciated its call for equal career opportunities and equal political rights for women. Her sense of justice as well as her repressed anger at the unequal treatment accorded her in contrast to her brother must have been aroused by these ideas, for she quickly applied them to the plight of Jewish women in Jewish custom and law. Her interest in German feminism coalesced with her deeply felt identity as a Jew. The relative successes of German feminists in improving women's status encouraged her to attempt to right what she considered the injustices against Jewish women. Her specific interest in the traffic in women grew out of the German movement's concern with abolition and white slavery as well as her own knowledge of Jewish prostitution.

Breuer described one of Anna O.'s essential traits as "sympathetic kindness."[23] She would related many stories about taking care of sick people while she sat with him. Bertha Pappenheim consoled and cared for the outcasts and urged others, particularly Jewish leaders, to "become conscious of their responsibilities."[24] She persistently goaded the all-male Jewish establishment to provide a centralized welfare organization for the needy. In 1916 she wrote an article for a widely read German-Jewish newspaper in which she demanded a national Jewish welfare association.[25] Such a body was created during the following year—the *Zentralwohlfahrtstelle der Deutschen Juden* (Central Welfare Association of German Jews), and she was elected its deputy vice president. The result of her crusading efforts in establishing modern Jewish social work was, in part, that she felt unpopular with Jewish leaders, particularly those in her home territory of Frankfurt, whom she pressured incessantly. Pappenheim's zeal and devotion were respected and even admired by the male authorities, but she was disliked by many, and it is certain that these feelings were mutual.

Breuer was as impressed with Anna O.'s willpower as later associates were with Bertha Pappenheim's. The very first paragraph of Breuer's case study concluded: "Her will-power was energetic, tenacious and persistent; sometimes it reached the pitch of an obstinacy which only gave way out of kindness and regard for other people."[26] It was her own strength and stubborn determination—often in the face of female indifference and male condescension—which allowed her to organize the Jüdischer Frauenbund (League of Jewish Women).[27] The Jüdischer Frauenbund, (referred to hereafter as Frauenbund), a German-Jewish feminist organization, was very much a product of her turbulent experiences and special leadership talents. She founded it and made it into a popular and articulate advocate of women's interests, attracting a membership of more than 50,000 women. Sympathetic associates described her as "absolutely uncompromising in causes she believed were just," and "rather dictatorial" at times. She was therefore "terribly uncomfortable for people who did not understand her" or, one might add, who did not agree with her.[28] Not having her way—particularly with the male establishment—made her angry and sarcastic. Pappenheim's strong will led to some conflicts even with colleagues in the *Frauenbund*. She was impatient and, some thought, importunate.[29] She threatened to resign four times from the Frauenbund executive board when her suggestions were opposed and twice succeeded in doing so.

Her fight against white slavery and prostitution among Jews was another example of her persistence. Only resoluteness (and self-righteousness) supported her in the face of severe criticism from those who refused to acknowledge the existence of this vice among Jews. She took an active part in every international conference on this subject, both Jewish and nondenominational, between 1902 and 1930. She regularly petitioned rabbis to modernize Jewish marriage and divorce laws, which, she felt, hurt women and led to prostitution. Despite constant disappointment—most of her letters to rabbis and government agencies remained unanswered—she continued her battle.[30]

The inner strength noted by Breuer in Anna O. was an inspiration to Pappenheim's friends and associates. Large numbers of women were attracted to the Frauenbund by the strength and determination of its vigorous leader. Pappenheim was aware that she could influence and inspire others. In fact, some of the more independent remained apart precisely because they disdained such powerful leadership.[31]

Breuer, in his case study, remarked on the intensity of Anna O.'s emotions. She never simply ''liked'' someone or something, but ''adored'' or was ''passionately fond'' of the recipient of her affection. Co-workers were later impressed with the powerful, compelling nature of Pappenheim's feelings and her fiery eloquence. The vice president of the Frauenbund wrote: ''A volcano lived in this woman, it erupted when she was angered . . . but . . . she only fought about things that were directly involved in her goals . . . She felt . . . the tragedy of these battles . . . Her fight against the abuse of women was almost a physically felt pain for her.''[32] She approached all her crusades with vehement conviction. Her own burning anger, no longer held back as in her youth, had found a socially respectable outlet in the fight for women's rights. It was a weapon Pappenheim turned to when her sarcasm or Viennese charm failed to achieve the goals she desired. Her happiness, too, was intense.[33] Martin Buber's thoughts on Pappenheim point to her passionate nature: ''Bertha Pappenheim was a person of passionate spirit. Didn't she have to become severe, not hard, but strict . . . and passionately demanding, because all was as it was . . . ?''[34]

Pappenheim maintained exacting religious and moral standards in her adult life, the result of a strictly religious upbringing and what Breuer described as a ''puritanically minded'' family. She was an observant Jew, and she insisted that all JFB homes and clubs maintain Jewish dietary laws, despite the fact that most members were not Orthodox. Although her attitudes toward ''moral'' matters were typically Victorian, they were seasoned with sympathy and understanding. In her crusade against immorality, Pappenheim, like Josephine Butler and other reformers, never condemned the females involved in prostitution or sexual promiscuity. Isenburg, Pappenheim's pet project, was a home founded to help girls whose ''physical, intellectual, or ethical''[35] makeup had been ''damaged''. Her harsh moral condemnation was directed at a society that neglected to educate and care for these girls. Her attitudes toward sex, although certainly not liberal, were not puritanical either. In a letter to a young convict, Pappenheim worte: ''It is not the worst thing to have made love with a boyfriend in adolescent passion.''[36] She considered married women more qualified to run Isenburg, because they ''understand sex life and . . . therefore are neither too strict nor too lenient with the girls.''[37]

A full picture of Pappenheim is incomplete without mentioning other personality features which Breuer did not note. Those who knew her commented on her charm and graciousness.[38] She invited her co-workers at Isenburg to her nicely decorated home once a week for an evening of conversation and companionship. Her sense of humor was remarked upon by her friends and foes. She often joked at her own expense. In 1936 Pappenheim composed ironic and witty obituary notices of herself for various periodicals, especially those which had frequently opposed her.[39] Her humor also informed her feminism as well as the topic of marriage as it applied to her. While on a trip to survey conditions leading to white slavery in Eastern Europe, Pappenheim met an old antique dealer who wanted to arrange her marriage to ''a nice professor who is a widower.'' Pappenheim maneuvered around the issue and wrote a friend, ''thus I escaped another *Schidduch* (arranged marriage).'' She promised that if she passed that way again she would see whether the antiques were still available and whether ''the professor was still to be had!!''[40]

From a social historian's viewpoint, there are probably two main reasons why Pappenheim never married. The first, and obvious one, was that she developed her symptoms at 21, an age when many women got married. While one could argue that this ''sickness'' was her only means of escaping the arranged marriage that was most likely her fate, it is more probable that her crisis interfered with the marriage traditions of her era. Young bourgeois woman married between the ages of 20 and 25. With a generous dowry, a 26-year-old could still find a mate. But by 28, one was already an ''old maid'' and well beyond the marriage market.[41] Thus the period of her illness, which probably lasted several years beyond her known treatment, interfered—purposely or accidentally—with normal marriage patterns. Second, and probably more important, Bertha Pappenheim was an extraordinarily strong and intelligent woman who would have been unable to accept a subordinate relationship—the only kind available to nineteenth-century women—in marriage. She would have had to subsume her own ideas, personality, and interests to those of her husband and to her marriage. Few women, with the exception of Josephine Butler, had spouses willing to be equal partners. Many feminist leaders, in fact, chose between marriage and woman-oriented activism, just as other women chose between motherhood and careers. In the nineteenth century it was impossible to contemplate reconciling both.

Pappenheim never mentioned regretting her celibacy. In sacrificing a home life to help Jewish women, she drew support for her life-style from the prevailing Victorian code, which granted dignity and offered incentives to unmarried women engaged in ''social motherhood.''[42] She did miss being a mother and openly admitted that much of her activity was surrogate motherhood. Her bouts of loneliness—''I am not necessary for nothing and to no one''[43]—were counterbalanced by the pure joy she experienced with children. She was convinced that ''Women who have to miss the happiness of real personal motherhood may have an opportunity for spiritual motherhood, if they go the quiet way of helping children and adolescents whose actual mother may fail.''[44]

The first trace of Bertha Pappenheim as a mature adult came from a book of short stories written by her in 1890 under the pseudonym Paul Berthold.[45] Entitled *In the Secondhand Shop,* the book was an expression of the writer's concern for the poor and her love of children.[46] The 1890s saw the blossoming of the German women's movement. Pappenheim embraced the ideals of German feminism, particularly its emphasis on education and full citizenship for women. In 1899 she published a play entitled *Women's Rights,* which stressed the political, economic, and sexual exploitation of women. That year she also published a translation of Mary Wollstonecraft's *A Vindication of the Rights of Women.*[47] Wollstonecraft, the eighteenth-century English feminist, maintained that women should be men's companions, not their playthings. Intellectual comradeship was the main basis for a fulfilling relationship between husband and wife. To this end she sought equality of education for boys and girls. Her main point was that women had human rights. Pappenheim admired her charm and courage and hung a picture of the Englishwoman in her living room.

The 1890s also witnessed Pappenheim's commitment to active social work. She began by dishing out soup to poor Jewish immigrants from Eastern Europe. Her interest in helping the needy, particularly women and children, gradually deepened. She organized a small Jewish nursery school, sewing classes, and a girls' club. In 1895 (the year Breuer and Freud published the case of Anna O.) Pappenheim accepted the position of housemother in an orphanage for Jewish girls. She remained in that position for twelve years, gathering valuable experience as an adminstrator and educator. At this time Pappenheim became increasingly aware of the desperate situation of Jews in Eastern Europe, especially of Jewish girls. She wrote a short pamphlet *The Jewish Problem in Galicia,* in which she maintained that their poor education led Jewish girls to poverty and vice in their later years. She repeated her message in another pamphlet, *On the Condition of the Jewish Population in Galicia.*[48] The growing wave of Jewish conversions also plagued Pappenheim. In 1902 she wrote a short story for a Jewish literary publication on the theme of conversion.[49]

Her concerns for the social welfare of Jews and women led her to found Weibliche Fürsorge (Care by Women), a Jewish women's society, in 1902. This society was not a traditional charity. Instead, she hoped to apply the goals of the German feminist movement to Jewish social work. She also wanted to introduce new social work techniques. She taught her followers to investigate cases, keep systematic records, and take periodic surveys to discover new areas of social need.[50] In 1902 Pappenheim attended her first conference on white slavery. Distressed by the number of Jewish girls who fell victim to the traffic in women, she advocated a plan for sending Jewish women to Galicia and Poland to warn of the dangers of the traffic and to improve the material and moral conditions of the poor.[51] In 1903 she journeyed to Galicia and Western Russia to seek ways in which German Jews could best aid their coreligionists in the East.[52] Pappenheim took several more study tours, in 1907, 1911–1912, 1926, and 1935. Her most well-known publication, *Sisyphus Work,* was a report on prostitution and white slavery in Eastern Europe and the Middle East.

Her experience with Care by Women encouraged Pappenheim to call for larger, national Jewish social welfare organizations. She felt Jewish charities were outmoded in their methods as well as their organization and warned that religious "good deeds" were becoming social "misdeeds" as a result of the unplanned nature of Jewish social work.[53] Maintaining that doles were demoralizing, she urged that programs be created to train people to help themselves. Further, Pappenheim remarked on the conspicuous absence of women in the leadership of Jewish charities and accused the Jewish establishment of "underestimating the value of women's work and trifling with their interest by refusing to admit them as equal partners."[54] Some of the best Jewish women were instead turning to German feminism as an outlet for their energies. She demanded a reform in the overall position of women in the Jewish community and in Jewish social service. Not surprisingly, she met with strong male resistance.

Pappenheim began to convince women of the need to form their own national organization. She turned exclusively to women, because she felt that "men always and in every situation follow their private interests."[55] She expected women to volunteer their services, because, among other reasons, Jewish middle-class girls and women had time to spare, needed no reimbursement (in the years when the Frauenbund began), and would be educationally and socially enriched by their experience. She envisioned an organization that would protect Jewish girls; extend modern social work techniques; fight for women's political, education, and career equality; and, in general, represent all Jewish women. The fact that Protestant and Catholic women had their own national organizations encouraged Pappenheim in her pursuit of a similar association for Jewish women. The convention of the International Council of Women, which met in Berlin in 1904, provided the opportunity for Pappenheim to meet with several other Jewish activists. There they founded the Jüdischer Frauenbund and elected Pappenheim as its first president. She held her post for twenty years and remained on the board of directors of the organization until her death.

To Pappenheim, the Frauenbund was not just another organization but one which rested on "an ethical and spiritual foundation." Her high expectations of the Frauenbund's capacity to bring about reforms caused her to travel frequently, lecture widely, and work tirelessly on its behalf. The Frauenbund built homes, health facilities, and dormitories for women; offered them vocational training courses and set up schools and employment services; organized

girls' clubs and dowry clubs; staffed railroad and harbor outposts to help travel-
ing women (in what was commonly considered a preventive measure against
white slave trafficking); and lobbied for women's equality in the Jewish community and German nation.[56] The organization did not attain the power Pappenheim would have desired for it. Yet, she was not wholly dissatisfied with her
achievement, considering it an auspicious beginning.

The attitudes toward the role of women with which Pappenheim guided the
Frauenbund were similar to those of the German feminists of her era. She
stressed the need for women's autonomy and equality so that women could
become better citizens. She demanded the opportunity for women to develop to
their individual potential, suggesting that they could better serve their community if they were fulfilled human beings. And Pappenheim's feminism, like
that of Helene Lange, was deeply imbued with veneration for marriage and
motherhood. On the one hand, she insisted that every female child be given the
same educational and career opportunities as every male child and that every
woman be allowed full participation in the political, cultural, and economic
spheres. On the other hand, she believed in the sacredness of the family and insisted that every woman first fulfill her responsibilities as a wife and mother.
Neither she nor most of her feminist contemporaries would have asked that
husbands or governments assume any of the traditional household or childrear-
ing functions; in fact, she probably would have opposed government intervention in the form of day care. Thus she placed an insuperable burden on married
women, particularly those with children, who responded to her call for equality.

Pappenheim tried to combine her feminism with her deeply felt religious
identity by arguing that all of her feminist activities were meant to strengthen
the Jewish population in Germany and in Europe. She organized the Jewish
women's movement in order to invigorate Jewish life by teaching women about
their religious heritage and by fighting for women's rights within the Jewish
community. Equality was an end, but it was also the means by which women
would return to Judaism. The same was true with regard to Pappenheim's efforts to help children and mothers. *Kinderschutz* (the protection of children) and
Mutterschutz (the protection of mothers) were key elements of German feminism
as well as programs through which Pappenheim hoped to strengthen the Jewish
community. Isenburg, the home for unwed mothers, was the one institution
that embodied all of Pappenheim's basic goals: to protect and educate Jewish
women; to help unwed mothers, prostitutes, or other victims of a society of
double standards; and to instill in girls the spirit and joy of Judaism. Pappenheim's participation on the board of directors of the major bourgeois German
feminist organization was also a reflection of her feminist and Jewish consciousness. She believed that if women with a clear sense of Jewish identity
worked within a nondenominational context, they would help combat anti-
Semitism through personal interaction. Above all, she hoped for religious
tolerance.

Although Pappenheim insisted that feminist reforms would strengthen Judaism, in fact her Jewish faith and her feminist convictions frequently stood in opposition to one another. For example, she worried that Jews were not emotionally involved enough in their religion and wrote Martin Buber that "many Jews in terrible spiritual need reach for 'their Goethe' before 'their Bible.'" She wished Jews would emulate Christians for whom the Bible was "a path to God."[57] (She added, "to God, not to HIM.") This emotional view contradicted the rationalism of her attitudes on the rights of women. To her dismay, she found that it was extremely difficult, if not impossible, to combine a literal and integral acceptance of the Bible with reformism. Orthodox Jews, who agreed with her religious views, were adamantly opposed to her feminism, while progressive Jews were more likely to accept her feminist programs, but preferred Buber's conception of the Bible, which she disliked. She was never able to resolve this dilemma to her satisfaction.

During her busy years as an activist, Pappenheim still found time to write. Although her literary talents were limited, her works were another part of her crusade against injustice. In 1910 she translated the *Memoirs of Glückl von Hameln* from Judeo-German into German.[58] She was a distant relative of Glückl (1645–1724) and admired her ancestor's piousness and strength, as well as her efficiency, charm, and motherliness.[59] In 1913 and 1916 Pappenheim published a three-act play and several short stories. The themes of the stories, anti-Semitism, Jewish life in Eastern Europe, and conversion, were areas of ever increasing concern to her.[60] Her play *Tragic Moments* was a vehicle for Pappenheim to voice her anxiety regarding anti-Semitism, white slavery, and the needs of young mothers. She expressed her largely negative opinions of Zionism through her main characters.[61] Her identity as a religious Jew, a patriotic German, and a feminist left her with little patience for Zionism. She worried that its exponents were anti-Orthodox, and her attachment to Germany convinced her that she already had a homeland. She particularly distrusted Theodor Herzl, the "latter-day Jewish saint," because she suspected his Jewishness to be of relatively recent vintage.[62] She attended Zionist conventions but "found no possibility of going along, or empathizing, with them." Their women's organizations, she noted, were completely subordinate to the male Zionist establishment. She was deeply dismayed by their lack of concern for the problems of women.

Pappenheim's antipathy to Zionism can also be traced to her attitudes concerning motherhood. She feared that Zionists intended to break up families, and wrote: "Zionists . . . considered all those women's duties which I regard as absolutely essential . . . as negligible." She particularly disliked their "collective breeding and raising of children," maintaining that a healthy family should bring up its own offspring.[63] Her tenacious belief in the importance of the nuclear family made her inflexible regarding Zionist plans in the 1930s to ship German-Jewish children to Palestine.[64] Her distrust of Zionists led her to exaggerate the risks of separating young people from their families in the face of the very real threat posed by the Nazis.

One gains the impression from Pappenheim's local, national, and international efforts that no matter how fast she ran, she was still in the same place; the poverty, vice, exploitation and inhumanity that she fought remained. She consoled herself by achieving admittedly small victories—she called them "holy small deeds" (*heilige Kleinarbeit*)—in the battle to defend Jewish women. Pleased as she was with the girls' clubs, scholarships, health facilities, and cultural contributions of the Jüdischer Frauenbund, as she aged she was "driven by fear" that she would "not . . . accomplish what she felt called upon to do." Despite her age and failing health she continued to write for women and to work for the Frauenbund explaining that she could not tear herself away from any aspect of Jewish women's work without giving up a piece of herself. In those years, she translated the *Mayse Bukh,* a collection of stories widely read by eighteenth-century Jewish women, and the *Ze'enah U-Ree'nah,* or woman's bible. Her activities focused on the protection of children. In 1928 she suggested that a "world collective guardianship" be founded to care for all abandoned and neglected children.[65] In 1934, at the age of 75, she personally delivered several of her small charges to an orphanage in Glasgow. She wrote two long essays that year in which she decried the historical role of Jewish women and pleaded for their education.[66] Her rage at the "sin committed against the Jewish woman's soul and thus against all Judaism" had not abated.

It might be supposed that her strong Jewish identity would have made Pappenheim more alert to the dangers of Nazism. It was precisely her self-conscious Jewishness (and her strong feelings for Germany) which clouded her perception of German anti-Semitism. Taking a certain amount of anti-Semitism for granted, she did not appreciate its real danger until 1930, and like other German Jews she relied on the constitution for her protection. Even when Hitler destroyed the constitutional state, Pappenheim's first reaction seems to have been that the forcible return of Jews to their faith was not an entirely negative phenomenon. Underestimating the nature of German fascism, she discouraged mass emigration and argued that Jews still had a place in Germany. She did not admit her error until after the Nuremburg Laws in 1935.[67] In this regard she displayed no less insight than most German Jews.

In the summer of 1935 Pappenheim was hospitalized for a tumor, which later proved to be fatal. Soon thereafter she began to understand the perils of the political situation and the urgency of emigration for Germany's Jews. In the spring of 1936 she visited Isenburg for the last time. Desperately ill, she was summoned by the Gestapo to explain an anti-Hitler remark made by one of the children. After her encounter with the police she never left her bed. Her close friend, Hannah Karminski, the executive secretary of the Frauenbund, stayed with her until she died. Seven days before her death she dictated a prayer in which she declared her readiness to die and asked God to give her peace.[68]

Death spared her from the agony of the worst of the Nazi maelstrom. She died at Isenburg on May 28, 1936. At her request, the funeral was small and there were no eulogies. The rabbi read Psalm 121, her favorite. It clearly expressed Pappenheim's strong and simple faith in God and her belief in the righteousness of her crusades. In her last will, written in 1930, Pappenheim hoped that those who visited her grave would leave a small stone, "as a quiet promise... to serve the mission of women's duties and women's joy... unflinchingly and courageously."[69]

Notes

1. Helene Lange, *Lebenserinnerungen* (Berlin: F. A. Herbig, 1921), pp. 87–88.

2. Sigmund Freud and Josef Breuer, *Studies on Hysteria,* translated by James Strachey (New York: Avon Books, 1966), p. 56.

3. *Ibid.,* p. 47.

4. The newest information on the period between 1882 and 1895 is in Albrecht Hirschmüller, "Physiologie und Psychoanalyse in Leben und Werk Josef Breuers," in *Jahr buch der Psychoanalyse,* Bern, 1978, Beiheft 4. See also recent research by Ann H. Jackowitz, "Anna O., Bertha Pappenheim and Me," in *Between Women,* ed. by Carol Ascher, Louise de Salvo, and Sarah Ruddick (Boston: Beacon Press, 1983).

5. Henri Ellenberger, "The Story of Anna O.: A Critical Review with New Data," *Journal of the History of the Behavioral Sciences,* vol. VIII, No. 3, July 1972; Ellen Jensen, "Anna O—A Study of Her Later Life," *The Psychoanalytic Quarterly,* XXXIX (1970): 269–293 (including a bibliography on Anna O); Richard Karpe, "The Rescue Complex in Anna O's Final Identity," *The Psychoanalytic Quarterly,* vol. 30, 1961.

6. H. W. Frink, in Mary P. Ryan, *Womanhood in America* (New York: New Viewpoints, a Division of Franklin Watts, Inc., 1975), p. 276.

7. Ryan, p. 276; Mara Mayor, "Fears and Fantasies of the Anti-Suffragists," *Connecticut Review,* VII, No. 2 (April 1974): 64–74.

8. Joan N. Burstyn, *Victorian Education and the Ideal of Womanhood* (London: Groom Helm, 1981); Deborah Gorham, *The Victorian Girl and the Feminine Ideal* (Bloomington: Indiana University Press, 1983); Martha Vicinus (ed.), *Suffer and Be Still: Women in the Victorian Age* (Bloomington: Indiana University Press, 1973).

9. Gerda Caspary, *Die Entwicklungsgrundlagen für die Soziale und Psychische Verselbständigung der bürgerlichen deutschen Frau um die Jahrhundertwende,* Heidelberger Studien, vol. 3, Heft 5 (Heidelberg: Verlag der Weiss'schen Universitätsbuchhandlung, 1933), p. 33; Jürgen Zinnecker, *Sozial-geschichte der Mädchenbildung. Zur Kritik der Schulerziehung von Mädchen in bürgerlichen Patriarchalismus* (Weinheim and Basel: Beltz Verlag, 1973), p. 98.

10. Gabriele Reuter, in her best seller, *Aus Guter Familie:Leidensgeschichte eines Mädchens,* depicted such women in a sympathetic but chilling manner. While some of her characters found "perfect" happiness in an "ideal" marriage, others lived with

headaches and nervous tensions and still others went insane (17th ed., Berlin: S. Fischer Verlag, 1908).

11. Fanny Lewald, *Für und Wider die Frauen,* 2d ed. (Berlin: Verlag Otto Janke, 1875), pp. 3–20, *passim.*

12. John Stuart Mill commented on the "nervous temperaments" of many women of his era. He understood these to result from "nervous energy run to waste." *The Subjection of Women* (New York: Frederick A. Stokes Company, 1911), p. 131. See also Carroll Smith-Rosenberg, "The Hysterical Woman: Sex Roles and Role Conflict in Nineteenth Century America," *Social Research,* XXXIX, No. 4 (Winter 1972): 652–678; Jan Goldstein, "The Hysteria Diagnosis and the Politics of Anticlericalism in Late Nineteenth Century France," *The Journal of Modern History,* (June 1982).

13. Carroll Smith-Rosenberg, "Puberty to Menopause: The Cycle of Femininity in Nineteenth Century America," in *Clio's Consciousness Raised* (New York: Harper Colophon Books, 1974), pp. 23–37; Ann Douglas Wood, "The 'Fashionable Diseases': Women's Complaints and their Treatment in Nineteenth Century America," *Journal of Interdisciplinary History,* IV (Summer 1973): 27.

14. Glen Petrie, *A Singular Iniquity: The Campaigns of Josephine Butler* (New York: Macmillan, 1971). An abolitionist was someone who tried to abolish the regulation of prostitution.

15. Jane Addams, *Twenty Years at Hull House* (New York: James W. Linn, 1938).

16. Eve Merriam, ed., *Growing Up Female in America: Ten Lives* (New York: Dell, 1971), p.67.

17. Katherine Anthony, *Feminism in Germany and Scandinavia* (New York: Henry Holt, 1915), pp. 242–243, emphasis added.

18. Hedwig Wachenheim, *Von Grossbürgertum zur Sozialdemokratie* (Berlin: Colloquium Verlag, 1973), p. 3.

19. Alice Salomon in Elga Kern, ed., *Führende Frauen Europas* (Munich: Verlag Ernst Reinhart, 1929), p. 6.

20. Freud and Breuer, *Hysteria,* p. 55.

21. Dora Edinger, *Bertha Pappenheim: Freud's Anna O* (Highland Park, Ill.: Congregation Solel, 1968) p. 16.

22. Bertha Pappenheim, *Sisyphus-Arbeit* (Leipzig: Verlag Paul E. Linder, 1924), p. 90.

23. Freud and Breuer, *Hysteria,* p. 55.

24. *Blätter des jüdischen Frauenbundes: Für Frauenarbeit und Frauenbewegung* (Berlin) (hereafter cited as *BJFB*), July 1936, p. 11.

25. *Allgemeine Zeitung des Judentums* (Berlin) (hereafter cited as *AZDJ*), December 22, 1916, pp. 600–601.

26. Freud and Breuer, *Hysteria,* p. 55.

27. Rahel Straus, *Wir Lebten in Deutschland: Erinnerungen einer Deutschen Jüdin* (Stuttgart: Deutsche Verlags-Anstalt, 1962), p. 151.

28. Werner collection, Archives of the Leo Baeck Institute, New York (hereafter cited as ALBI), #3079 (35).

29. She apologized to her friends for her impatience, explaining: "There is an impa-

tience of youth which cannot wait to mature to do great deeds, and there is an impatience of age, which is harder to bear, because it fears that it will never see the completion of its work, of its life's duties." Straus, *Wir Lebten in Deutschland*, p. 258. See also, Pappenheim, *Sisyphus-Arbeit II* (Berlin: Bethold Levy, 1929), p. 49.

30. Pappenheim, *Sisyphus II.*

31. Margaret Edelheim-Mühsam, private interview, October 23, 1974, New York.

32. *BJFB*, July 1936, p. 8.

33. Edinger, *Pappenheim: Freud's Anna O*, p. 29.

34. *BJFB*, July 1936, p. 2.

35. Else Rabin, "The Jewish Woman in Social Service in Germany," in *The Jewish Library*, ed. by Leo Jung (New York: The Jewish Library Publishing Co., 1934), p. 300.

36. *BJFB*, July 1936, p. 16.

37. *BJFB*, June 1937, p. 2.

38. Pappenheim collection, ALBI, #54 (50), and Werner collection, ALBI, #3079 (35); *BJFB*, July 1936, p. 23.

39. *BJFB*, July 1936, p. 28.

40. Pappenheim collection, ALBI, #33(9).

41. Marion A. Kaplan, "For Love or Money: The Marriage Strategies of Jews in Imperial Germany," in *Leo Baeck Institute Yearbook* (London: Secker & Warburg, 1983).

42. Ryan, *Womanhood*, p. 235.

43. Pappenheim, *Sisyphus I*, p. 161.

44. Edinger, *Pappenheim: Freud's Anna O*, p. 60. Such thoughts were common among unmarried women engaged in "social motherhood." See Kathryn K. Sklar, *Catherine Beecher: A Study in American Domesticity* (New York: W. W. Norton, 1966), p. 167.

45. Pappenheim may have used a pseudonym to avoid calling attention to herself because of her recent move to Frankfurt or because she feared that any notice might expose her recent past. Further, many women used male pseudonyms in order to get published and avoid publicity.

46. Paul Berthold (Bertha Pappenheim), *In der Trödel-bude: Geschichten* (Lahr: Druck und Verlag von Mortiz Schauenburg, 1890). One of Pappenheim's favorite pastimes was to rummage through secondhand shops.

47. Paul Berthold (Bertha Pappenheim), *Frauenrechte* (Dresden: 1899), and *Eine Verteidigung der Rechte der Frau—Übersetzung aus dem Englischen* (Dresden: Verlag Pierson, 1899).

48. Paul Berthold (Bertha Pappenheim), *Zur Judenfrage in Galizien* (Frankfurt: Knauer, 1900); Pappenheim, *Zur Lage der Jüdischen Bevölkerung in Galizien* (Frankfurt: Neuer Frankfurter Verlag, 1904).

49. Pappenheim, "Ein Schwächling," *Jahrbuch für Jüdische Geschichte und Literatur*, ed. Verbande der Vereine für jüdische Geschichte und Literatur in Deutschland (Berlin: Verlag von Albert Katz, 1902), p. v.

50. *BJFB*, July 1936, p. 7. See also Ruth R. Dresner, "Bertha Pappenheim: The Contribution of a German-Jewish Pioneer Social Reformer to Social Work: 1859–1936," unpublished Master's thesis, Fordham University, 1954.

51. For the history of Jewish prostitution, see Edward J. Bristow, *Prostitution and Prejudice: The Jewish Fight against White Slavery, 1870-1939* (Oxford: Oxford University Press, 1983).

52. *The Jewish Association for the Protection of Girls and Women: Report, 1902* (London: Burt & Sons, Printers, 1902).

53. *AZDJ*, December 22, 1916, p. 602.

54. Ottilie Schönewald, unpublished memoirs, #356, ALBI, p. 16.

55. Pappenheim collection, ALBI, #331 (9).

56. For further information, see Marion A. Kaplan, *The Jewish Feminist Movement in Germany: the Campaigns of the Jüdischer Frauenbund, 1904-1938* (Meriden, Conn.: Greenwood Press, 1979), trans. and revised as *Die jüdische Frauenbewegung in Deutschland* (Hamburg: Hans Christians Verlag, 1981).

57. Letter from Pappenheim, March 18, 1936, in *Martin Buber: Briefwechsel aus sieben Jahrzehnten,* ed. by Grete Schaeder, (Heidelberg: Verlag Lambert Schneider, 1973), II: 587.

58. *Judeo-German was the forerunner of modern Yiddish.* For an English version, see *The Memoirs of Glückl von Hameln,* trans. by Marvin Lowenthal (New York: Schocken Books, 1977).

59. George H. Pollock, "Bertha Pappenheim's Idealized Ancestor: Glückel von Hameln," *American Imago,* XXVIII (1971).

60. Pappenheim, *Kämpfe: Sechs Erzählungen* (Frankfurt: Verlag von J. Kaufmann, 1916).

61. Pappenheim, *Tragische Momente* (Frankfurt: Verlag von J. Kaufmann, 1913).

62. Dora Edinger, ed., *Bertha Pappenheim: Leben und Schriften* (Frankfurt: Ner Tamid Verlag, 1963), p. 112.

63. *Ibid.,* pp. 112-114.

64. *BJFB,* October 1936, pp. 6-7.

65. Pappenheim, *Sisyphus II,* p. 61.

66. Both essays, "The Jewish Woman" and "The Jewish Girl," are reprinted in Edinger, *Pappenheim: Freud's Anna O.,* pp. 77-90.

67. (See her short story, "Die Erbschaft" (the Inheritance), *Frankfurter Israelitisches Gemeindeblatt,* July 1933, p. 277. Edinger, *Pappenheim: Freud's Anna O.,* p. 21. These laws deprived Jews of the rights of citizenship and forbade, among other things, marriages or sex between Jews and "Aryans."

68. The poem seemed to indicate that Pappenheim was finally at peace with herself after years of fighting. In Hannah Karminski, unpublished memoirs, ALBI, #301. The poem was translated by Lucy Freeman, *The Story of Anna O* (New York: Walker & Company, 1972), p. 170.

69. *BJFB,* July 1936, p. 39. Jews traditionally leave a small stone when they visit a grave.

Anna O.: Female, 1880-1882; Bertha Pappenheim: Female, 1980-1982

11

Anne Steinmann

Anna O.'s importance in the history and development of psychoanalysis is well known. Just as well known is the refrain in the literature on Anna O. that her life as a complete woman was handicapped because her culture, time, and sex did not favor individual fulfillment through the accomplishment of personal goals, and that her world was not conducive to her developing and activating marked intelligence, an intelligence to which Breuer himself gave tribute:

> She possessed a powerful intellect which would have been capable of digesting solid mental pabulum and which stood in need of it—though without receiving it after she had left school [Breuer, 1895, p. 21].

Anna O. was handicapped not so much by her culture as by the neurosis whose cure she invented and worked on with Breuer. Her cure was not completed; if it had been, she might have become another Helene Deutsch, a pioneer female psychiatrist.

Anna O. was raised in an Orthodox Jewish family. Since she was female, and in spite of her superior capabilities, her education was halted at the age of 16, as was the custom in such a family. Further frustration was added when at age 21 she was placed in the position of nurse to her adored dying father, with devastating results to her physical and emotional health. Anna O.'s breakdown and Breuer's subsequent treatment of her are well documented.

What is impressive about discoveries—scientific, biological, geographical, all discoveries—is how so often great discoveries and remarkable insights come about almost accidentally. If Anna O. had not broken out into her painful symptoms and had not been treated by Breuer in her particular time and place (Taine, 1863), she would not, could not have been the comparatively fulfilled woman she later became.

Note the *comparatively fulfilled*. Anna O. was a woman of her time and culture, the 1880s. In the 1980s, all other things being equal, if Anna O. had undergone a completed treatment of her neurotic condition, she might very well have become a more richly fulfilled woman. Breuer, as Freud recognized, relieved Anna O.'s physical symptoms only. He did not finish his job. She never did receive true insight into the real causes of her breakdown. They had never been brought to light.

As this chapter develops, we will do what TV and film do so well—juxtapose, flash the same characters back and forth between different centuries. Imagine how Joan of Arc would function today. Would she picket against Vietnam? Would she be another Patty Hearst? What would Catherine the Great achieve today? What would Anna O. be like today? We push the button on the TV set, and we jump a century. We will examine Bertha Pappenheim's psychotherapeutic treatment in 1980.

For the moment, however, we will stay in the 1880s. The "talking cure" alleviated Anna O.'s paralyzing physical symptoms, but it had an additional effect as well. It was the realization of what we will call here "a double sense of identity"—double in the sense of identity as a nurturing individual, one who achieves through the other, together with identity as a self-achieving individual, one who fulfills oneself through one's own accomplishments.

One must free oneself from seeing Anna O. simply as the historic subject and object of Breuer and Freud's study on hysteria. One must see Anna O. whole, as a young woman of the last part of the nineteenth century. Although Anna O.'s formal education had ended at age 16, she was a quick and avid learner and continued to educate herself. No matter how closeted she was by the religious orthodoxy of her family, she could not have helped but absorb the intellectual ferment of her time. Like a true Viennese, she must have visited the coffee houses, enjoyed the theater and music, read the journals and books of her day (Jensen, 1970, p. 274), and engaged in general discussions about what was going on around her. She knew the English language well. Later in life she translated Mary Wollstonecraft's book *A Vindication of the Rights of Women*. She was a creature of her time, and it was a rousing time. Certainly her achieving self was fostered by the excitement of what was occurring in the world around her during this last part of the nineteenth century. It was an age that provided the soil for her double sense of identity. In Ellen Jensen's opinion, Anna O. "fought to realize herself and . . . this happens only when one feels on firm ground" (Jensen, 1970, p. 276).

Anna O. was born the year Darwin published *The Origin of the Species*, in 1859. Ideologically, Darwin questioned the pat certainty of this peopled Victorian world that believed that what had been would always be and would continue to be forever. Long before, in 1542, Copernicus had told the world that the earth was just another planet revolving around the sun; things were not as people believed, that the earth was supreme and the sun revolved around it. People were shaken and at first denied what to them was unbelievable heresy. Now, Darwin's evolutionary doctrines questioned man's primacy. He postulated that man was not unique, that all life descended from common ancestors. The story of Adam and Eve was a fable. What followed then? Much of the Bible was myth, and particularly the Book of Genesis. Heresy was again shaking the world.

Another blow now descended on this formerly secure globe. In 1867 Karl Marx, in the first volume of *Das Kapital*, formulated a dynamic theory of social change. He denied man's inviolable position in a social hierarchy. The aim of life for men and women would be truly a dynamic one—to move toward a classless society.

Before Anna O.'s birth the Industrial Revolution already had profound effects on the life of the family and women's roles in it. Power-driven machinery revolutionized the family life of women and men. Industry became depersonalized. The factory was the central entity, not the people who worked there. For rural women, work and home were now separated, and the distances between the two were greater than for women who worked in the cities. Machines began to perform many household duties. At the same time, children who formerly were educated at home were now educated away from home, at school. Women felt deprived of responsibility for their household and children.

The lives of middle-class women assumed an emptiness they had rarely known before. They were in a machine economy. They were now economically useless (Klein, 1946). This uselessness is deftly illustrated in Jane Austen's *Pride and Prejudice* (1813), where getting a husband was the primary goal of the main characters. The middle-class woman no longer was head and director of a working household. Her former purpose in life as the important member of home and family was gone, without a replacement.

Before the Industrial Revolution the middle-class woman, Chaucer's Wife of Bath, if you will, could fulfill herself as an achieving individual and as a family woman at one and the same time. What she achieved as a family member, how she performed, was recognized and valued. She was important to the life and financial wellbeing of her immediate family and thus to the life and economy of her larger family, the society. Consequently, she felt important to herself. She was a whole person with a double identity, fulfilling her emotional needs in the family and achieving as an individual in her work. For most women these identities fused, the double identity was one.

The Industrial Revolution destroyed all this. Curiously enough, however, this upheaval of a former life-style gave birth to a new concept of individualism and change that was to be immensely stimulating for women. In spite of the machine and a conformity that was encroaching on their lives, they started to think of themselves as individuals, as people apart from their families, as persons not just dependent on men. Middle-class women began to fight for the right to work, higher education, and political freedom (Klein, 1946). Anna O. was born and matured in the midst of these dramatic changes.

For Anna O., growing up into her twenties in a home where traditional values for women were strong, woman's place was in the home. That was her narrow, inbred, single identity, set up by the tradition that the female should be a nurturing family-oriented woman. Woman's goal was to help the *other* achieve. And in Orthodox Jewish families, women were in a more subordinate position than in some other civilized cultures. Thus in spite of her wishes to continue her education, it is not surprising that her brother went on to law school and she was chosen to nurse her dying father. The single-identity female role of Anna O.'s ultratraditional culture should not be confused with the fused double identity of family orientation and self-achieving of pre-Industrial Revolution females, nor was it self-achieving in an individual sense—separated from the other. However, as Breuer states, "she was bubbling over with in-tellectual activity" (Breuer, 1895, p. 21). Certainly she must have caught some of the excitement of the revolutionary thinking and philosophy of individualism and change of her time.

Ellen Jensen notes that Bertha felt on "firm ground" (1970, p. 276). Bertha P. reached firmer ground because of her discovery of the "talking cure" treat-ment and Breuer's pursuit of it. "Patient and doctor shared . . . one discovery: the cathartic treatment. This highly intelligent and determined young woman, with the sympathetic assistance of a physician, actually treated herself" (Karpe, 1961, p. 6).

Bertha Pappenheim began her social work officially in 1895, the year that Anna O.'s history appeared. Could she have read about herself? At any rate, it was in that year that she was appointed director of the Jewish Orphanage for girls in Frankfurt. Here she demonstrated her double identity; it was not a divided identity. She fostered her nurturing identity by having the girls learn all about running a household large or small, but she also exposed them to a better education than that which was prevalent at that time. She said, "Our time makes the imperative demand: everything in the private household, the cells of the state, which the impoverished world needs, are recognized and nursed in order that it may recover from the damages of our time" (Jensen, 1970, p. 279). What is Anna O. revealing? That she is a person of her time. Her double identity is revealed—her nurturing identity and her self-achieving one as a woman with a purpose in her world. However, we will show in discuss-ing the 1980 completed treatment how Anna O. might now be able to achieve a richer nurturing identify as a mother and wife together with her self-achieving identity.

Before discussing the 1980 treatment of Anna O., it would be well to discuss the relationship between Anna O.'s life story and the life stories of women of the 1980s—one hundred years later. This writer is fortunate in having had as a mother a woman who bore her double identity as a nurturing and self-achieving woman gracefully and for the most part quietly. This writer was also fortunate in having had forceful women and sensitive men as teachers and mentors. Her feeling of the rightness of woman's double identity—and, by the way, the rightness of man's double identity—led her to a study of appropriate female and male roles in a changing society that has encompassed much of her own achieving working life. Through a foundation called Maferr (Male-

Female Role Research), she has been in charge of furthering research on feminine role perception and behavior for more than twenty-five years. During this whole period Maferr's research noted that women faced severe ambiguities in contemporary society (Maferr Bibliography, 1980). Should they proceed with self-achieving interests to which they were exposed one hundred years after Anna O., or should they conform to the stereotyped image of the female which presented itself to Anna O.—and which, of course, is still with us? The conflict for today's well-educated woman is clear: an inner tension created by two opposite and opposing needs, to "do her own thing" and at the same time to be "ultrafeminine," to be a homebody, to be the "other" of the male. Even today, many women are unable to reconcile this conflict in their own lives. Many still face daily tensions and anxiety because of their difficulty with this sex role dilemma.

In our times there are many Anna O.'s who are ambivalent in their double identity as self-achieving women and home-oriented nurturing women. These Anna O.'s were further confused when Betty Friedan, the author of *The Feminine Mystique*, ordered them, for their own good, to get out of the kitchen and follow in the path of World War II's "Rosie the Riveter" (Friedan, 1963).* Friedan, in her zeal to liberate women from suburban kitchens, failed to see that Rosie the Riveter was on her job as a replacement for the man who was not available at that time. When the men returned from the service, many women—some reluctantly, some defiantly—returned to the home. Although the women had not yet merged their two roles, they had proved their capability in the workplace. While the men were out of the industrial world in a frightening world of war, Rosie, at home and on the job, clearly demonstrated that she was quite a worker in areas that had been considered man's territory. About ten years after World War II, when automation increased rapidly and male strength was no longer needed for many jobs, and preciseness and dependability were required, Rosie and her daughter began to move into the job market. The double role came into being once more. But with a difference. This time, unlike pre–Industrial Revolution times, the achieving work role was separated from the nurturing family role. Distance from the home was one of the factors that made a fusion of double identities difficult.

It is well at this point to discuss the concept of double identity, as used here, and the concept of divided identity. The two concepts are employed often in the analysis of both female and male roles without noting a distinction between the concepts. Divided identity is a strict division in the understanding and following through on one's sex role. The concept of woman's double identity is seen here as a merging and fusing of a self-achieving role with a family-oriented nurturing role. An interesting example of such fusion is the well-known writer of American Civil War times, Harriet Beecher Stowe. She functioned as a woman secure in her double identity. She was both self-achieving and family-oriented.

*During World War II women engaged in jobs undertaken formerly only by men. Some of these jobs were in the steel industry, and this is where the name developed.

This was possible because she could write at the kitchen table with the dinner meal cooking on the stove, her numerous children surrounding her, and still write a definitive novel of her time, *Uncle Tom's Cabin*. Her place of work was in her home. She had no sense of divided identity, no conflict. Her double identity was secure. Anna O. attained a double identity of self-achievement and nurturing. However, unlike Harriet Beecher Stowe, who was able fully to fuse her roles, Anna O.'s restricted situation and also her interrupted psychotherapy did not permit a complete double-identity fusion.

It is engaging to read an article in the July 5, 1981, *New York Times Magazine* by Betty Friedan. She has at this late date come out for a double identity for women. She writes, "We have to break through our own feminine mystique now and move into the second stage, no longer against men, but with them." She further notes, again at this late date, what Maferr's research has demonstrated for over a quarter of a century:

> The true potential of women's power can be realized only by transcending the false polarization between feminism and the family. It is an abstract polarization that does not exist in real life. For instead of the polarization that has plagued the women's movement in the last few years and prevented the very possibility of political solutions, new research shows that virtually all women today share a basic core of commitment to the family and to their own equality within and beyond it, as long as family and equality are not seen to be in conflict [Friedan, 1981, p. 15].

Bertha Pappenheim, Anna O., transcended her feminine mystique (the notion that women can find fulfillment only by limiting themselves to their roles as wives and mothers) in a mature, commonsense manner. She wrote and published. Her works include an original play, *Women's Rights*, and a translation of Mary Wollstonecraft's *A Vindication of the Rights of Women*. She worked as a social worker, helping orphans and wayward girls. Certainly Anna O. deftly put into action her double identity. But that is not the whole truth. Lucy Freeman writes, "She could have married, there were men over the years who had proposed, but she had felt no need to marry, her need was to help the persecuted and exploited" (Freeman, 1972, p. 105). When we discuss Anna O.'s 1980 therapy we shall not pass over lightly that "she had felt no need to marry."

A concept of divided identity, as opposed to the concept of double identity, is used often by feminists in describing the stresses modern women undergo in trying to combine their roles as individuals and as nurturers of the family. The psychiatrist Alexandra Symonds, in a keynote address to one of the largest gatherings of women in medicine held in the United States, suggested that female physicians' lives were much more stressful than those of their male counterparts. One of the reasons: "The female physician has a divided sense of identity when she combines profession and home. A man does not have this divided sense of identity when he becomes a doctor; on the contrary, his identity and sense of self is now fulfilled. Men in our culture are able to fuse their work identity with their personal identity, while women cannot'' (*New York Times*, April, 13, 1981, p. B11).

It is the deep feeling of this writer that if women could accept the concept of double identity rather than rail against divided identity, their lives would be richer and fuller for themselves and possibly more comfortable than the lives of their male counterparts. Double identity enriches; divided identity by definition conflicts. The way our society as organized today, it is more difficult for women to realize both roles. Men can count on women to take care of the home and the children while they are at work, thus avoiding the divided identity problem. For women, however, there is no given and in general men have not been asked to take on double identity roles: It is the women who must struggle to find the right balance between their personal and professional lives. It is well to note that men in our culture lose much that is creative and joyous in life because their work identity tends to take precedence over their personal, family identity. Because they necessarily work outside the home, and sometimes at a distance from their families, they become more and more removed from their nurturing role. In recent times women are experiencing similar difficulties in fusing their double identities, and perhaps even to a greater degree, because the nurturing role has always been expected of them.

Double identity signifies a double gift of life's resources. Women must use their achieving talents to organize their life-styles so that their double identities will work *for* each other, rather than conflict. Anna O. used her organizational ability to fulfill her nurturing needs. As a woman undergoing therapy today she would get insight into her biological nurturing needs as well as her social nurturing needs.

It is relevant at this point to discuss the Maferr research on feminine roles. The Maferr Inventory of Feminine Values (1966), one of the instruments used in the research, is based upon the double concept of women's role. The *traditional* family-oriented concept of the feminine role is that the woman conceives of herself as the ''other,'' the counterpart of the man and children in her life. She performs a nurturing role. Her achievement is to help others achieve. Her distinguishing feature is that she fulfills herself by proxy (Steinmann, 1963). The *liberal* concept of the feminine role is held by the woman who embraces a self-achieving orientation. She strives to fulfill herself directly by realizing her own potentialities. Her distinguishing feature is that she seeks fulfillment through her own accomplishments. Using these concepts as the basis for the study, the inventory seeks to understand cross-culturally which role women want to realize, and which one they believe the men in their lives want them to fulfill.

The basic hypothesis of the research is that women of different professional and life status, of different ages, of varied ethnic backgrounds and national origins, will still share specific values and beliefs regarding feminine roles and behavior. Among these is the desire to combine in harmony both duties related to the family and worthwhile self-achieving activities outside the family context. Another is the belief that men desire an extremely family-oriented woman, a woman who derives her major satisfactions from her role and responsibilities as wife and mother.

To test this hypothesis, the Maferr Inventory of Feminine Values has been administered to samples of women and men deliberately selected to vary on psychosocial variables.

In a Maferr study of women and men on a cross-cultural level, the data supported the initial hypothesis. Women of varied backgrounds were found to share specific values regarding feminine roles and behavior. In addition, the data reveal that women worldwide currently are attempting to approach the new double identity. Most of the women sampled indicated on the Maferr inventory that they perceive themselves to be well balanced between self-achieving (liberal) and family-oriented (traditional), although there do tend to be relative cultural differences within each sample, where the highly educated and/or professional women see themselves as more self-oriented and self-achieving.

However, while most women indicate that they are becoming pretty much what they would like to be, they do not believe that men approve of their new roles outside the family. One hundred years after Anna O. nursed her dying father, women still perceive that men do not accept a woman's self-achieving role. Cross-culturally, women indicate that they think that the men in their particular cultures desire a woman who is extremely nurturant and places her own personal growth and development second to the family. Women still report that there are stereotypes and restrictions of one sort or another to block or limit their total development. Although women appear to be moving toward the combination of self-achievement and familial responsibilities, they continue to feel frustrated by the various discriminatory practices designed to hinder their progress and freedom. This frustration in women must be recognized by men and resolved for their own male well-being. When a man recognizes a woman's frustration and then communicates with her, and she with him, he deepens his insight into himself as well as his insight into her frustrations. He becomes more understanding of her as an individual and as a female and more understanding of of himself as an individual and as a male. Our society is in a transitional period. Men and women must keep on working to find each other, and to get in touch with each other's true feelings.

The disparity in the understanding of self and in the understanding of the other usually reflects a lack of communication. (This is not simply a male-female problem, of course. Breakdown in communication is a global problem of today's society.) The research data suggest that one factor which might contribute to the male-female confusion in role concept is woman's push toward higher education. The Maferr studies have shown that as women's level of education rises, the gap in communication between the sexes seems to become greater. In this light it is significant to note that in Anna O.'s culture, higher education for women was not considered. To alleviate the problem, then, do we curtail education for women? Of course not; that is a ridiculous regressive solution. What needs to be done is to raise levels of education within society as a whole, and particularly among men, as to the content, cause, and possible solutions for discrepancies in masculine and feminine role concepts.

In sum, the male-female research tends to indicate that the conflict for women attempting to combine both family and self-achieving roles exists; it is not just a plank for women's liberation. It was a problem that existed for Anna O. in 1880. It is still a problem shared by women and men today. Men too are conflicted in this area of trying to combine family and self-achieving roles, to achieve a double identity.

This conflict will remain until both men and women change their static and stereotyped attitudes about male and female roles that do not benefit them. Further, the conflict will remain until social institutions change to make it easier for men and women to communicate and understand each other better in the context of their double roles.

In this regard, Anna O. was ahead of her time. The "talking cure" released her from her physical symptoms. She could then develop into the accomplishing woman she later became; fulfilling her self-achieving needs as well as nurturing her home-oriented and family needs. Her family were the children she cherished, the wayward girls she felt close to. Her home was wherever her girls were. Her achieving needs were fulfilled by the organizations she built to take care of her people. She wrote, she thought, she worked on projects to satisfy her needs for accomplishment. She said that she loved justice more than love. She came to terms with her double identity, basing her self-achievement on her giving, caring, nurturing, family-oriented feelings. The orphanage harbored her many children. For her, her real family was larger than husband and children. Truly she had achieved a larger extended family.

She did not marry or live with any man. We do not know what happened between 1883 and 1895. How did she deal with her instinctive sexual feelings? Did she deal with them directly, or did she sublimate them? If she did, what is wrong with sublimation? Nothing, if she had the insight to understand it. In the 1980s, with in-depth therapy, Anna O. would come to understand her motivations.

How would this therapist treat Anna O. today so that she not only would be free of physical symptoms but also would understand the roots of her emotional upsets and be free to fulfill her biological nurturing needs as well as her social nurturing needs? Since this therapist is a female psychoanalytically oriented clinical psychologist in 1980, and not a physician in 1880, as was Breuer, Anna O.'s treatment would differ in some important ways from the treatment described by Breuer and Freud.

Breuer, as physician for the family, was called in because of Anna O.'s very severe cough. However, he quickly saw that physically she suffered from more than the cough. The symptoms, as Freud notes, were as follows:

1. Rigid paralysis, accompanied by loss of sensation of both extremities on the right side of her body;
2. The same trouble from time to time affected her on the left side of her body;
3. Eye movements disturbed and her power of vision was subject to numerous restrictions;
4. Difficulties over posture of her head;
5. Severe nervous cough;
6. Aversion to taking nourishment;
7. Unable to drink for several weeks in spite of a tormenting thrist;
8. Powers of speech reduced, to the point of being unable to speak or understand her native language;
9. Subject to conditions of "absence," of confusion, of delirium, and of alteration of her whole personality [Freud, 1909, p. 10].

Breuer's finding that Anna O. was subject to conditions of "absence," confusion, delirium, and alteration of her whole personality clearly led to a diagnosis of hysteria, and, as Freud notes, "we coined the term 'hysterical conversion' " (Freud, 1909, p. 10).

Cases of hysterical conversion are rarely seen today. However, if a therapist were to be called in to treat Anna O. today, one would probably be called in by the family physician. After examining her thoroughly and ruling out any physiological causes for the symptoms, the family physician would surmise that the disturbance was psychological, and the case would be transferred to the therapist. Now here we are in 1980, not 1880. How does one proceed to help this young woman who is suffering so much?

Breuer visited Anna O. daily. The average psychotherapist today does not visit a patient daily except in a hospital or sanatorium setting. However, there are many innovations in therapy today. A book called *Handbook of Innovative Therapy* discusses at least sixty-four therapies in some depth (Cosine, 1981). At least one therapy, devised by Landy and Dahlke, calls itself "Twenty-four-Hour Therapy" (Cosine, 1981). It is just that. The patient is with the therapist and an assistant or assistants on a twenty-four-hour daily basis. In a certain sense Breuer was with his patient almost every day. When he had to leave her, he left her with a consultant. Even if he couldn't be with her, he made her feel that he was within reach, so that it was equivalent to twenty-four-hour coverage. Anna O.'s feelings for Breuer seemed to be reciprocated by him. Evidently, there was strong transference and countertransference.

Now Anna O. is being treated in 1980. The medical doctor has put her in the therapist's hands. The members of Anna O.'s family would be seen in depth, and the therapist would try to learn as much as possible about their family life. Breuer's treatment would be followed and extended even further. Anna O. would free-associate, as Bertha Pappenheim did with Breuer, and "each symptom would disappear after [Anna O.] had described its first occurrence" (Breuer, 1895). Breuer discovered that in talking through each symptom the symptom resolved itself. According to Breuer, this was in accordance with his diagnosis of hysterical conversion. The patient practically cured *herself* in 1880. She invented the "talking cure."

In 1980, once the physical symptoms had abated, the basic technique would be psychoanalytically oriented psychotherapy. Anna O. would be asked to remember specific events relating to her childhood. What were her childhood illnesses? Who took care of her—her mother, her father? Does she remember being held, kissed, read to? She would be asked to free-associate whatever came to mind about her father's role in her life and her mother's role. Jones (1953) called her mother "somewhat of a dragon." This relationship would be explored. What were her feelings about her mother's role as a housewife? What was discussed at home? There would be talk about the relationship of father and mother. What did Anna feel about her brother, about his intelligence, then about men in general? We would work on the repressed thoughts and feelings behind the neurosis, which climaxed into hysterical conversion while she was in the role of nurse to her dying father.

Today the therapist would be quickly aware of the transference phenomenon. Would Bertha Pappenheim react to a female psychotherapist in the same way as to a male therapist? Although at one time all psychoanalytically oriented therapist believed that the sex of the therapist made no difference in the transference, this therapist has never believed that this is true for all cases. It is considered that Anna O. might have a more affirmative transference to a female therapist, because she would be working with a role model who was both achieving and female. Instead of the transference to a male therapist, a father figure, to whom she already had an ambivalent relationship, there would be the thorough examination of the transference to the female therapist. She would have to continue to explore her feelings toward her mother, who never went beyond the housewife role. Then she would see the therapist as a working woman, fulfilling her need for self-achievement. Further, with a female therapist it is quite unlikely that Anna O. would experience the hysterical childbirth (pseudo-cyesis) she did when working with Breuer, as her sexual fantasies would be explored directly. This time the therapy would be completed, without the flight of the therapist. Countertransference issues would not be as relevant for this therapist as they may have been for Breuer. Anna O. would grow to experience a feeling of strength in her new understanding of her relationships to her mother, her dying father, whom she loved but did not want to take care of, and her brother, whom she resented for being able to continue his studies.

Since Bertha Pappenheim was a woman ahead of her time in 1880, in 1980, if her therapy were thorough and successful, she would probably be, at age 21, liberated and career-oriented. If the transference to the female therapist as a role model were meaningful to her, it would be difficult for her to accept second place in her home, no matter how pressed by her family to observe ultraconservative regressive values. Anna O.'s schooling ended when she was 16, while her younger, less intelligent brother was educated to become a lawyer. Today,

Anna O., if she did not decide to enter medical school, would probably have entered law school and surpassed her brother in her studies, judging by the list of scholarly achievements which she did actually accumulate later in life. Today she probably would not accept the "onerous chore" (Hollender, 1980, p. 798) of nursing her father. The family was wealthy. She could feel free to love her father while a trained nurse cared for him, and she could continue her studies with impunity.

Thirteen years, from 1883 to 1895, are unaccounted for in Anna O.'s life. Today, if she had successful therapy, perhaps those years would be as full of accomplishments as her later life was. Her analysis would open up a deeper understanding of herself and her needs as a professional woman. Her achieving identity might encourage her to seek further fulfillment in a helping profession as a means of enriching her active, inquiring mind. Also, through working with a female therapist, Anna O.'s strong feminist feelings might come into being while she was still a young woman, and her intuitive feelings might be allowed to develop warmth and softness. And by exercising her sensitive feelings and experiencing a freedom from the discipline of her intellect, she might become able to allow herself to relate to a man.

The aim of therapy with Anna O. would be to bring to her consciousness the feminine and masculine qualities in her personality, to help her relate to a man, not "hysterically" as she did with Breuer, but with a free, open emotional empathy.

Anna O. was a strong-willed person. Her resistance would be quite strong and it would take some work to break it. Her transference to the female therapist might break the resistance more easily than with a male therapist. She would see the female therapist operating from a double identity—nurturing and achieving. Anna O. would be helped to see that it is possible to be a housewife, mother, and family member and at the same time to be a creative achieving individual.

That this achievement could very well be attained by Bertha Pappenheim today is illustrated by the following: On Saturday, October 17, 1981, there appeared in the *New York Times* a photograph of Ellen V. Futter, age 32, president of Barnard College (youngest president of a major college in the United States), with her infant daughter of 3 weeks, Anne Victoria Shutkin, at a baby shower, surrounded by students possibly only ten years younger than President Futter. The accompanying article noted:

> There was once another president of Barnard who got pregnant, but she never had a baby shower. Her name was Emily Jane Smith Putnam, and when she told the board of trustees in 1901 that she was to give birth, she was promptly dismissed. Miss Futter said yesterday that when she told the board, they were ecstatic. "They thought it was just a terrific symbol for a women's college," she said [Quidlen, 1981, p. 27].

President Futter has succeeded in fulfilling her double identity. An added point of interest is this comment by President Futter: "He [her husband] will want a full report of this."

Anna O.'s therapy—her "talking cure"—would not be performed through trial and error as it was in the early days of psychology in the 1880s. Just as she did with Breuer, today she would use each physical symptom as a starting point associated with painful moments in her past, reliving them in order to assess the true reasons for her physical and emotional discomfort. However, the major difference in the 1980 therapy would be the transference to the female therapist and uninterrupted treatment. A present-day therapist would not be scared off, as Breuer was, by certain transferential and countertransferential issues. Today Anna O. would be encouraged to talk out her feelings about men in greater detail—perhaps coming to understand her identification with her father's intellectual ability, and thus the traditionally more "masculine" side of her self. Today a therapist would be dealing with a modern reality, full of choices that Breuer did not have to work with in the repressed atmosphere of Vienna in the 1880s. Anna O. could be channeled into a society with more opportunities for women seeking to fulfill their double identity.

As one reads about Bertha Pappenheim and her real accomplishments in dealing and working with women, young girls, and children, one gets no insight into her feelings toward men. Although Breuer characterized her as asexual, claiming that "the sexual element in her make-up was astonishingly undeveloped" (Breuer, 1895, p. 21), it is clear that her incipient sexuality was trampled in the transference phenomenon and perhaps later frightened into silence by Freud's sexual theories. Although as Karpe (1959) intimates, Anna O. had unrecognized homosexual tendencies, this therapist rejects that notion, and believes instead that Anna O.'s sexuality was sublimated into her work against immorality. Today this female therapist and Anna O. would explore sexual questions from the beginning of treatment. Might a result of this exploration be that Anna O. could combine her identity as an organizer of extended families with the nurturing identity derived from her own biological offspring?

It is hoped that Anna O.'s therapy today would help make her not a "comparatively fulfilled woman" but a more completely fulfilled woman. However, there are still obstacles. More than twenty-five years of Maferr research demonstrates the fervent desire of women to fulfill both individual self-achieving needs and home-oriented nurturing needs. Even now these needs are not secured. There have not been enough profound changes in the organization of our society to guarantee women the possibility of fulfilling both needs. In many cases the desire for self-achievement is not enough to assure that home life will be attended to. Further, for some women self-achieving needs predominate, for others home-oriented demands take the ascendancy. The balance between the traditional and liberal needs varies according to age, time, socioeconomic level, and culture. It always has been so. A homeostatic identity is difficult to attain. However, the riches of the double identity are well worth struggling for.

References

BREUER, J., and FREUD, S. (1893–1895). *Studies on Hysteria.* vol. II. London: Hogarth Press, 1955.

FREEMAN, L. *The Story of Anna O.* New York: Walker, 1972.

FRIEDAN, B. *The Feminine Mystique.* New York: W. W. Norton, 1963.

FRIEDAN, B. Feminism's next step. *New York Times Magazine,* July 5, 1981, pp. 14, 15.

FREUD, S. *Five Lectures on Psycho-Analysis.* Delivered on the occasion of the celebration of the twentieth anniversary of the foundation of Clark Universty, Worcester, Massachusetts, September 1909 (1910). Standard Edition, vol. XI.

HOLLENDER, M. H. The case of Anna O: A reformulation. *Amer. J. of Psychiat.,* 137:797–800, 1980.

JENSEN, E. M. Anna O—A study of her later life. *Psychoanal. Quart.,* 39:269–273, 1970.

JONES, E. *The Life and Work of Sigmund Freud* (vol. I: *The Formative Years and the Great Discoveries, 1856–1900*). New York: Basic Books, 1953.

KARPE, R. The rescue complex in Anna O's final identity. *Psychoanal. Quart.,* 30:1–27, 1961.

KLEIN, V. *The Feminine Character—History of an Ideology.* New York: International University Press, 1946.

KLEMSRUD, J. Women in medicine find a need for support. *New York Times,* April 13, 1981, p. B11.

LANDY, E., and DAHLKE, A. E. Twenty-four hour therapy: A personal renaissance. In R. J. Corsini (ed.), *Handbook of Innovative Psychotherapies.* New York: John Wiley & Sons, 1981.

Maferr Bibliography. New York: Maferr Foundation, Inc., 1980.

Maferr Inventory of Feminine Values, The. Developed originally by Alexandra Botwin, PhD, San Francisco. Revised and copyright, 1966, Maferr Foundation, Inc. (Male-Female Role Research), New York.

QUINDLEN, A. At Barnard, teddy bears in the deanery. *New York Times,* October 17, 1981, p. 27.

STEINMANN, A. A study of the concept of the feminine role of 51 middle-class American families. *Genetic Psychol. Mono.,* pp. 275–352, 1963.

TAINE, H. *Histoire de la litterature anglaise* (4 vols., 1863–1864; English translation, 1883, History of English Literature). New York: Fredrick Ungar Publishers, 1965.

The Case of Anna O.: Aggression and the Narcissistic Countertransference

12

Hyman Spotnitz

The annals of psychoanalysis indicate that major problems have centered around the theoretical approach to aggression. Early illustrations are the particular elements of the Greek myths on which psychoanalytic formulations on the Oedipus complex and narcissism are based. In both instances the transgressions of the child are emphasized and those of the parent are ignored.

In other words, Oedipus is viewed as a man who killed his father and had sex with his mother, and his guilt, Freud points out, ''was not palliated by the fact that he incurred it without his knowledge and even against his intention'' (1913, p. 68). Attention is not called to the fact that the parents (to defeat the prediction of the oracle Tiresias that their son would one day kill his father) put the infant out to die. Similarly selective use is made of the myth of the handsome Narcissus; he is focused on as a youth who loved himself to a pathological degree and pined away gazing at his own reflection in a pool of water. But a study of the Narcissus myths reveals that a great deal of hatred existed between his parents. His mother, having been raped by his father, was consumed with unconscious hatred for Narcissus, the product of that rape, and deeply concerned about his future (Spotnitz, and Resnikoff, 1976). Psychoanalytic literature has given relatively little attention to the problems of parents who have hostile feelings for their children.

It is my impression that the parents' hostile feelings are absorbed by the children, who may have difficulty handling such feelings. When the children are vulnerable, they develop that pathological pattern of dealing with unwanted feelings that we refer to as the schizophrenic reaction.

Schizophrenic and other patients with preoedipal problems demonstrate two different types of transference states in the course of analytic therapy, oscillating between them. In the first type, which Freud recognized and which is now identified as object or oedipal transference, the patient relates to the analyst as a separate object. In the second, more primitive type—the narcissistic or preoedipal transference—a patient with indistinct ego boundaries tends to relate to the analyst as a part of himself. The working concept of narcissistic transference has recently come into prominence; many investigators have contributed to its development (e.g., Spotnitz, 1969; Kohut, 1971; Kernberg, 1975).

In response to the narcissistic transference reactions of a severely disturbed patient, the analyst tends to develop a narcissistic or preoedipal countertransference. In that state, feelings induced by the patient become fused with the analyst's own feelings and seem to him to be entirely unrelated to the patient. The key to the effective treatment of schizophrenic, borderline, and seemingly hysterical patients like Anna O. is, in my experience, understanding of the feelings induced by the patient and the ability to distinguish them from one's own feelings (Spotnitz, 1979).

When Breuer treated Anna O. a century ago, he was not aware of the phenomenon of transference, which is now regarded as the essential mechanism in psychoanalytic therapy. Some time after the treatment had ended, Breuer disclosed to Freud that Anna O. had confronted him with a phantom pregnancy (pseudocyesis) on the final day of the treatment. Freud then called attention to the universal nature of transference, thus overcoming Breuer's objections to reporting the case (Jones, 1953). Freud did not, however, call Breuer's attention to countertransference. The case of Anna O. antedated the first published reference to the counter-phenomenon by nearly three decades (Freud, 1910).

Here is a clinical illustration.

When I was 35 years old, I became involved in a case that put me on the road to acquiring a deep understanding of schizophrenic individuals. Like Anna O., the patient was a charming woman in her early twenties; I also recall her in the present context because of the sexual problem in the case and because of the uncertainty surrounding the diagnosis. The hospital where I was working admitted her as a hysterical patient; a few days later her condition was diagnosed as manic-depressive psychosis, and some months later as catatonic schizophrenia. Since the hospital staff knew that I wanted to study and work with schizophrenic patients, the case was assigned to me.

An interesting coincidence occurred in the course of that relationship. I became aware of feelings for this attractive young woman and sensed a desire to make her pregnant. At that very time she began to talk about the circumstances surrounding her breakdown. (In the light of our present understanding, I would say that she transferred desires to conceive a child, inducing similar desires in me. In the context of this narcissistic transference-countertransference situation, she was reliving her feelings for her husband.)

She stated that she had become psychotic as a result of having sexual relations with her husband when they were practicing coitus interruptus and he failed to withdraw successfully. (At her insistence they had agreed to wait a year before having a child, and her husband told me that he had no intention of making her pregnant against her wishes.) She said, ''That bastard husband of mine was really trying to make me pregnant. That was not a mistake. It was intentional, his idea of tricking me.'' Then, out of guilt, suppressed rage, and remorse, she became psychotic.

As the patient continued to verbalize her feelings, she came to recognize that, despite her conscious resolve to put off raising a family, she unconsciously wanted to become pregnant and had apparently induced that desire in her husband. As soon as she understood the situation, she demonstrated that she really wanted to have a child. Our warm relationship terminated in her wish to return to her husband and have several children with him.

Since that first successfully handled case, I have worked mainly with pre-psychotic and postpsychotic schizophrenic patients, with those suffering from psychosomatic conditions, character disorders, hysterias, and compulsive neuroses. The overall clinical diagnosis is not, as in physical medicine, a determining factor in their treatment. The psychotherapy is based on one's immediate diagnostic impression of the patient, which may change from moment to moment. The therapist modifies his interventions accordingly.

In treating someone like Anna O. today, some accommodation would be made for the presence of any severe mental or bodily symptoms such as Breuer initially observed in that young woman. The patient would either begin psychotherapy in a hospital or be escorted to and from the therapist's office by a hospital attendant or relative (Spotnitz, 1981). But whatever the clinical diagnosis, I would conduct the treatment on the same general principles.

The first principle is that there must be no action in the treatment sessions; the patient must not act and the analyst must not act. They must be able to feel all their feelings and not act on them in their relationship. If you are going to work with schizophrenic or psychotic patients who go into rage reactions and want to attack you, who may come at you with knives or guns—both of which I have faced—you will have to forestall action. For the beginning therapist, the safest way to do this is to have the patient lie on the couch. I permit my seriously ill patients to get up from the couch when they want to do so, but I try to help them return to it expeditiously. Until they do return, I usually do not intervene to facilitate the resolution of their resistances to verbalizing their negative feelings.

Some patients like Anna O. have great difficulty getting on the couch and remaining there throughout the analytic session. They may get terrified when they don't see the analyst because of the feeling that he does not exist, a feeling that is characteristic of the narcissistic transference. A patient in that state, as already indicated, tends to induce a narcissistic countertransference in the analyst. For example, in reaction to the patient's feeling that the analyst does not exist, the analyst may experience feelings of indifference or no feeling whatsoever for the patient. Many analysts who work with schizophrenic patients complain of a total lack of feeling for them without being aware that this is a familiar constellation of the narcissistic transference-countertransference situation.

In the preoedipal relationship between child and mother, the child's ego boundaries are indistinct; where one person ends and the other begins is not experienced by the child. In the narcissistic transference state, the patient may feel that the analyst is part of himself. Distinct feelings of separateness and distinct feelings of the other person's existence are lacking. Whereas a patient in a state of object (oedipal) transference senses that "I am I" and the analyst is "someone else," a patient in the narcissistic (preoedipal) state of transference experiences the feeling that "I exist and I don't know whether there is anyone else." That attitude, though it appears to be total self-absorption, is typical of the narcissistic state.

One patient brought this out dramatically. She said, "I talk to you in your office once a week, and the rest of the week I talk to you all day, twenty-four hours a day. The results I get from talking to you at home twenty-four hours a day are much better than the results I get when I'm in the office with you." With patients who sense that they are relating to the analyst when he is absent, or who sense him as nonexistent when he is with them, the analyst gets to feel that what he does as a real person is relatively insignificant. The attitudes conveyed by such patients make him feel like a very inconsequential human being.

These patients have strong desires to be destructive to the analyst because, when the transference fully evolves, they experience him as wanting to destroy them. In other words, they tend to transfer the aggressive feelings they experienced with their parents, and they tend to experience in the other person the aggressive feelings their parents had for them. The patients may need to be convinced that, no matter how you feel, you are not going to act on your feelings but on your understanding of the total situation.

The next instruction one gives such patients is what Anna O. told Breuer. They are embarking on a "talking cure," nothing else. Talking is all that goes on between patient and analyst. There is to be no physical contact. I don't expect an analyst to pass this test 100 percent, but in working with an acting-out psychotic patient, the analyst should earn an A grade for "no physical contact." The less one touches the patient, the less danger there is of his acting out. It is also true that the less danger there is of the patient's acting out, the less objectionable it is for the analyst to touch the patient once in a while—for example, to shake hands or assist the patient in putting on his coat. But if there is any real danger of psychotic acting out by the patient with you as the victim, physical contact is by all means to be avoided.

In 1880–1882, Breuer did not follow this dictum. His report on the case of Anna O. (Breuer and Freud, 1893–1895) refers to different forms of physical contact between them. He frequently touched her hand. He gave her massages. He restrained her forcibly at times. He fed her. He took her riding in his carriage. Presumably such physical contact helped to set up the problem of pseudocyesis (false pregnancy) in which the relationship between the two culminated just a few hours after Breuer thought he had completed the treatment.

Having established the principles that there is to be no action in the therapeutic sessions and that the patient is to verbalize his immediate feelings, thoughts, and memories, the analyst applies himself to resolving the resistances to communicating freely that the patient is experiencing. Ultimately everything that goes on between them in the course of the relationship is verbalized and eventually discussed—that is, when discussions are therapeutically indicated.

In 1880–1882, what were not verbalized and discussed were the transference feelings that Anna O. directed toward Breuer, and Breuer's countertransference feelings for Anna O. It is quite evident from reading the case report that Anna O. experienced a wide range of feelings for Breuer. Moreover, one encounters numerous references, explicit or implicit, to his emotional reactions to Anna O. He did not, however, seem to attach significance to these reactions at the time; no reference is made to their having been discussed with the patient. And when Breuer later discussed the case with him, Freud apparently explained that whatever feelings Anna O. had for Breuer were transference feelings and that whatever feelings Breuer had for Anna O. were appropriate to the situation.

Some thirty years later, however, in a brief reference to the case of Anna O., Freud stated, ''After the work of catharsis had seemed to be completed, the girl had suddenly developed a condition of 'transference love'; he [Breuer] had not connected this with her illness, and had therefore retired in dismay'' (Freud, 1925, p. 26). Subsequently Freud's biographer Ernest Jones disclosed the name of the patient and details of the occurrence that had been so disturbing to Breuer (Jones, 1953).

Breuer thought he had cured Anna O., but on the day he had brought the treatment to a close, he was called back to minister to her again. On returning to her home, he found her in the throes of a fantasied childbirth. She exclaimed, ''Dr. Breuer's baby is coming'' (Freeman, 1972, p. 56). Imagine the effect of that pronouncement on an upright and dedicated physician! All he had tried to do was to help a charming, brilliant young woman become a healthy person, and here she was accusing him, vividly, of having made her pregnant. Not only that, but she was ''delivering'' his baby right there before him!

I have been trying to puzzle out why and how Breuer's ministrations produced Anna O.'s psychological pregnancy. In the course of investigating various dates cited in the history of the case, I encountered what impresses me as an interesting coincidence.

Anna O.'s propensity for repeating what happened between her and her father—repeating it a year later—is discussed in Breuer's report on the case as follows: ''She lived through the previous winter day by day. I should only have been able to *suspect* that this was happening, had it not been that every evening during the hypnosis she talked through whatever it was that had excited her on the same day in 1881, and had it not been that a private diary kept by her mother in 1881 confirmed beyond a doubt the occurrence of the underlying events. This reliving of the previous year came to its final close in June, 1882. . . . Thanks to the diary I knew what was happening'' (Breuer and Freud, 1893–1895, p. 33).

Anna O.'s fantasied pregnancy, it has been disclosed, occurred on June 7, 1882. What happened the year before that ''untoward event,'' as Freud later referred to it?

To reconstruct what had happened from the facts as we know them today, the patient's psychological pregnancy occurred precisely a year after Breuer's wife became pregnant; their daughter Dora was born on March 11, 1882. Whereas it took Frau Breuer nine months to deliver their baby, Anna O. produced her psychological baby in a few hours! It is my impression that, having sensed Breuer's feelings at the time he made his wife pregnant, Anna O. a year later imagined that she too was creating a child for Breuer. The spectacle that confronted him must have been even more shocking because of his awareness of her inclination to repeat ''whatever it was that had excited her on the same day in 1881.'' After hypnotizing her for the last time, he fled from the house and had nothing further to do with her.

Anna O., on the other hand, felt like a woman who had actually been raped and then deserted by her husband-to-be. We can understand, then, why Anna O., or Bertha Pappenheim, after recovering her health, devoted the rest of her life to taking care of women who had actually been so victimized. Taking care of children, including some orphaned in pogroms in Eastern Europe, was another major concern for Anna O. She gained renown as the first social worker in Germany (Freeman, 1972).

A troublesome aspect of the narcissistic countertransference, as many analysts will attest, is that they don't experience themselves as being in that state when they are. Time and time again, while working with preoedipal patients, I have felt like getting rid of one as incurable, or felt that maybe I ought to marry that wonderful female patient or have a homosexual affair with an attractive male, before recognizing that I was being swayed by the induced feelings. Unless you are alert to the possibility that feelings that you experience as your own and that seem to have nothing to do with the patient may actually be the patient's feelings, that danger exists.

Over the centuries, the phenomenon of emotional induction appears to have contributed to society's dismal handling of those suffering from acute mental illness. One explanation of why these individuals have been mutilated, shackled, sexually abused, burned at the stake, even killed, is that they felt that they deserved such mistreatment and induced those feelings in the people around them.

Years ago, when I served as consultant to a casework agency, I was told over and over again by caseworkers, ''I would like to dismiss this patient'' or

"I would like to transfer this patient to another worker." The case under discussion usually turned out to be that of a preoedipal patient with indistinct ego boundaries who wanted to be eliminated, but the caseworker thought that dropping the patient was his own desire.

One of Dr. Breuer's problems in working with Anna O. was that he did not know that he had countertransference feelings toward her. He did not know that she might have aroused sexual impulses in him and that he might have experienced desires to make her pregnant. Finally, however, he recognized that he had hostile wishes for her; he confided in Freud that he wished Anna O. were dead, rationalizing that death would put an end to her terrible suffering (Jones, 1953).

Breuer never experienced Anna O. as having been his collaborator in a great scientific discovery. Together they opened the door to the analytic cure of schizophrenia.

In the 1980s, when you work with a patient like Anna O., you may anticipate experiencing feelings which appear to have nothing to do with the patient but which are actually induced by him. If you don't recognize that these are feelings that the patient had for a mother or father in the first few years of life or that the patient's mother or father had for the child, you cannot treat the patient successfully. These feelings are not necessarily reported or interpreted to the patient. But when the patient is able to function comfortably on the couch and wants to communicate with the analyst, the analyst can begin to investigate why the patient does not communicate his feelings for the analyst and the feelings the patient imagines the analyst is experiencing for him.

These patients usually demonstrate an intense need to deny that the analyst experiences hostile feelings or sexual feelings toward them. They have a terrific need to deny anything "bad" about the analyst, denial that may take years to investigate and undo. Eventually the patient has to be asked, "Do you think I have sexual feelings for you? Do you think I would like to conceive a baby with you? Do you think I feel like harming you?" Such questions are investigated in the course of the long-range treatment required to help the schizophrenic patient become a mature, well-adjusted personality.

If the goal of the treatment is limited to the removal of symptoms, that can sometimes be accomplished in less than five years. But the process of effecting complete change in the character structure and immunizing the patient against a relapse into psychosis requires anywhere from five to twenty years. And then, who knows if all this effort has been worthwhile? Often I ask myself that question. But if their parents love such children, they are willing to do whatever is necessary to assure their recovery.

The final questions I want to address myself to are these: Why did Breuer and Freud fail to recognize the narcissistic countertransference? Why did they not recognize that Breuer may have experienced feelings for Anna O. that foreclosed complete success in treating her? Why was the subject of countertransference so long neglected in the literature?

It is quite clear that in the dawning years of psychoanalysis, it was considered improper for an analyst to have countertransference feelings for a patient, just as parents were not supposed to have incestuous feelings or murderous feelings toward their offspring. For an analyst to sustain and admit that he experienced such feelings for a patient would have been regarded as shameful. Thus the analyst's need for self-approval and social approval may have retarded progress in facing the problems implicit in the countertransference. It is my impression, however, that unless you have real feelings for the preoedipal patient, unless you're aware of these feelings, and unless you engage in emotional communication with the patient, it is virtually impossible to help the patient appease his maturational needs and become an emotionally mature individual.

Another question begs for an answer. Why are we analytic therapists so terrified of the feelings we tend to experience when we work with such patients? Many of us are afraid to recognize these feelings and to face them. We are often afraid to investigate how these feelings operate in our work. In my view, the feelings aroused in us by patients like Anna O. are of such a primitive nature that they threaten the foundations of our personality structure. We need thorough self-analysis and also social understanding and support in order to tolerate such feelings comfortably and to communicate them effectively to our preoedipal patients.

We are willing at times to have positive feelings for our patients; what are particularly intolerable, and much disapproved of, are hostile feelings. We do not wish to experience such reactions to the emotionally disturbed individuals who need our help, and whom we are dedicated to helping. When we do experience such emotions, we try to rationalize them. Sooner or later, we may get to feel that a patient ought to be put out of his misery and advocate euthanasia.

Nevertheless, when these feelings are recognized and verbalized and the resistance state between the patient and the analyst is resolved, the patient is in a position to experience a full recovery from the processes that preserved the illness, and ultimately to be immunized against its return.

References

BREUER, J. and FREUD, S. (1893–1895). *Studies on Hysteria*. Standard Edition of the complete Psychological Works of Sigmund Freud, vol. II. London: Hogarth Press, 1955.

FREEMAN, L. *The Story of Anna O*. New York: Walker and Company, 1972.

FREUD, S. (1910). *The Future Prospects of Psycho-Analytic Therapy*. Standard Edition, vol. II. London: Hogarth Press, 1957.

FREUD, S. (1913). *Totem and Taboo*. Standard Edition, vol. XIII. London: Hogarth Press, 1955.

FREUD, S. (1925). *An Autobiographical Study*. Standard Edition, vol. XX. London: Hogarth Press, 1959.

JONES, E. *The Life and Work of Sigmund Freud*, vol. 1. New York: Basic Books, 1953.

KERNBERG, O. F. *Borderline Conditions and Pathological Narcissism.* New York: Aronson, 1975.

KOHUT, H. *The Analysis of the Self.* New York: International Universities Press, 1971.

SPOTNITZ, H. *Modern Psychoanalysis of the Schizophrenic Patient.* New York: Grune & Stratton, 1969.

SPOTNITZ, H., and RESNIKOFF, P. The myths of Narcissus. In H. Spotnitz, *Psychotherapy of Preoedipal Conditions.* New York: Aronson, 1976.

SPOTNITZ, H. Narcissistic countertransference. *Contemp. Psychoanal.,* 15:545–559, 1979.

SPOTNITZ, H. Ethical issues in the treatment of psychotics and borderline psychotics. In M. Rosenbaum (ed.), *Ethics and Values in Psychotherapy.* New York: Free Press, 1981.

The Family Therapy of Anna O.: Other Times, Other Paradigms

13

Donald A. Bloch

This chapter grows out of an invitation to participate in a meeting occasioned by the centenary of the treatment of Bertha Pappenheim, known as Anna O., generally held to be the first patient treated by psychoanalysis. Readers of this volume are fully aware of the importance of her treatment in the history of psychoanalysis and are acquainted as well with her circumstances, symptomatology, and treatment by Josef Breuer. As a family therapist, it is my intention to discuss how I would treat Anna O. in the light of current theories of etiology and treatment.

My last contact with the Anna O. case took place thirty years ago when I was a student in the Washington Psychoanalytic Institute. After completing my analytic training and practicing for a time, I began to move away from analysis and toward the center of my professional interests: human psychosocial contexts, with particular emphasis on families and family therapy.

The ground rules for discussing the way Anna O. would be treated by a family therapist today are unclear, most particularly as to what data are to be used. I naturally reread the original Breuer-Freud chapter in *Studies in Hysteria;* my memory had retained few of the details of the case. It was impressive to revisit the struggles of Breuer, to understand the confusing welter of images presented to him by his patient. The writing was clear and forceful (Freud's influence, one suspects); the story was gripping. But I was in a state of considerable dismay when I completed reading the chapter. There were only the tiniest scraps of information about the patient's family. She had a mother whom she spelled in the care of her dying father—and a brother. Not even ages were mentioned.

In the light of the fact that Bertha Pappenheim is a minor historical figure, it would have been possible at that point to undertake additional historical research and, based on this, to offer some thoughts on the dynamics of the Pappenheim family. I chose another route. The ground rules under which the first part of this chapter was written were that only information unquestionably available to a family therapist at the time of actual contact with the family would be used; there would be no inferential or post hoc reconstructions. Given those rules, what did I have to work with?

The original Breuer chapter focuses almost entirely on Bertha's care of her father, who lay gravely ill. With the information available at the time when Breuer was first consulted,* I believe that a family systems therapist might have dealt with the situation somewhat along the following lines.

In the opening scene of the real Anna O. drama, Breuer was invited to make a home visit, and thus was provided with an unparalleled opportunity to see the family in its own natural setting. (It should be noted that such a home visit is rarely part of the therapeutic armamentarium of the present-day psychotherapist, who most likely would ask to have the young woman come or be brought to his office for the initial consultation, or would have had her hospitalized.) It seems to me that the opening phases of the treatment of this family would have taken place in their home, and certainly should have taken place there so as to include the father in the treatment.

At the time of Breuer's first contact with the family, it could not have been known that the father would surely die, although it must have been clear he was profoundly ill. In any case, there would have been little doubt in the family therapist's mind as to the gravity of the situation. My intuition is that the onset of Bertha's acute symptomology coincided with her sensing the final hopelessness of her father's situation; perhaps he no longer fought the illness, perhaps his spirit had broken and he had become hopeless about his own recovery. Family members monitor their own and others' physiological and psychological states; often subtle changes in these suffice to disequilibrate the family system.

Thus it would have been immediately evident, as it was, I am sure, to Breuer, that this was a family crisis. In the consultation the introduction to the presenting problem, Bertha's symptoms, would have been lengthy, and we may imagine the therapist attending to this moderately carefully. At the same time he would have been occupied with another issue, that of making a map of the family system. The first task would have been to ascertain the answer to the apparently simple question "Who are the members of this family?" The answer most certainly would have been "The three of us, and in addition a son, Wilhelm." On inquiring about the present whereabouts of Wilhelm, the therapist would have been told that he was at the university and planning to enter the legal profession. (In modern times, aided by prior telephone discussion, the brother would almost certainly have been invited to the first meeting.)

This first, most important mapping task is to identify the components and boundaries of the *relevant* family system. I underscore the word "relevant,"

---

*Is is a fair guess that Breuer knew something about the Pappenheim family pedigree, and that they in turn knew about him. The wealthy Jews of Vienna were few in number, and the community was close-knit. They would be expected to choose their physicians with care; their patronage in turn was much sought after.

meaning by that the persons and subsystems for whom the symptomatic behavior fulfills an essential function. Robyn Skynner has termed this the "minimal sufficient network" (Skynner, 1976 p. 291), and the identification and assembling of this network are foundation tasks for the family therapist. My guess is that in attempting this, the therapist would have almost immediately discovered an important piece of the problem, as well as one of the major resistances of the family. The dialogue might have gone something like this:

THERAPIST: (on being told that Wilhelm was at the university): Ah yes, ah well, I am glad to hear that he is well. It would be necessary for him to be part of our therapeutic work, and I look forward to meeting him.

MRS. P.: But, Doctor, he is entirely well. It is for my daughter that I have summoned you.

THERAPIST: Indeed, I understand this. However, my experience is that all members of a family have a contribution to make to understanding the nature of a family's problems, and I am certain that Wilhelm, because he loves his family, most certainly will wish to do whatever he can to help the family deal with these trying matters.

We may be certain that the therapist, as this conversation goes on, is visually scanning all persons present, most particularly watching the daughter, Bertha, for signs as to the significance of pieces of information. Would she have allowed an enigmatic smile to play across her face as her mother came forward with the next comment?

MRS. P.: Doctor, I fear you do not understand me. I am not in the least bit worried about Wilhelm. It is Bertha whose care I wish you to undertake.

An experienced family therapist would see this issue as critical. Two children are being held in polar positions by the family's system, one well, the other ill. Bertha can be thought of as a kind of scapegoat. Wilhelm's absence from therapy is a case of what family therapists speak of as the "absent-member maneuver." Using the desire of the family to have the benefit of his assistance and hoping that it may outweigh the profound resistance of the system, the therapist decides to take a decisive stand and says:

THERAPIST: Madam, I am delighted to hear that Wilhelm is doing so well; it must be a great source of comfort and satisfaction to you to know that in these trying circumstances. However, my experience is that I must have the assistance of all members of the family if I am to carry out the work with any hope of success, and so I must insist. I hope you will oblige me in this matter.

Had this outrageous suggestion been made in 1880 and had Mrs. Pappenheim consented to it, we might today be celebrating the hundredth anniversary of the first case of family therapy. My guess, though, is that she would have thought to herself, "Such a strange man. I certainly will have nothing to do with him. I hear there's a nice Dr. ——— down the street who has been having very good results with difficult cases. I will see if he will undertake the care of my Bertha."

It is obvious that such a conversation would never have taken place in those days, although perhaps one might be just a bit curious about the *present* infrequency of such interchanges. It is, I think, of consequence to note that by pressing this issue, the therapist would rapidly have made evident the asymmetrical structure of the family, particularly in regard to the sex roles of the children. On a historical-cultural note, we might guess at least that this is one of the reasons family therapy could not have been invented in that cultural environment. It would have inevitably challenged the sex role assumptions then prevalent—unlike psychoanalysis, which was able to go on with its work assuming them to be in the very nature of things.

But let us assume a consent from Mrs. Pappenheim. The problem the therapist must now address is a clear continuation of the question, "Who are the members of this family?" He or she must decide how to format the treatment, mapping what the actual arrangements should be, who should be included, where, and how. Granted that all four members of the family must in some way be included, two of them are bedridden and one may be dying. Let us imagine that they can meet at the bedside of the father. There are other major concerns, one of which is the question of the probable outcome for the father: Will he die, linger on, or perhaps recover? In regard to Bertha, are we dealing with an acute problem, a chronic problem, or an acute outbreak on a base of chronicity? Early on in treatment the family therapist must attempt to assess the chronic vulnerability of the family in the interest of treatment planning. In family therapy, diagnosis and therapy are seen as a single process. The very organization of the information-gathering procedure has a therapeutic impact. If, as was the case with Bertha Pappenheim, the identified patient is the target of an individualized diagnostic study, the effect is to agree with the family system's definition of the nature of the difficulty, i.e., that it is a personal, individual difficulty rather than a feature of the functioning of the family system. Beyond this, all interviews are at the same time diagnostic and therapeutic. Hypotheses both small and large are advanced, tested, discarded, or acted upon at the *process* level.

Perhaps I can illustrate this better by turning to a task that should most certainly have occupied the family therapist no later than the second session: the construction of a genogram. Doing this would, I believe, have considerably advanced the understanding of the family problem.

The genogram is a graphic representation of the multigenerational family tree. It records the membership of a family over several generations, together with some of the significant events of the family history. My custom and that of many family therapists is to undertake such an exercise quite early on in the work, in the first or second session. Collecting the needed information is, for the most part, nonthreatening; relationships and events that are affectively charged may quickly be located, and some of the multigenerational structure of the family will become evident. Through constructing a genogram, it is also possible to form a preliminary impression of the legacies and unresolved issues passed along from earlier times, as well as those generated in the family system at hand.

Thus, after establishing the membership of the family sessions to be held at the bedside of the father as including mother, daughter, and son as well, and after a preliminary canvass of the overall situation, including the perception of each member of the family of the problem, the therapist would have invited them to help him construct a genogram.

As Lucy Freeman tells us, the mother was "the former Recha Gold-schmidt, daughter of one of the wealthiest families of Frankfurt. Bertha's father, a banker, was a cousin of the Warburg family of international bankers" (Freeman, 1972, p. 63). Given our self-imposed limitations, that is all we have for the families of origin of Bertha's parents. It is a tiny fragment, indeed, from which to construct a meaningful picture, but our attention is most certainly directed to the wealth and power concentrated in these two families, as well as to their ethnicity. One wonders whether the marriage of Recha and Sigmund Pappenheim was a love match; it most certainly was arranged and approved, and could be called, in Augustus Napier's phrase, "a marriage of families." But the most striking finding generated by the genogram is the discovery that Bertha, who is always in the psychoanalytic literature spoken of as an eldest daughter, was in fact for a good part of her childhood a middle child—indeed, that she was both a *replacement child* and a *survivor*.

The facts are these: In 1849 a daughter, Henrietta, was born, the first child of this family. The second, in 1853, was Flora. Both died—Henrietta at the age of 17, when Bertha was 7 years old, Flora at the age of 2, four years before Bertha's birth. Let us revisit the chronology. Married for a year, the young couple have a daughter, Henrietta, in 1849; they have a second, Flora, in 1853. Then disaster strikes, and the worst, though commonplace, fears of a family at that time in history are realized. Just as Flora begins to toddle around at the age of 2, she dies. But life must go on, and four years later, in 1859, when Henrietta is 10, Bertha is born. Once again the household contains two daughters, who are joined a year and a half later by the fourth child and first boy, Wilhelm. Thus Bertha goes through all her formative developmental phases as a middle child, with a sister 10 years older than herself and a brother one and a half years younger.

Then, there is a second major calamity: In 1866 Henrietta, now 17 and about to become a young woman, is stricken almost certainly by infection—perhaps the tuberculosis that killed their father—and dies. Bertha, the replacement child, is now the eldest, the only daughter left of three.

Without overdramatizing this series of events, it is, I feel, hard to overestimate their importance. This family was an intensely close unit. Look, for example, at Bertha and her mother keeping the dying husband and father at home, caring for him *themselves* even though they most certainly had ample money and servants. We know about the pain and anxiety over the father's illness and death; surely, pain and anxiety would not have been any less as

2-year-old Flora lay dying or, twelve years later, when 17-year-old Henrietta came to her end.

These preceding deaths must have certainly potentiated and intensified the searing sense of gloom and despair associated with the illness of the father. It is not hard for us to imagine the degree to which the family system was stressed by these events. Family systems research has emphasized the powerful effect on other family members and the family relationship system of such losses in family membership. And Bertha, as both replacement child and survivor, must have been especially the focus of such stress. Seen in this light, to my eye at least, there is a striking similarity between the more flagrant symptoms of Bertha and those of modern Holocaust survivors. Death was in the air for the Pappenheim family. In 1880, when Bertha became 21, it was a social unit that soon would have lost half its membership.

As you know, I have tried in this exercise to include only those facts that indisputably would have been immediately available to the therapist at the point of initial contact with the family. All these facts were known, or could easily have been known (assuming the appropriate paradigms were available) at the end, let us say, of an initial two-hour diagnostic-therapeutic consultation. From this point forward, it is no longer possible to proceed quite so easily: The responses of the family system to the joining of the therapist with the family define and change, to some extent at least, the very configuration one proposes to treat. The paradigm generates a format and a line of inquiry, and the very substance of the inquiry, in this instance the problem of Bertha and her family, changes in the process. Treatment begins at the moment of the first contact. Inquiring about Wilhelm, for example, changes the family's view of the problem, and including him in the session has a major impact.

How would a family therapist proceed? What follows is a search of one possible line of therapeutic action. It should be remembered that family therapy is a rapidly growing and changing body of theory and technique.

First and foremost it would be necessary for the family therapist to turn his attention to the issue of despair, impending death, and the history of pain and loss suffered by the family. The family's response to the death of Henrietta and Flora, any associated affective blocks, and any failure of mourning that may have occurred in regard to these events would all be of great interest. The therapist might conduct an exploration through the genogram of losses (unknown to us) both parents may have suffered in the course of their own growing up, as well as the patterns of identification they may have had with their children by virtue of such things as being in a similar sibling position.

It seems likely that the therapist might begin to make some structural moves designed to equalize the roles of the two children and to reinforce the generational boundaries, since it would seem evident that the permeability of these boundaries was excessive. It seems a good guess that Bertha was overprotected by her parents.

Thus the therapist might focus on these issues: the mother-daughter fusion from which Bertha was bowing out by assuming patienthood, and, second, the sex role skewing associated with Wilhelm's developing career as a lawyer and Bertha's developing career as a patient. My first major intervention under these circumstances would be to attempt to move Wilhelm back into the family.

The specifics of how this might be accomplished, of course, depend so much on the symbol systems of the people involved that my suggestions here can only be illustrative. One might consider such things as having Wilhelm take instruction from his sister on how to be a good bedside nurse to their father; one could urge the employment of paid nurses and insist, for reasons of health, that Bertha take a university course (to get her out of the house, as it were).

I would be monitoring the degree to which this replacement child was being groomed by the family system to replace her dying father and, on some long-term basis, would be carefully attending to Bertha's mother's ties with her own generation, so as to improve her lateral support system and make it possible for her to disengage from her daughter. Above all, I would ignore Bertha's symptoms as much as possible and would reemphasize all of the functional competence I could find, feeling confident that more such would soon become evident.

I would like to permit myself one final illustrative suggestion—a suggestion about what a family therapist would *not* do, given a system with the Pappenheim family's powerful propensity for inducting persons into replacement roles. *I* would most certainly wish *not* to be in the position of substituting for this soon-to-be-dead father. I would count on the fact that seeing the Pappenheims as a family (rather than seeing Bertha alone) would substantially reduce the intensity of the transference and countertransference, and thus avoid some of the later twistings and turnings that were associated with Dr. Breuer and the actual treatment venture.

There are, of course, severe limits to this exercise. In the time when Bertha Pappenheim lived and suffered, a new paradigm, psychoanalysis, and an associated intervention technology were evolving, a process being repeated in our own time with the family systems paradigm. It is of more than passing interest to note that the Vienna of those years was the location for the metaphysical and epistemological studies of Mach, Wittgenstein, and others. Indeed, it was in those very years and in that bubbling cauldron of intellectual excitement and innovation that modern definitions of these subjects were set forth.

Epistemology is firmly rooted in language and culture; what we can think about and how we can think about it today are functions of our social contexts. What Bertha Pappenheim could think about and how she could think about it were functions of her social contexts in precisely the same way. I say contexts since we now see these to be multiple and complexly layered—the dyads of Bertha and her mother, Bertha and her father, Bertha and Dr. Breuer, and so on. As in all lives, these relational patterns contextualize each other and make a feltwork that itself is built, with other elements, into a hierarchy of contexts. Among these contexts are the larger societal definitions of sexuality and gender. Hapsburg Vienna was notable for the extent to which it defined sexuality and sex roles differently for males and females. The Pappenheim family was constructed by (and was part of) these powerful forces. Small wonder that these contexts were almost unbearably conflictual for Bertha, especially in the light of the other issues raised above.

Language is always metaphorical, and, we should add, it is always an operator. Language is a behavior in an interactional context. The choice of communicative mode must satisfy the needs of the particular setting.

In Bertha's instance we may guess that her symbols, in order to be effective interpersonal operators, needed to conceal as they revealed. Thus the family systems therapist approaching her florid imagery would search for its meaning not only as a representation of inner stored information—memories, if you will—but also as understood from the effects it had in the interpersonal system. I have suggested that one of those meanings was to move her from the untenable position of fusion with her mother and replacement for her dead sisters and soon-to-be-dead father into the more integrative position of "patient."

From this vantage point in history, with the complete life of this remarkable woman set out before us, what can be learned that might aid us in our choice of paradigms? The most striking pattern to my eye is the enormous extent to which she was contextually defined. Who indeed, seeing her half paralyzed and tortured by phantoms in the months before her father's death, would have guessed at her wit and tenacity, her courage and stamina as they were revealed in other circumstances?

Other times, other paradigms. True enough, but we may look back over this century full of admiration for this talented woman, talented in her illness and in her life, and we may admire as well the young doctor who was compelled to listen to her.

References

FREEMAN, L. *The Story of Anna O.* New York: Walker and Company, 1972.
SKYNNER, A. C. ROBIN. *Systems of Family and Marital Psychotherapy.* New York: Brunner/ Mazel, 1976.

Anna O.: An English Object Relations Approach

14

Gerald J. Gargiulo

If Anna O.'s concerned mother and ailing father called upon an analyst today, what would take place? The analyst, undoubtedly, would respond by asking the parents to bring the distraught young woman into the office on a certain date, for a certain period of time, and for a stated fee. The patient would see other patients in the waiting room (the analyst would not to go to her home), she would note the relative impersonality of the analyst's office, and she would be addressed by someone who evidenced in his tone of voice no signs of parental anxiety or possible unconscious annoyance at Anna's symptoms. All of this is quite obvious to us, the inheritors of Freud's legacy, but in its very commonality it contributes to a particular setting which would match the ''private theater'' in Anna O.'s internal world with a distinctive therapeutic theater outside her. The analyst, in all likelihood, would respond to the patient's dramatic communications (hysterical symptoms) by seeing her as frequently as feasible; no medication would be prescribed.

The analyst would have to know internally, however, whether the seemingly psychotic symptoms were something he could comfortably allow to unfold or whether he would have to rush to understand and resolve them as soon as possible. Only if the analyst was comfortable with the primitively symbolic nonrational elements inside himself could he allow the play to go on in a way that might allow its successful finale. Such an approach is particularly congenial to analysts who follow an English object relations model.

It is a truism that without the living patient before one—without the personal presence, the movement of the eyes, the tone of the voice, and the carriage of the body—it is difficult to have the emotional confirmation integral to an analysis. It is not merely metaphor which led Freud (1901–1905) to observe that the unconscious spills out from ''every pore of the body'' (pp. 77–78). The historical information about Anna O., as is well known, is truncated, and although Jones (1953), Ellenberger (1970), and Pollock (1968) have augmented our knowledge, we are essentially dealing with a literary work filtered through Breuer's defense structure. Even with all these caveats, however, the case is worth discussing. Clearly no attempt is being made to offer an empirically verifiable hypotheses—actually none need be made.* Interpretations that offer a patient new personalized internal meanings with a consequent new mode of experiencing the self are worthwhile. The value of a psychoanalytical historical reconstruction is not in its exact verifiability or its intellectual correctness, as obviously important as these considerations are. From an object relations standpoint the primary issue is the subjective (personal aliveness) as well as objective (usable externality—play and work) experience(s) of reality that a particular line of interpretation and therapeutic interaction makes possible for a *particular* patient.

Before discussing the case in any detail, I would like to elaborate on these thoughts and give a very brief summary of what has come to be known as the English object relations school.

Major English authors who have written in this area, within the Freudian tradition, include Fairbairn (1954), M. Balint (1979), D. W. Winnicott (1958, 1965, 1971), H. Guntrip (1973), and M. S. Kahn (1974). Such writers as these have worked with patients on what is called a preoedipal level of personal development. Actually, Freud's theory of neurosis, with its oedipal conflict core, presupposes the existence of a person capable of using adult language and of experiencing interpersonal and therefore psychological conflict. Freud's theory of the mind and his consequent technique follow from such metapsychological presumptions. Classical Freudian technique suggests a one-person psychology, namely the patient within the treatment. Even when such preoedipal stages as oral, anal, and phallic are spoken of, these are approached through the oedipal model of personal emotional existence, articulated by the patient's language manifesting his or her conflict. The emphasis, again, is on the individual's pathology. The English school, on the other hand, has focused on those emotional and developmental issues which go into the making of a person, as it were. They have worked with patients whose use of language does not have the same emotional import and meaning as that of neurotically conflicted individuals; patients, that is, who feel empty or dead inside or who do not (emotionally) know that they have an inside. And using such terms as "schizoid problems" (Guntrip), "basic fault" (Balint), and "true self–false self" (Winnicott), they have attempted to understand the developmental issues that give birth to the psychological person.

Within the actual treatment setting, the technical approach of this school reflects an appreciation of the role of the analyst as a contributing factor in the patient's developmental maturation, reflecting a sensitivity to the mode of ob-

*In such a literary work as this, we are attempting to understand the patient through the metaphor of interpretations, as it were. There is a logic to understanding interpretations known as hermeneutics. It is a perspective to which the noted French philosopher Paul Ricoeur (1974), has made us particularly sensitive. His phenomenological philosophical perspective is alluded to here since it one of the implicit conceptual frameworks in my discussion of the case. Cf. particularly Ricoeur (1977).

ject relatedness which emerges in the treatment. Such an approach to patients precedes any understanding of the patient in terms of instinctual unconscious conflicts and their consequent resolution through verbal interpretation. Believing that individuals come to experience themselves as real through progressively relating to other individuals and not primarily through instinctual expression,* the English school has charted areas of the mind not available to a more classical practitioner. The type of patient and the issues addressed in classical therapy with neurotics are radically different from those having to do with healing a most basic split in the psyche.

From another perspective we might note the difference of approach by saying that in classical psychoanalytical treatment the area of the patient's regression is handled very cautiously and is understood frequently as a defense, as a resistance, and potentially, if not actually, as pathogenic. The patient's regression as a positive contribution to the therapeutic process is hardly ever spoken of. In the object relations school, on the other hand, regression, in all its forms, is spoken of and used much more extensively, with particular emphasis on the analyst's role and use of regression.

Now to return to the patient, Anna O., to see where our line of inquiry might take us. Given the severity of her symptomatology—difficulty in speaking in coherent syntax, numerous physical conversion symptoms, extreme difficulty with vision—one could understand her parents' alarm. Furthermore, the apparent splitting of her social response into a good self and a bad self, more like a 3½-year-old naughty child, must have been puzzling and extremely disconcerting to this well-to-do, middle-class Viennese family. Her alternating selves had been obvious to the patient and she complained of going mad. The family, probably out of a mixture of unconscious anxiety and ignorance, assured her that she was not. Her moods, we are told, changed rapidly; she would hallucinate black snakes which were her hair, fingers, and various ribbons, yet she would catch herself and attempt to reassure herself of the objective reality of the world around her. Furthermore, as Breuer wrote, "At moments when her mind was quite clear she would complain of the profound darkness in her head, of not being able to think, of becoming blind and deaf, of [as mentioned above] having two selves, a real one and an evil one which forced her to behave badly, and so on" (Breuer and Freud, 1893–1895, p. 24).

Anna had a brother younger by one year and an older sister who died at the age of 17 when Anna was 8 years old. Actually, she had had two older sisters, the first of whom died even before she was born. She related all of the family history, Breuer indicates, in a manner that showed her educated concern and a clear intelligence. She spoke of her extreme concern for her father, who seemed gravely ill; she spoke of how she had gotten worse herself through taking care of him; she made passing, almost casual reference to her brother; of her mother she spoke not at all.

---

*It is the emotionally cohesive person who experiences instinctual drives as personal; otherwise they are experienced as external persecutory impingements.

Today, of course, since we have been so formed by Freud's theories, it is difficult to imagine Anna, as the daughter of an educated, wealthy Jewish family, living in a cosmopolitan center, expressing such oedipal metaphors in such an obvious way. Such issues would be addressed, of course, but within the broader context now available to us.

For the first few sessions, at least, our "literary" Anna would sit opposite me; I would not ask her to use the couch, initially, since I would want to retain eye contact with her. I would want Anna to see me until I was sure that she could use not seeing me as a way of understanding herself and *not* as a way of collapsing into herself. There is a difference, as Winnicott (1958) makes particularly clear, between a patient experiencing regression in the sessions, which is a goal, and withdrawal, which is an unproductive process.

In addition to the description of symptoms above, particularly Anna's inner darkness, we can take Breuer's remarks (1895) as a further summary of the presenting symptoms. He says:

> In one of these states she recognized her surroundings; she was melanchony and anxious, but relatively normal. In the other state she hallucinated and was "naughty"—that is to say, she was abusive, used to throw cushions at people, so far as the contractures at various times allowed, tore buttons off her bed clothes and linen with those fingers which she could move, and so on. At this stage of her illness if something had been moved in the room or someone had entered or left it (during her other state of consciousness) she would complain of having lost some time and would remark upon the gap in her train of conscious thoughts. Since those about her tried to deny this and to soothe her when she complained that she was going mad, she would, after throwing the pillows about, accuse people of doing things to her and leaving her in a muddle, etc. [p. 24].

In speaking with Anna, I would attempt to convey, more by tone than by verbal content, that I was not interested in finding out something about her. I would question her as to her experiences of herself during her daytime and nighttime daily activities. I would not respond to her as an oddity to be cured, but in fact would take her statements at face value and try to see if they had any additional meanings which could help her understand herself in a wider framework than that which had been, so far, available. I would go on to tell Anna that I understood why she spoke of herself as going mad, since her external behavior was evidencing a splitting of which she was aware. The only thing that would be questioned would be the tense of her statements, i.e. that she was going mad. I would mention that she was, with this fear, remembering having gone mad; that is, remembering a break in her sense of continuity-of-being, which occurred in her earliest childhood. Such a break in the sense of who one is, is what we frequently refer to as "going mad." Given Anna's subsequent development, her education, her mastery of languages I would postulate that the (maddening) early event(s) had happened and that she recovered, but the recovery did not completely heal the initial break(s). Her reactions to her father's severe illness and her hallucinations all pointed to a disruption in the knitting together of her inner world and her interaction with the external world.

I would watch her physical reactions to our sessions very carefully, judging whether our interactions had any calming effect on the flamboyance of her symptoms. Was she able to focus her eyes in a more centered manner, for example? Were my remarks making some sense out of an inner experience of chaos, by enabling her to have the conviction that she was understood. Or, on the other hand, were my remarks possibly being experienced as intrusive, thus fostering more anxiety, with a consequent failure of the patient to be self-observing? If she were not able to use what I said, I would say to her that there was a great deal happening to her, that we could try to understand together what may have caused her present condition, and that anything I said was tentative. I would convey all of this in a simple, direct manner of speech.

If, on the other hand, there was more of a capacity to look at herself, which I suspect would be the case with Anna O., I would then go on to a second major motif, namely, that her conduct betrayed, and her sense of self indicated, that she was a ''bad'' self and a ''good'' self (Anna's words). After asking her (over many sessions), for her associative musings on what she meant by these words, I would respond by speaking about her split experience of herself. I would be aware that we would be dealing with an issue which Winnicott speaks of as a loss of personal ''continuity of being,'' occurring anywhere from 18 months to 48 months of age. I would convey to Anna that such splitting arises from conflicts having to do with love and hate; with using and being used. Winnicott (1971) has postulated that a child goes from ''relating'' to an object out of need to ''using'' an object, which is the emotional acknowledgment of separation. ''Using'' an object entails mastery of aggression in terms of negotiating effectively with the outside world. Balint (1979) speaks of the same developmental process when he speaks of the child's ''work of conquest'' vis-à-vis the important persons in his emotional world.* The progressive achievement of personalization, which such a ''work of conquest'' implies, precludes the excessive splitting which Anna manifested.

After a relatively short period of time, having had her speak about what was going on at home and after judging, as noted above, the effect of my words on her, I would ask Anna to use the couch. I would see her a minimum of three times a week and, depending on her capacity to use these sessions, would eventually increase these to four sessions a week. I would not answer the phone during her sessions. I would answer her in most of her initial questions unless I sensed an oedipally inquisitive or narcissistically demanding question, in which case I would simply ask what she thought might be behind such questions. Other questions, as general as this seems, would be responded to, that is, if the

---

*Balint goes on to state that in his judgment Anna O. was a case evidencing a malignant regression (in contradistinction to a regression in the service of a new beginning—one of recognition). I suspect that his diagnosis, in this case, reflects his respect for Breuer. There are too many variables in the case to make such a negative judgment.

question applied to her. If they applied to me, I might give some personal information but not intimate information. If my initial diagnosis was correct, I would be addressing a sense of herself by speaking to her, since the darkness inside her head would not be served well by creating a darkness between patient and analyst, i.e., my silence. This area of therapeutic interchange is most open to misunderstanding and probably defies description. Being unable to reproduce a tape of the sessions, I will presume the reader senses that I would not be conducting the sessions as if they were educational classes. Rather, this therapeutic process would be attempting to aid the growth of what André Green (1975), the contemporary French psychoanalyst, calls "the analytic object." Such an object relations perspective involves more of a mutuality than is usually recognized in classical analysis. In attempting to describe what he means by an analytic object, Green writes that

> . . . in the end the real analytic object is neither on the patient's side nor on the analyst's but in the meeting of these two communications in the potential space which lies between them, limited by the setting which is broken at each separation and reconstituted at each new meeting . . . the analyst does not only unveil a hidden meaning. He constructs a meaning which has never been created before the analytic relationship began [p. 12A].

This meaning which arises out of this particular object relations situation, that is, from the interface of this particular patient with this particular analyst, is an essential normative factor in aiding the patient's personal integration and personalization. I would speak, therefore, more than one might expect in a classical analysis, since I would be speaking to the early mothering environment, alluded to above and still present within Anna, which, in its presumptive absence (or intrusive presence), was the context for this child's mind slipping into darkness and for the splitting in her experience of personal integration evidenced by a failure to speak.* Whether historically (when Anna was a young child) the mother's presence was one still beclouded by mourning for her lost child or her mother's presence was that of an intrusive disciplinarian, the effect could be the same. Namely, these would be cumulative interruptions in her personal sense of continuity of being.

Anywhere from six to eight months into the treatment I could let the couch, the regularity of appointments, the office, and my presence do more of the holding in terms of the good mothering environment, thereby allowing my own comments increasingly to recede into the background. But of silence and of listening, of clarifying and of repeating, it is hard to write, particularly without the living patient. Psychoanalysis is a humanistic science; we interact with people and not diagnostic categories. I emphasize this in order to put in context the

---

*Breuer (1895) notes, for example, that Anna "lost the power of speech (a) as a result of fear, after her first hallucination at night, (b) after having suppressed a remark another time (by active inhibition), (c) after having been unjustly blamed for something and (d) on every analogous occasion (when she felt mortified)" (p. 40).

apparent exclusive verbalizations that the literary format of this presentation might lead one to believe would occur.

In addition to the issues of integration and personalization, we can hypothesize obvious disciplinary difficulties, as mentioned above, in Anna's early environment. Of course a child is not a tabula rasa upon which the environment simply writes a message for better or ill, since a child's innate biological and psychic mechanisms actively respond to what they are given. In the course of her development, Anna probably did have great difficulty holding together good-mother-loved, bad-mother-feared—anywhere from 18 months on. It is only, as mentioned above, when a child can go from relating to an object to using an object that the successful coming together of a person happens, and we can presume that Anna's later symptomatology betrays that this was not successfully accomplished. That is, Anna never experienced as a very young person that mother-world could survive her hatred and come back, after a while, not only surviving but smiling. In this regard, D. W. Winnicott (1971) notes:

> In the sequence one can say that first there is object-relating, then in the end there is object-use; in between, however, is the most difficult thing, perhaps, in human development; or the most irksome of all the early failures that come for mending. This thing that there is in between relating and use is the subject's placing of the object outside the area of the subject's omnipotent control; that is, the subject's perception of the object as an external phenomenon, not as a projective entity, in fact recognition of it as an entity in its own right. . . [p. 89].

Summarizing, Winnicott notes one of the positive developmental functions of aggression in the service of personal integration when he says:

> Study of this problem involves a statement of the positive value of destructiveness. The destructiveness, plus the object's survival of the destruction, places the object outside the area of objects set up by the subject's projective mental mechanisms. In this way a world of shared reality is created which the subject can use and which can feed back other-than-me substance into the subject [p. 94].

Such a resolution of love and hate, we might note, is not only a developmental process but an experience healing any previous interruptions in the sense of one's continuity of being. The analysis, as we have indicated, would be structured so as to foster such a resolution's coming about by means of a regression, which would unravel the primitive thoughts and feelings that were the force behind Anna's splitting of her experience of herself into good and bad, sane and mad, past and present.

Prior to Anna O.'s resolution of these issues, she would manifest what is referred to as part-object identifications. This is confirmed and exemplified by another one of Anna's symptoms, namely her hallucination that her hair and fingers were black snakes. This hallucination clearly suggests to me Medea, the murderous mother, and therefore I would use it as an associative backdrop for listening to Anna. (A possible fantasy of Anna's: "Who killed my oldest sister?'') The murderous mother is the unused mother, the unseparated from mother, and therefore, the frightening mother-self; the part-object mother, not whole and integrated. This merged with aggressor mother—the person who took care of her and her older dead sisters. All of these aspects of the murderous mother fantasy, not merely its possible occurrence, would be explored.

Having explained to Anna that there were leftover fears from childhood about the death of her sister(s), that the unintegrated good self and bad self were understandable phenomena having to do with a progressive integration of her self in dialogue with the mother-environment, and that a break in one's sense of continuity of being would give rise in adulthood to a fear of madness to come and to a subjective sense of a great inner darkenss—having said all that in a context of respect for this troubled person, I would expect some noticeable alleviation of symptoms and, more importantly, some growth in her experience of personal aliveness. Only when, however, the isolation of her inner darkness could be overcome—and here we are talking about a considerable amount of therapeutic time—could Anna begin to leave the hysteria of her symptoms, those manic distractions from the developmentally aborted task of finding out and creating who she was as a person.

Needless to say, out of all this work there should be some marked improvement in Anna's condition.* If the treatment went well, the patient would gradually allow a more basic, more primitive level of dependency to come to the fore in reference to the analyst. Thus one could conjecture that the subsequent death of her father, while being experienced as a serious event, would not have to precipitate a destructive psychic withdrawal. Given the regressive context of the treatment, I believe Anna would talk about her pain as well as cry for her lost lover-father. The lover aspect would clear up eventually, I believe, but *not* solely by an interpretation of an oedipal involvement. The validity of a preoedipal interpretation could be tested by seeing whether it cleared up this apparent oedipal issue. That is, I would say to Anna that she most likely used her relationship with her father for unconscious defensive purposes via overidealization and overidentification—to ward off her part-object ''bad'' mother. (This defensive process might explain why she had done so well in school and why she may have been particularly frustrated with her life at home and jealous of her brother.) Although there was probably a sexualization of this defensive process, Anna's pathology had more to do with her relationship with her mother than with an oedipal attachment to her father. The role of father would then be understood not so much as an oedipal figure but rather the needed father person of childhood who protects against the bad witch Medea (the split-off part-object mother). If this line of thought was correct, and Anna was able to hear it, she would be able to allow more primitive fantasies to emerge in analysis. Consequent upon this line of thought, addressing another of Anna's symptoms, I would say to her that what was important to remember was not

---

*Sometime during the first year I would have requested a physical examination as a general practice, and to rule out any organicity in this case.

only the incident of a dog drinking from her glass, but the fact that this may well have signified for her a breaking into a civilized mode of life of what Anna would consider primitive unintegrated oral aggressivity—the oral aggressivity of the bad-mother-witch.

As mentioned above, if this line of thought and interpretation were correct, Anna would not get markedly worse at the death of her father. Furthermore, having talked to the angry self of childhood who did not know what to do with her aggression, Anna would not have to be hospitalized, since some of her severe splitting would have been alleviated. If a feeling of safety in the analysis was internalized, she would not have to conduct her own analysis—for example, by stating the date when she would be cured. Rather, she could let the analyst and analysis serve as a needed protective shell enabling the "darkness" inside her to be confronted and, not manically, via her symptoms, fled from. Thus Anna's symptoms would be understood not primarily as mnemic symbols of particular traumatic experiences, as Freud (1910) postulates, but as attempts to cope (in a manic way) with the deadness of the dark space within her. By the analytic process, Anna would be attempting to reach "a new beginning" to use Batlint's (1967) term. This would occur if she was able to remain in treatment and tolerate the encounter, via transferences, with the bad-mother self without deteriorating repetitively into reenacting split-off love/hate object relations.*
As the darkness within her began to resolve itself, the frantic quality of her symptoms, with their strong narcissistic hysterical flavor, could be dealt with more directly by saying to Anna that such frantic maneuvers "her splitting" were a distraction from the "madness" within her. Furthermore, her symptoms perpetuated an experience of herself which incapacitated her in handling aggression. In addition, I would mention that it was possible to find a way of negotiating life without finding mortification everywhere.

The fundamental issue in my analysis with Anna O. would be how to facilitate her being a real (emotionally alive, centered) person. The treatment today would be guided by the metaphor of the internal journey whereby Anna could find the safe quiet place from which she could meet the world, with all its frustrations and limitations, without recourse to primitive defenses. Winnicott (1965) warns us of certain dangers in this type of work and of the developmental issues involved for the patient when he says:

> More dangerous, however, is the state of affairs in an analysis in which the analyst is permitted by the patient to reach to the deepest layers of the analysand's personality because of his position as subjective object, or because of the dependence of the patient in the transference psychosis; here there is danger if the analyst interprets instead of waiting for the patient to creatively discover. It is only here, at the place when the analyst has not changed over from a subjective object to one that is objectively perceived, that psychoanalysis is dangerous, and the danger is one that can be

---

*Such a deterioration would indicate what Balint calls a malignant regression; while a capacity to tolerate what had been said to her in the service of experiencing and overcoming the darkness would indicate a regression in the service of recognition.

avoided if we know how to behave ourselves. If we wait we become objectively perceived in the patient's own time, but if we fail to behave in a way that is facilitating the patient's analytic process . . . we suddenly become not-me for the patient, and then we know too much, and we are dangerous because we are too nearly in communication with the central still and silent spot of the patient's ego organization [p. 189].

The other side of this quiet spot, as I have mentioned above, is madness—the madness that comes from repetitive impingements on one's sense of continuity of being and being-taken-care-of, prerequisites to integration and personalization. In aiming at the darkness in Anna's head and the self behind the split selves she showed to the world, we would be attempting to get to the deepest elements of her personality. Winnicott (1958) notes, for example:

> The analysis of the hysteric (popular term) is the analysis of the madness that is feared but which is not reached without the provision of a new example of infant care, better infant care in the analysis than was provided at the time of the patient's infancy. But please note, the analysis does and must get to the madness, although the diagnosis remains neurosis, not psychosis [p. 100].

To elaborate the case any further without the actual Anna O. is to speculative to be pursued. I have discussed some of the major themes which would preoccupy my thinking in working with an Anna O. Of course, what would actually occur in the spontaneity of the meeting of the patient and her unconscious with the analyst and his unconscious is impossible to predict. The actual treatment flows from such a living relationship. In the tone of voice or body movement, the patient can be telling the analyst that no interpretations, no matter how correct, can be heard; or, on the other hand, a signal can be given that something must be said. Sometimes the minor bodily movements of the analyst, as Musad Khan (1974) has written, will affect the patient's capacity to use a particular session.

I have attempted to show where the analysis might go, following some of the themes of the English object relations school. To say that we might, in following this approach, be seeing farther than Breuer and Freud is not a statement of their limitations but rather of their achievements. That Breuer was perhaps overly frightened by an eroticized transference is not evidence of an intellectual or characterological timidity; that Freud was not so frightened, in his work with similar cases, can be understood as his having had the time and perspective to reflect on Breuer's experience. His vantage point was different, and so he handled things in a different way. The primary danger for analysts today would not be a possible eroticized transference/countertransference reaction, but rather the analyst's overactivity via interpretations, hindering the patient from finding the quiet center within the self, with all the madness that might be involved in such a journey. For the analyst to allow the patient to find his or her madness is for the analyst to allow such madness to be refound in himself. D.

W. Winnicott has cautioned analysts repeatedly about ignoring that quiet, centered, solitary place out of which one arises as an emotionally alive person, in their haste to do and figure out all kinds of "therapeutic" things. In Anna O.'s case, only when one can get beyond any symptom appraisal of the situation do the dynamics become clear. That Anna accomplished as much as she did with her life is testimony that she got more from Breuer than he indicates.* That she had to write, as Ellenberger (1970) indicates, so many of her own obituaries at the end of her life, so obsessively, means there was still a part of her that was lost and that Anna was looking for—right up until her death. Of course the question remains, have we found Anna O.?

References

BALINT, MICHAEL. *The Basic Fault*. New York: Brunner/Mazel, 1979.

BREUER J., and FREUD, S. (1893–1895). *Studies on Hysteria*. Standard Edition, vol. II. London: Hogarth Press, 1955.

ELLENBERGER, HENRI F. *The Discovery of The Unconscious*. New York: Basic Books, 1970.

FAIRBAIRN, RONALD D. *An Object-Relations Theory of the Personality*. New York: Basic Books, 1954.

FREUD, S. (1901–1905). *A Case of Hysteria*. Standard Edition, vol. VII. London: Hogarth, 1953.

FREUD, S. (1910). *Five Lectures on Psycho-Analysis*. Standard Edition, vol. XI. London: Hogarth Press, 1957.

FREUD S. (1915). *The Unconscious*. Standard Edition, vol. XIV, London: Hogarth Press, 1957.

GREEN ANDRÉ, The analyst, symbolization and absence in the analytic setting. *Int J. Psycho-Anal.*, vol. 56, part I, 1975.

GUNTRIP, HARRY. *Psychoanalytic Theory, Therapy and the Self*. New York: International Universities Press, 1973.

JONES, ERNEST. *The Life and Works of Sigmund Freud*, vols. I, II, and III. New York: Basic Books, 1953, 1955, and 1957.

KHAN, MASUD M. *The Privacy of the Self*. New York: International Universities Press, 1974.

POLLOCK, GEORGE H. The possible significance of childhood object loss in the Joseph Breuer–Bertha Pappenheim (Anna O)–Sigmund Freud relationship. *J. Amer. Psychoanal. Ass.*, vol. 16, no. 4, 1968.

POLLOCK, GEORGE H. Bertha Pappenheim's pathological mourning. *J. Amer. Psychoanal. Ass.*, volume 20, no. 3, 1972.

POLLOCK, GEORGE H. Bertha Pappenheim: Addenda to her case history. *J. Amer. Psychoanal. Ass.*, vol. 21, no. 2, 1973.

---

*Not withstanding all the serious limitations of Breuer's treatment, it is obvious that he was a good object for Anna O.; he spent many hours with her, gave her a good deal of personal attention, and genuinely wished her well. He was a concerned authority figure in her life—while her father was dying.

RICOEUR, PAUL. *The Conflict of Interpretations*. Evanston, Ill.: Northwestern University Press, 1974.

RICOEUR, PAUL. The question of proof in Freud's psychoanalytic writings. *J. Amer. Psychoanal. Ass.,* vol. 25, no. 4, 1977.

WINNICOTT, DONALD W. *Collected Papers*. London: Tavistock Publications, 1958.

WINNICOTT, DONALD W. *The Maturational Processes and the Facilitating Environment*. New York: International Universities Press, 1965.

WINNICOTT, DONALD W. *Playing and Reality*. New York: Basic Books, 1971.

Conclusion

Melvin Muroff

> Although the goal of scientific explanation is sometimes defined as the discovery of the necessary and sufficient conditions for the occurance of phenomena, we have had repeated occasions for noting that this ideal is rarely achieved even in the most highly developed branches of natural sciences [Nagel, 1961].

Who could have predicted one hundred years ago that Breuer's interest in asking Anna O., under hypnosis, how she felt rather than telling her to feel better would evolve into a major therapeutic system for helping emotionally conflicted people? Or that, furthermore, in the masterful hands of Freud, it would become a complex system for understanding human behavior? Freud's insights into the functioning of the mind moved Breuer's "simple" hypnotic technique into a vital, living body of knowledge called psychoanalysis. Today it is recognized as a phenomenon influencing all mankind. On all levels of life it is now usual for people to discuss day-to-day mundane events using some form of psychoanalytic terminology. Much of our understanding of how and why governments and leaders behave as they do rests frequently on variations of psychoanalytic thinking and assumptions. The infant psychoanalysis is no longer just a treatment modality for emotional disorders but now is, as an adult, a major force in understanding, explaining, and coping with the common everyday behaviors occurring within and among people.

There are many apparent similarities found through out the preceding pages' discussions of "today's treatment of Anna O.," and the differences in the psychotherapeutic positions range from the subtle to the dramatic. Therefore, before we conclude, remember that all which was written in the preceding pages is a tribute to the original work done with Anna O., the first reported case using a dynamic psychological treatment to help an individual with an emotional disturbance. Also, and most significantly, these chapters are a dedication to the treatment method itself, psychoanalysis. At this time we celebrate its life of one hundred years. Psychoanalysis is no longer an embryo or, for that matter, an immature infant. As with other growing, developing, and living organisms, it is frequently difficult to recognize the infant in its present-day adult form.

The comparison of Anna O.'s treatment in 1880 with present-day therapeutic interventions has made for fascinating reading. How we may understand and resolve her problems today reflects the tremendous and complicated growth of psychoanalysis. After one hundred years there exists more than just one dimension for the treatment of Anna O. As we have read, the more rigid, classical analytic approach is still the treatment of choice for many therapists. This therapeutic position, now considered to be conservative especially in face of the current emphasis on brief therapy, states that it is basic to the system to remain within the given vigorously prescribed analytic structure. To conduct therapy, one needs to recognize and analyze the existence of the unconscious phenomena of transference and countertransference within the treatment setting. Many of those following this path become adamant and often reactionary when changes are suggested. On the other side are those who claim that analyzing these two variables is not in itself "sufficient." They urge psychoanalysis to change from its outdated position, one which is no longer too relevant, to concepts about treatment more representative of the current experimental research. They are concerned that adherence to old structures is too restrictive, and they wish for further growth. There is concern that the adult psychoanalysis will become too feeble, especially if it continues to depend only on its rigid grasping onto the past ideas.

These therapists calling for a change present the "new" insights into human behavior and hope that psychoanalysis will use them to go beyond explaining behavior on the basis of only intrapsychic, unconscious functioning. They press for analysts to be more flexible, to continue their growth by including the new experimental data especially on interpsychic, social interaction dynamics. There are a few others, and they are a minority of extremists, who insist that psychoanalysis is very old and that its time is over. They are the purists and usually represent the biological experimental position for understanding human behavior. Often they state this position very discreetly by indicating that psychoanalysis has become too costly, there are fewer analytic trainees, it is not cost-effective as compared with other forms of current treatments, its results are not verifiable, and so on. Garfield (1981) has indicated that psychoanalysis has been "over sold" and that the importance of psychoanalysis is decreasing in favor of briefer, more verifiable forms of psychotherapy. Strupp (1976) criticizes psychoanalysis for having a "closed shop mentality," and he, like Cooper and Michels (1978) indicates it will die if it does not keep up with the current psychotherapeutic data. There are even a few in this group who whisper that the infant psychoanalysis should have been aborted at the onset. Sometimes angrily, they indicate that its development has set back, sidetracked, psychiatry during the past one hundred years. For them, psychoanalysis is much too speculative, not founded on substantiated evidence. They emphasize "systematic scientific research" as the only way for collecting data on human behavior. It is their contention that we are now just beginning to know and understand that all "mental" disturbances have a biological, physiological basis, and the most extreme among them hold that it is not in any way psychologically determined. In this approach the treatment of Anna O.

would consist mainly in discovering how her brain functioned electrochemically, how chemical inhibitors affected her behavior, and even how nutrition determined what she was. Today this particular point of view rests on the technology of computers, drugs, EEG printouts about brain waves, ECT impulses to the brain, and other similar ''medical'' methods for helping the mentally ill.

After one hundred years, given such an extreme diversity of opinions as to how to help Anna O., where are we in our understanding of the dynamics in the diagnosis and treatment of her condition? As we have seen, the answer to this question depends on who answers it. There are those who claim we have moved quite a distance and others who believe we've moved hardly at all. Some therapists see psychoanalysis as a highly respectable science, while others, reluctantly perhaps, more or less accept it but insist that it is not scientific. All agree that there still remain many unanswered questions in our understanding of emotional disturbances.

To distinguish any one treatment modality from another as best for Anna O. is like finding the most suitable path for a person lost in a forest. Anna O. is lost in the forest of her mind, and the task of the analyst and/or therapist is to help her find an appropriate path out. How this is done depends on how well the analyst or therapist knows the intricacies of the forest and where he believes she should be when she ultimately does find her way out.

Anna O., lost and alone in her forest, considers many possible ways out. She uses all her acquired skills and knowledge of woodsmanship. She quickly and painfully discovers that she does not possess adequate knowledge or have the skill to find her way out. Alone, she tries and tries but is not successful, and she gets more confused. In desperation she resorts to ways of protecting herself from the real and imagined terrors of the forest. In this effort she uses whatever she has available, appropriate or not, to defend herself. Just when all looks hopeless, an experienced guide appears. At first she tests whether she can depend on him and trust that he knows a way out. This accomplished, she follows the path selected by him and hopes it will take her out of her forest.

This is how it was in 1880. Breuer was the guide who appeared to help Anna O. Now, however, one hundred years later, she has many available guides, and each is suggesting his own particular path as the necessary, efficient way to go. One guide says, ''Let us use the sun,'' another says, ''We'll use the moss on the side of the trees''; some suggest other familiar and even untried methods as means of getting out. Interestingly, it is possible that all of the suggested paths may help Anna O. out of her forest. Yet each guide requests that she prefer his path. An examination of all the possible ways of going tells her that they do go in different directions and thereby also lead to very different exit points. A few of the paths crisscross with one another; some apparently lead back to where she started. There are a few that tempt her to make further excursions into the forest, going directly away from any exit point. Also, there are some paths that are interesting and exciting but do not seem to take her to any exit. Then there are paths that look very promising, but the guides appear inexperienced and not too sure of where they will take her. She is swamped with choices. All the guides are convincing and very persuasive that using their path out is the true one and best for her. It is difficult for her to decide. What is certain, however, and different from one hundred years ago, is that there does exist more than one way out. Anna O. can accept the guide who proposes medication as the true path, or the one who offers a short-term here-and-now therapy path, or the one who involves her in working in a group and/or with her family, or the one who dictates a change in food habits, e.g., less use of sugar and watching zinc and magnesium levels. There is the holistic path that combines several of the others. Anna O. can use the path that involves mainly the interaction between herself and the guide, or she can still select the more traditional analytic-couch route, or even the one she used one hundred years ago, hypnosis. These are a few of the paths available to her at this time.

Since there are so many paths, all going in somewhat different directions, it is clearly evident that they take Anna O. to different exit points. Now the problem becomes more obvious. Each guide, with his unique therapeutic persuasion, has a preferred exit point, a particular way for leaving the forest, and he is strongly urging Anna O. to go in his direction if she wishes to be "cured" of her illness. Therefore, the path she takes must depend on where she wishes to be when she leaves the forest—on what she wishes to cure. In order to select an appropriate path, she needs to know which exit point she wishes to reach. The making of this decision in itself raises perplexing but interesting questions. If she is confused, how can she decide which exit point is best for her? Who, then, should make the decision for her? These and similar vital, and perhaps ethical, questions remain to be answered. "Part of the patient's difficulties are seen to be caused by his lack of awareness of significant portions of his behavior and of the events that influence him. His disorder *prevents* him from making sound judgment about what is wrong and what the objectives of therapy should be" (Ford and Urban, 1963, p. 663).

The psychoanalytic path used most frequently is called the "cathartic cure" (Ellenberger, 1972; MacMillan, 1977), and it has been well traversed. It is criticized for being too long, too costly, and maybe even leading Anna O. in the wrong direction, one which may not cure or even alleviate her mental illness (Berelson and Steiner, 1964). Essentially its route leads to a destination having the name of "awareness of unconscious functioning." There are considerable doubts in the minds of many clinicians as to whether this place is exactly where Anna O. should be. It is their contention that helping her only to become more conscious of her unconscious conflicts may not actually cure her (Horwitz, 1976). They say this path may help her understand herself but in itself does not take her out from her forest, help her to function appropriately in society; other traditional paths are necessary. Ford and Urban (1963) recognize this important issue in their discussion of the goals of psychotherapy and speak of "three general opinions . . . Freud, the Ego-Analysts, Dollard and Miller, Wolpe, and Adler all view the therapist as an expert whose task is to determine what is wrong and what is required to produce a change. . . . A second opinion (Rank, Rogers, Horney, Existentialists) argues that the patient must select goals of treatment . . . Sullivan represents the third opinion . . . the therapist and the patient should agree explicity on some goals towards which they both can work; agreement about what they will try to accomplish is a precondition to effective therapy'' (p. 663).

For many the old analytic road map is seen as too speculative and not adequately developed experimentally or scientifically. There is questionable proof that is has rescued anyone lost in a forest. McGee and Saidel (1979) say that ''two other most important trends affecting the evolution of behavior therapy were: the development of the social learning theory of psychopathology as a viable alternative to the disease or medical model; and a growing dissatisfaction with psychoanalysis and psychodynamic psychotherapies because of their alleged inefficacy'' (p. 73). A comparable, more extreme position is taken by Berelson and Steiner (1964): ''There is no conclusive evidence that psychotherapy is more effective than general medical counselling or advice in treating neurosis or psychosis'' (p. 287). Eysenck (1952) is more specific in his comments: '' . . . these data . . . fail to prove that psychotherapy, Freudian or otherwise, facilitates the recovery of neurotic patients.''

The development of psychoanalytic thinking has been devoid of any exact scientific methodology and therefore impossible to validate experimentally. Again, as Ford and Urban mention, '' . . . no measurement, however, is involved in Freud's procedures of verification, no careful controls are established so that others can reproduce the conditions under which Freud made his observations. In fact . . . the accuracy of his data records must be suspect'' (1963, p. 175). Thus for many it is not possible to factually determine if this particular path can help people like Anna O. find their way out of their forest. The more scientific investigator, with his insistence on controlled experimentation, using such techniques as double-blind studies among others, usually views the Anna O. data as inadequate and insufficient to substantiate any meaningful conclusions. As indicated above, there are some who suggest that any form of psychotherapy has questionable results. DeCharms, Jerome, and Wertheimer (1954) follow Eysenck: ''We feel that the only conclusion which can be made at this point is that we have as yet no data on the basis of which to evaluate the therapeutic effects of psychotherapy'' (p. 233). Perhaps this position is too extreme and harsh. It is necessary to understand that the scientific method in itself may not be as exact as many would like to believe; it too is based on ''logical'' assumptions. Nagel (1961) describes four types of explanation for scientific data. Let us briefly examine them and then decide if the analytic methodological path is or is not scientific.

First, the deductive model: '' . . . in explanations of this type the premises state a sufficient (and sometimes, though not invariably, a necessary) condition for the truth of the explanation'' (p. 21). This model requires the acceptance of premises, which then leads to forming logical conclusions concerning collected data. As with all scientific systems, psychoanalysis depends on basic assumptions. Rapaport (1960) mentions four early Freudian assumptions: psychological determinism, unconscious psychological process, unconscious psychological forces and conflicts, and psychological energies and their origin in drives. As with all science, if one accepts the validity of the given underlying assumptions, then one must accept the logical conclusions derived from them. The issue is not about the conclusions, but about the acceptance of the assumptions. There is no doubt that in the case of Anna O. Freud's insights were based on and developed from those assumptions mentioned by Rapaport. For many, these still underlie their analytic explanation of Anna O.'s unusual behavior.

Second, the probabilistic explanation, "encountered when the explanatory premises contain a statistical assumption about some class of elements, while the explicandum is a singular statement about a given individual member of that class" (Nagel, 1961, p. 22). Psychoanalysis is notoriously without statistical mathematics. It is rare to find studies with a sample size of an N more than 1. However, as seen in our review of Anna O., many statements are made as to the probability of an event happening. It is true that an N of 1 does not lend itself to any statistical analysis of data, yet an N of 100 or more, in itself, is also not totally reliable, since it too depends on probability and the concept of probable error. At the same time, most investigators feel reassured if the N is large and if the experiment can be repeated. But many agree with Rapaport's opinion of the use of statistics when he states, " . . . it expresses (statistical analysis) and fosters a disregard for theory, and it is thus a major obstacle to theoretical advancement" (1960, p. 144). Although the statistical analysis of data is not usual in psychoanalytic research, its conceptual model is represented and used in many related areas of research. The dynamic psychoanalytic interpretation of behavior has been used frequently to explain experimental, large-N data found in medical and psychological research. Sometimes the study is not particularly related to psychoanalysis itself, e.g., Groffman's (1978) mention of Anna O.'s conversion reaction and the correlation between visual disturbance and personality characteristics.

Third, the functional or teleological explanation: " . . . explanations take the form of indicating one or more functions (or dysfunctions) that a unit performs in maintaining or realizing certain traits of a system to which the unit belongs or stating the instrumental role an action plays in bringing about some goal . . . . they employ such typical locutions as 'in order that,' 'for the sake of' and the like" (Nagel, 1961, p. 23). Teleological explanations answer "why questions by referring to a behavioral action in terms of the goal of the action itself. Why did Anna O. develop her unusual symptoms? To repress undesirable, unacceptable thoughts and wishes. The symptoms have a goal or a purpose. Much of psychoanalytic thinking, as well as most research in other fields, e.g., biology and physics, utilizes some form of teleological thinking to explain data.

Fourth, the genetic explanation: " . . . the task of genetic explanation is to set out the sequence of major events through which some earlier system has been transformed into a later one . . . such explanations will therefore necessarily contain a large number of singular statements about past events in the system under inquiry" (*ibid.*, p. 25). This form of collecting scientific data is most familiar to those involved with psychoanalysis: the analyzing of developmental data to explain and understand current normal or abnormal behavior; e.g., Anna O.'s illness resulted from her unresolved attachment to her father, the conflicted relationship with her brother, a fixation on an earlier stage in her infantile development, and so on. Each, or a combination of any, is an example of the genetic explanation of data. The case study, with its dependency on early childhood developmental data, uses primarily the genetic explanation when it reconstructs the psychological intrapsychic dynamics of the individual. To a large degree, this genetic method may be considered the cornerstone in the development of psychoanalytic theory.

This brief, oversimplified view of scientific methodology indicates that the system psychoanalysis is scientific. The "scientific" analysts contend that they do follow basic scientific methodological principles. They have their basic assumptions; e.g., Anna O.'s illness resulted from unconscious forces reflective of repressed sexual wishes and/or hostile aggressive impulses; or she did not improve with Breuer because he was not aware of countertransference reactions. They use the concept of probability, although not statistically; e.g., if Anna O. talks, it is probable that she will make conscious repressed unconscious conflicts within her which can be resolved and lead to her cure. If an individual experiences an unresolved trauma at age 3, it is probable that the socialization process will be an area of difficulty in her later years of life. The teleological and the genetic explanations are more easily accepted as part of the psychoanalytic scientific methodology. Teleologically, Anna O.'s illness had a purpose, mainly to protect her from unacceptable ideation and wishes. The genetic explanation is self-evident. Few today disagree with the assumption that the early environmental influences directly affect child development and result in molding the adult.

Still, in a true Talmudic tradition, one may yet say psychoanalysis is not scientific. The scientific purist insists that much of psychoanalysis is speculative; it is founded on ideas that defy quantification, it is devoid of a systematic theoretical formulation for its data, and its data cannot be verified through repetition of the "experiment." Both sides are correct. The conflict is easily resolved if it is understood that the two sides are taking different paths to get Anna O. out of her forest. Further, they start out with very different intentions as to where they hope to take Anna O. when they do find their way out of the forest. They start with different thoughts about what is to be treated. The pure scientific group, accepting only experimentally validated paths, searches for the exit point which involves understanding the internal, biological-physiological-chemical functioning of the individual organism. It uses the experimental paths to get there. The psychoanalytic scientists search for a totally different exit point and therefore use a different set of assumptions. These would involve paths that have data concerning the psychological growth and development of the organism. They also accept the biological paths but do not consider them the only explanations of behavior. The dynamic interplays of psychological forces seen as paths just as real as the more apparent biological ones but leading to a very different exit point.

In examining the various contemporary explanations of Anna O.'s illness and treatment, many different paths have been suggested. All of them converge into three major routes—the biochemical, the social, and the psychological. Although at times each may crisscross with the others, they have different exit points. Each has indicated that the treatment of Anna O. today depends upon a definite point of view based on different sets of assumptions as to the underlying cause and the treatment of her illness.

For the moment let us digress into an important, basic reality issue concerning Anna O. A brief note needs to be made about the question of her diagnosis. By now, most probably realize that this aspect of understanding Anna O.'s illness probably depends, to a large degree, on the therapist's ideas or point of view as to which exit point is desirable for the purpose of helping. Fink (1982) reports that it may not be possible for today's analysts to give Anna O. an approved diagnosis, or at least not possible to use the DSM III categories; analytic thinking is not represented in that system (p. 358). If the analyst is more neurologically-pharmacologically oriented, then the diagnosis could involve a DSM III label most likely related to some form of organic mental disorder and/or, perhaps, a schizophrenic disorder. For those more invested with the internal psychological process of Anna O., there could be a range of DSM III labels but each suggesting some form of developmental, anxiety, and/or "hysterical neurosis, conversion type, 300.11" (DSM Classification, 1980) emotional disorder. For culturally oriented therapists, there might be still some difficulty in finding the proper diagnosis in the DSM III and therefore, as a side issue, difficulty in collecting third-party insurance claims for treating Anna O. using their particular therapeutic technique. The diagnosis might be something like family disorganization, or some form of disturbance in the family "ego." However, most therapists working with families tend not to give a "group" diagnosis and instead "diagnose" the particular individuals within the family constellation. As most know, the problem of how to diagnose Anna O.'s emotional state is an open question, not only because of the fact that we do not have sufficient information from the past but also because the diagnosis depends largely on the point of view of the therapist working with Anna O.

Returning to the mainstream, we can see, as expected, that the biological position, although accepting the existence of the social and psychological factors, quickly eliminates their centrality. Psychological events are described as being secondary to biological functions. Fink writes (1974), "The psychological consequences of these biochemical events are decreased discrimination of sensory stimuli, altered perception, decreased short term memory and recall, mood elevation, and physiologic changes of increased appetite, weight, saliva- tion, sweating and heart rate'' (p. 14). Here the biochemical events are the cen- tral factors. If this path is taken to understand Anna O.'s difficulties, then it follows that her explicit psychological symptoms resulted from an internal biochemical brain syndrome. A further example of how paths may crisscross as they seek different exit points is also seen in Fink: ''Patients who habitually use denial and displacement as (psychoanalytic) defense mechanisms . . . will be viewed as hypomanic and 'improved.' The type of adaptation may be predicted from pretreatment psychological test performance and makes prob- able a more complete calculus of the relation of the brain neurohumors and behavior which may yet provide biochemical constructs (paths) for these 'psychologic' events'' (ibid.). Jarvik (1969) treats memory strictly as a chemical phenomenon: ''The only drug which seemed to impair matching behavior and which accelerated forgetting was scopolamine. This reenforces the notion that cholinergic mechanisms (paths) play an important role in learn- ing and memory'' (p. 145). There is no disagreement with these data nor any doubt that this biological path has merit; but it does not explain, nor does it pre- tend to, the psychological and/or social aspects in Anna O.'s condition. This position views Anna O. from the assumption that her symptoms are related to a biological brain syndrome and needs to be understood as such. In using this path, it is unnecessary to discuss or to work through such psychological factors as transference and countertransference. This view claims that these are ar- tifacts and that if one knew enough about drugs and brain functioning, today she would be quickly ''cured'' of her symptoms, if not of her illness.

The more psychological dynamic approaches suggested also differ and have two different major exit points: the *intrapsychic* and the *interpersonal.* The in- trapsychic, the examination and study of the internal psychological forces within the particular individual, is the more classical, traditional psychoanaly- tic Freudian explanation of Anna O.'s condition. This path discusses Anna O. in terms of transference and countertransference, narcissism and borderline states, object relations, and identity problems. At this time, the analytic posi- tion has moved on from Breuer's and Freud's emphasis mainly on develop- mental, historical data for explaining her unusual behavior. But in this ap- proach the underlying, essential path is the understanding of the dynamics of transference; the internal state of the individual. The main change in understanding and helping Anna O. would be in the more recent movements toward unraveling the therapist's countertransference reactions toward Anna O. Interestingly, even among this group of writers there is a difference in em- phasis. For some, the more conservative path dominates. Psychological issues are resolved through clinical observation. Theory, as such, is secondary to the understanding of behavior. The major path for helping Anna O. is to further understand her transference reactions encountered by her therapist. This point of view explores aspects of the intrapsychic functioning using data on drives, ego-adaptive functioning, infantile sexuality and levels of development, and other similar intrapsychic data. For those few holding this conservative position, constitutional theories dominate their explanation of behavior. Although they use psychoanalytic intrapsychic concepts, their purpose is to demonstrate the existence of a basic constitutional proclivity underlying all emotional disturbances. In the analytic group this position comes closest to postulating strong biological conditions as probable causal factors in Anna O.'s illness. The more adventurous analytic travelers have added other paths for understanding Anna O. All of them use some form of child developmental theory to explain the dynamics of Anna O.'s condition. Transference reactions, from early childhood experiences, attributed or directed to the therapist, are essential data for analysis.

To this they add on another ingredient, one which Breuer unknowingly experienced, the countertransference condition of the therapist. In their different ways, they all emphasize the need to understand the therapist's reactions to Anna O.'s data—the therapist's need to analyze and work on the countertransference reactions emanating from the treatment setting if Anna O. is to get better. For this group, treatment of Anna O. requires that the therapist not only work through her unreal "realities" but also his/her reactions to Anna O.'s unusual behavior. No longer is the therapist just the objective observer— the mirror of the patient or the nonexistent variable. The therapist is there and so is an essential element in the treatment milieu. If Anna O. is to get better, the therapist must resolve within himself/herself the feelings and thoughts provoked by the patient in the treatment situation. Underlying all this is an old dictum: all psychotherapists should be analyzed themselves so that they do not confuse their own problems with those of their patients. Above all, they should know how to use the countertransference data as an additional way to help Anna O.

The awareness of the significance of the therapist's countertransference reactions has opened many new, interesting, and perhaps entertaining paths leading to further understanding Anna O. This realization that the therapist's own character structure directly affects the patient's progress in therapy is not of recent origin. The position of the analyst was seen as important from the early beginnings of psychoanalysis. However, this role was downplayed; the therapist was to blend into the environment and not intrude into the analytic scene. He/she sat behind the patient and was not seen. Over the years the validity of this position has been questioned, especially since "object relations" phenomena do occur in the therapeutic situation. These data today are seen as critical and need to be examined and worked through with the patient. There are many adherents to this way of thinking, but not all have taken identical paths. They too have branched out in different directions, though most of them still depend on an *intrapsychic* frame of reference to explain interpersonal, social data. For example, in using the dynamics within a family group, many theorists expand the intrapersonal term "ego functioning" to also include a concept called "family ego." It is as though interactions within the family group had the same properties and dynamics found operating within the individual. In explaining behavior, it has been difficult for the analytic position to make the transition from using only the path of internal dynamics of the individual to also incorporating the path of social interaction. The analytic model has had its difficulties in explaining *interpersonal*, social behavior. The assumptions underlying the analytic concept of superego functioning imply the individual's relation with others (a social process) but do not adequately explain the dynamic interplay caused and affected by the fact that the individual is also in a group process.

Perhaps part of the problem is related to the fact that psychoanalysis itself is a product of its times and has been strongly influenced by its cultural soil. From its inception, the Darwinian model of individual differences has strongly influenced the psychoanalytic point of view. This approach dictated that investigators study the individual's unique internal dynamics as though they were separate and distinct from external variables. Therefore the unit of study consists of what is happening within the organism and how this behavior differs from the internal functioning of other individuals. This particular approach in working with Anna O. has two requirements: (1) knowing about her particular syndrome, and (2) knowing how her symptoms are reflective of her own internal process. Taken together this process necessitates looking for the specific details within the unit, Anna O., and then isolating and examining them as though they were distinct and separated, self-contained units themselves. In this approach Anna O. becomes a storage center housing a collection of discrete units. This form of reductionism frequently has difficulty in reassembling the isolated parts to form the original whole: collecting Anna O.'s symptoms may not lead us back to understanding Anna O. as a social interacting person. An exponent of Gestalt psychology would say the whole is more than the sum of its parts. Helping Anna O. demands seeing her as a totality and not merely as a collection of intrapsychic parts. It is necessary to know how she affects and is affected by other people within a social interactional system.

Recently, this form of thinking has caused a shift in emphasis away from the more individualized, internal dynamics to the dynamics of interpersonal relations. Other psychological paths are therefore suggested for understanding Anna O.'s unusual behavior. This had led to the development of other psychological models, most often based on theories of group process. No longer is the unit of study just the internal dynamics of the person; now it is also the behavior of the individual in a group and the behavior of the group itself as it affects the individual. There is an awareness that almost regardless of the individual's character structure, the influence of the group process on the individual and the dynamics within the group itself directly influence and determine the individual's behavior (Cartwright and Zander, 1960). It is stated that this social interactional approach does not concern psychoanalysis, which studies the *internal* dynamics of the mind. Analysis is concerned with understanding the meaning of Anna O.'s paralysis, her imagery of snakes, and what these tell us about the workings of her mind. It usually does not concern itself with Anna O.'s place in the family group, and if it did, it would study this only to further understand its influence on the unique workings of her mind. Of course this is a somewhat narrow, too sharp statement, for certainly most analysts today are tuned into more than just the inner workings of the mind. They are also occupied with understanding the individual in the context of his/her group affiliations. This is dramatically different from Breuer's or Freud's concept for treating the abnormalities of human behavior: working with the symptoms to find specific, and perhaps unconscious, problems.

At the present time there has been a move away from searching the internal functioning of the mind and probing the unconscious dynamics of the individual. This deemphasis on understanding the unconscious has led to a path which stresses the here and now. There is no need to study the workings of the mind, one needs to know and understand only the reality of the symptom. It is no longer important that Anna O. sees snakes or important to understand the unconscious nature of her paralysis. It is now possible to decondition Anna O. and thereby get rid of her disabling symptoms. Or, for that matter, to hypnotize her and tell her not to have these terrible symptoms. Have we returned to 1880, where again we are telling Anna O. to feel better instead of asking her how she feels? On the surface many of the more current approaches to treating Anna O. would have us believe that the ''doctor'' knows what is best for her and that this does not necessarily involve the need for her to understand the intricate meanings of her psychological symptoms. The ''doctor'' only needs to know about the manifest symptoms and how to get rid of them, all to be *done to* Anna O. and on a conscious level. The emphasis is on the doing and certainly not on any understanding of her behavioral dynamics. Again, Anna O. would be hypnotized and then told not to have any particular symptoms—just as one might get a person to break the smoking habit or get rid of fear of flying. An approach used more, and also an old one at that, would place Anna O. in a behavior modification setting and decondition away her obvious symptoms.

It is not appropriate to say which therapeutic technique is the better form of treatment, which path is the best way out of her forest. This depends on what we wish to accomplish. Is our goal to alleviate symptoms and to make the patient feel better, or do we desire to give the patient some form of self-understanding, to ''cure'' her underlying conflicts? The choice of the particular treatment path depends on which exit point we decide to reach in order for Anna O. to leave her forest of confusion. Again it is important to note, however, that the exit points do take us to different places and they are not necessarily equally good ones. If our purpose is to make Anna O. feel better, temporarily or permanently, perhaps the here-and-now exit point is adequate, and it may be quicker and less expensive in time and money. If our purposes are to understand her functioning and thereby help her know more about herself and to help her take command of her life by involving Anna O. in working with her own data, then a more dynamic, time-consuming path must be taken. Possibly this will take longer and be a more expensive way of leaving the forest, but the cost can be determined only by what one wishes to accomplish.

Perhaps, for psychoanalysis, these various here-and-now treatment paths are not its concern. Most present-day analysts are confronted and concerned with the issue of incorporating the psychological data of *interpersonal* dynamics with those of *intrapsychic* functioning. The concepts of group process have opened the door to massive amounts of new data which may be significantly related to unconscious, intrapsychic functioning. There is more in the treatment situation than just the important issue of countertransference and the place of the therapist in the "social" treatment situation. This is clearly apparent in the development and mushrooming growth of group and family types of therapies, each apparently relying on some form of group dynamics systems theory to explain the individual as well as group behavior.

The growing interest in group dynamics among psychotherapists as a dimension of the treatment process provides not only additional concepts but also a somewhat different language to describe behavior of the person. In child development the oedipal period is generally seen as a time when the child is in competition with the father for the mother, and this is frequently described as an *intrapsychic* process involving sexuality and id-ego conflicts and related to the formation of ego ideals. Group process language describes this phase of development differently, using the language and concepts of group dynamics: the oedipal phase is a time when the child is in competition with the father, who is seen by the child as an outsider, as someone who is alien to the child's autocratic, omnipotent, leadership position in his, the child's, psychological space. A study of child development would be phenomenological and then include all that is known about intrapsychic development and, in addition, the understanding of the conflicts involved in the struggle for maintaining leadership in a group. This requires knowing about such concepts as the qualities of leadership, the differences among autocratic, democratic, and laissez-faire types of leadership, the child's view how he/she phenomenologically experiences such interaction, and other similar psychological issues involved in the dynamics of group process. In turning attention to this type of material, the therapist has become more able to understand and to use the cultural-time aspect of behavior to further understand and help Anna O. cope with her emotional state.

Thus, current therapists would be able to treat Anna O. differently today than one hundred years ago. At the time, women were severely restricted to an "inferior" position. A woman who attempted to live on her own, like Anna O., who did not seek a goal of marriage and who had a professional career instead, was seen as *odd*, to say the least, and outside the context of the cultural conditions of the time. Today, with the cultural changes the world has undergone, minimal as they may be, Anna O. would fit in more easily. She would not be seen as strange for wanting a career and not necessarily needing a man or children to give purpose to her life. She would not need "treatment" for these "conditions." Today we are much more aware of the determining influence of the culture on the way people relate to one another and the need for the therapist to recognize two factors: first, the patient exists in a cultural context that in itself may not be a "treatable" condition, and second, the therapist himself or herself is constricted by his/her own cultural limitations.

We have come to the end of examining and reflecting on the status of psychoanalysis and how now we might treat Anna O. We have come a long way since she was seen one hundred years ago by Breuer and her illness further explained through Freud's insights. No longer is there just one analytic procedure available to help her, but many paths to do this. Which one is best, which path to take through the forest, depends on one's perspective of the forest and on the exit point one wishes to reach. Some of the exits available today did not exist and were not possible one hundred years ago. The growth and development of psychoanalysis have followed the world conditions. Now this oldster may have to make some decisions as to whether it wishes to incorporate some of the more cultural, group process forms of understanding Anna O.'s difficulties or to continue on its old and tired paths. Regardless of what psychoanalysis does in the future, it has directly affected not only how we treat emotionally conflicted individuals but also the world we live in. The early treatment of Anna O. developed tremendous, significant insights into the dynamics of the unconscious process of the individual's mind. The writers in this volume in varying degrees, accept this development; they all indicate that any current work with Anna O. still depends on some kind of an analytic explanation of behavior. Although most of them suggest an analytic model, they have added modifications dependent on their particular viewpoints and their understanding of the more recent data describing human behavior. The definitive answer as to how best to treat Anna O. is still elusive. Perhaps that is significant; perhaps it means that helping Anna O. today should not be the end in itself, but as it was yesterday, the beginning of increased understanding of how we humans cope with our personal conflicts as we encounter each other in the world.

References

BERELSON, B., and STEINER, G. A. *Human Behavior.* New York: Harcourt, Brace & World, 1964.

CARTWRIGHT, and ZANDER, A. (eds.). *Group Dynamics,* 3d ed. New York: Harper & Row, 1960.

COOPER, A. M., and MICHELS, R. An era of growth. In J. Brady and H. K. H. Brodie (eds.), *Controversy in Psychiatry.* Philadelphia: Saunders, 1978.

DeCHARMS, R., JEROME, L. and WERTHEIMER, M. A note on attempted evaluations of psychotherapy. *J. Clin. Psychol.,* vol. 10, 1954.

DSM III Classification, American Psychiatric Association, 1980.

ELLENBERGER, H. F. The story of Anna O: A critical review with new data. University of Montreal, Quebec, Canada. *J. Hist. Behav. Sciences*, July vol. 8, July 1972.

EYSENCK, H. J. The effects of psychotherapy: An evaluation. *J. Consult. Psychol.*, vol. 16, 1952.

FINK, MAX. Induced seizures and human behavior. In M. Fink, S. Kety, J. McGaugh, and T. A. Williams (eds.), *Psychobiology of Convulsive Therapy*. New York: Wiley, 1974.

FINK, PAUL. Psychoanalysis and academia. In J. O. Cavenar and H. K. H. Brodie (eds.), *Critical Problems in Psychiatry*. Philadelphia: Lippincott, 1982.

FORD, D. H., and URBAN, H. B. *Systems of Psychotherapy*. New York: Wiley, 1963.

GARFIELD, SOL. Psychotherapy: A 40 year appraisal. *Amer. Psychologist*, vol. 36, no. 2, 1981.

GROFFMAN, SIDNEY. Psychological aspects of strabismus and amblyopia. *J. Amer. Optometric Ass.*, vol. 49, 1978.

HORWITZ, LEONARD. New perspectives for psychoanalytic psychotherapy. *Bull. Menninger. Clin.*, vol. 40, no. 3, May 1976.

JARVIK, MURRAY E. The effects of drugs on memory. In P. Block (ed.), *Drugs and the Brain: Papers on the Action, Use and Abuse of Psychotropic Agents*. Johns Hopkins Press, Baltimore, Maryland, 1969.

MACMILLAN, M. B. The cathartic method and the expectancies of Breuer and Anna O. *Int. J. Clin. Exp. Hypnosis*, vol. 25, April 1977.

MCGEE, J. P. and SAIDEL, D. H. Individual behavior therapy. In J. Noshpitz (ed.), *Basic Handbook of Child Psychiatry*. New York: Basic Books, 1979.

NAGEL, ERNEST. *The Structure of Science*. New York: Harcourt, Brace & World, 1961.

RAPAPORT, DAVID. *The Structure of Psychoanalytic Theory*. New York: International Universities Press, 1960.

STRUPP, HANS H. Some critical comments on the future of psychoanalytic theory. *Bull. Menninger Clin.*, vol. 40, no. 3, May 1976.

Additional References

HOLLENDER, MARC H. The case of Anna O: A reformulation. *Amer. J. Psychiat.*, vol. 137, 1980, 797–800.

SUTHERLAND, J. D. Psychoanalysis as a form of psychotherapy. In M. Dongier and E. D. Wittkower (eds.), *Divergent Views in Psychiatry*. New York: Harper & Row, 1981.

Index

Index

Abortion, 19
Absent-member maneuver, 143
Addams, Jane, 104
Adler, Alfred, 12, 164
Adolescence, 63–64
Aggression, positive development functions, 155
Aggression and narcissistic countertransference, 132–139
Agoraphobia, 88, 94, 95
Alfieri, Count Vittorio, 99
Allegemeine Krankenhaus, 8
American Jewish Historical Society, 52
American Psychoanalytic Association, 36
Analytic approach, 74
Analytic model, 78, 174
Analytic object, the, 154
Analytic theory, 75
Analytic treatment method, 72, 73
Anhedonia psychomotor retardation, 93
Anna O.
  and abortion, 19, 20
  adolescence, 63–64
  aggression and narcissistic countertransference, 132–139
  analytic biography, 47–51
  and Bertha Pappenheim: an historical perspective, 101–114
  the case then and now, 34–41
  child psychiatrist, seen by, 59–70
  conclusions, 161–174
  cultural aspects, 52–58
  diagnosis, 42
  an English object relations approach, 149–159
  family therapy: other times, other paradigms, 141–148
  female, 1880–1882; female, 1980–1982, 118–131
  feminine role, 49
  her history, 1–23
  illness and treatment, explanations, 168–169
  insight, hindsight, and foresight, 26–32
  marriage, 108
  methodological problems, 27–29
  morphine addiction, 7
  nosology, 31
  Nazism, 20, 21
  psychoanalysis and group process theory, 71–83
  psychopharmacological treatment, 85–99
  and puberty, 62–63
  reflections on, 42–46
  sexuality, 49–50
  Zionism, 20, 21
Anorexia, 66, 69
Antianxiety agent, 89, 92
Antidepressants, use of, 87, 88, 93, 94, 99
Antipsychotic and antidepressant combined, 97
Antisemitism, 19, 21, 55, 102, 111, 112, 113
  manifestations, 53
  sources in Austria, 53
  in Vienna, 57, 58
Anxiolytic treatment, 90, 91, 94
Aronson, G., 40
Ativan, 90
Austen, Jane, 120
Ayd, Frank, 91

Baeck, Leo, 22
Balint, M., 150, 153, 157
Baruch, Chiam, 15
Basic fault, 150
Behavior modification, 172
Behavioral program, for child therapy, 70
Behavioral therapy, 165
Benecke, F. E., 11
Benzodiazepines, 91
Berelson, B., 164
Berlin Medical Journal, 10
Berliner, Cora, 22
Berthold, Paul, 14, 29, 109
Beta-adrenergic blocking agents, 92
Biochemical brain syndrome, 169
Bloch, Donald A., 141
Bloch, Rabbi, 55
Borderline and narcissistic conditions, treatment of, 42, 44–46
Borderline states, 69, 95
Bowlby, 60
Brahms, Johannes, 56
Brain syndrome, biochemical, 169
Brandeis University, 58
Breslauer, 7
Breuer, Dora, 13, 54, 137
Breuer, Joseph, 2–14, 16, 22, 23, 26–31, 34–36, 39, 42–44, 47–51, 67, 71–73, 81–83, 86–88, 90, 98, 99, 105–109, 118, 119, 121, 126, 127, 129, 130, 133–138, 141, 142, 147, 150, 151, 158, 159, 161, 167, 170, 172, 174
Breuer, Mrs. Joseph, 13, 137
Brief reactive psychosis, 97
Buber, Martin, 19, 98, 107, 112
Butler, Josephine, 104, 107, 108

Cafe Central, 12
Calordiazedoxidepozide, 91
Care by Women, 109, 110
Career identity, 64
Cartwright, 171
Case history data, absence of, 53
Cathartic cure, 162
Cathartic method, 10, 43

Centrax, 90
Charcot, Jean Martin, 8, 9, 34, 43
Chaucer, H., 120
Chemotherapy, 86
Child analysts, 35
Child development, 60, 79–81, 173
  conceptual model, 79
  and group process, 75, 82
Child and father interaction, 77, 80
Child psychiatry
  applied sciences of, 60
  diagnosis, 60, 66–67
  nature of, 60
  parental intervention, 70
  therapeutic approach, 69–70
  treatment, 61
  view of Anna O., 59–70
"Chimney sweeping," 10, 32, 34, 66, 93
Chlorpromazine, 86
Chlorpromazine haldoperidol, 95
Chmielnicki, Bogdan, 14
Clark University, 10
Coleridge, Samuel T., 10
Collective unconscious, 11
Conceptual models, 75
Condition seconde, 50
Complaints, obsessive-compulsive, 90–91
Conversion disorder, hysterical, 89
Conversion reaction, 166
Cooper, A. M., 162
Copernicus, 119
Corsini, R. T., 127
Countertransference, 9, 14, 30, 44, 73, 87, 88, 92, 127, 128, 130, 133, 138, 139, 147, 162, 167, 169, 170, 173
  narcissistic or preoedipal, 133, 134, 137, 138
  narcissistic and aggression, 132–139
Culture, influence of 173–174

Dahlke, A. E., 127
Darwin, Charles, 12, 119
Darwinian system, 75
Das Kapital, 120

Death, and family therapy, 146–147
DeCharms, R., 165
Deductive model, 165
Depression disorder, 92
Depression, reactive and endogenous, 92, 93
Der Judenstat, 56
Descartes, René, 10, 11
DeSwaan, 39
Deutsch, Helene, 118
Development, intrapsychic, 74–76
Dexamethasone suppression test, 69
Diagnosis, 89, 134
    of Anna O., 42
    in child psychiatry, 60, 66–67
    in family therapy, 144
Diagnostic and Statistical Manual III (DSM III), 22, 86, 89, 97, 168
Diazepam, 89, 91
Dickens, Charles, 34
Die Welt als Wille und Vorstellung, 11
Divided identity, 123–124
Dohm, Hedwig, 104
Dollard, 164
Dopamine, 99
Dora, case of, 55
Double identity, 120–124, 129, 131
    vs. divided identity, 123–124
Dr. Frankenstein, 14
Drucker, Paul, 52, 56, 58
Drug treatment, steps of, 88
Dukas, H., 32

Edinger, Dora, 19, 29
Efficacy, 91
Ego-analysts, 164
Ego development, 47
Ego dysfunction, 74
Ego functioning, 170
Ego and Id, 76
Ego organization, 158
Einstein, Albert, 32
Elizabeth von R., case of, 35
Ellenberger, H., 4n., 5–7, 11, 30, 149, 159, 164
Emmie von N., case of, 35, 43, 44

English object relations approach, 149–159
    technical approach, 150–151
Erikson, Eric, 60
Etrafon, 97
Eysenck, H. F., 165
Existentialists, 165
Expressive vs. suppresive therapy, 167
External ego, 79

Facial neuralgia, 7
Factitious disorder with psychological symptoms, 97
Fairbairn, 150
Family ego, 171
Family evaluation, 69
Family group characteristics and group membership, 76
Family therapy of Anna O.: other times, other paradigms, 141–148
    and death, 146
    and diagnosis, 144
Federation of Jewish Women, 17
Feminine Mystique, The, 122
Feminine role, 49
Feminism, German, 101–105, 109–111
Feminism, and hysteria, 103
    and mental illness, 103
Feminist movement, 14
Fink, Max, 168, 169
Floating-uterus concept, 9
Flow sheet for consideration of psychopharmacological treatment, 92, 96
Ford, D. H., 164, 165
Free association, 10, 127
Freeman, Lucy, 47, 49, 50, 123, 136, 145
Freiburg Welfare Department, 22
Freud, Anna, 35
Freud, Martha Bernays, 8, 54
Freud, Sigmund, 1, 2, 3, 5, 8–13, 17, 22, 23, 26–29, 31, 34, 36–40, 42–44, 50, 52–54, 57, 58, 71, 72, 75–78, 83, 99, 105, 109, 119, 126, 127, 130, 132, 133, 135–138, 141, 149, 151, 152, 157, 158, 161, 164–166, 172, 174

Freudian techniques, 73
"Freud's Case Studies," 31
Friedan, Betty, 122, 123
Furer, M., 78
Futter, Ellen V., 129, 130

Garfield, Sol, 162
Genogram, 144, 145, 147
German culture, Jewish identification with, 55
German fascism, 113
German Federation of Women's Organizations, 17
German National Committee to Fight White Slave Traffic, 18
Gill, M. M., 36
Goethe, Johann von, 10
Goals of therapy, 67
Greek mythology, psychoanalysis and, 132
Green, André, 154
Groffman, Sidney, 166
Group dynamics, 173
Group membership, characteristics of family group, 76
    and leadership, 80, 81
    as a regressive phenomenon, 77
Group process, 171
    approach to child development, 82
    approach to transference, 82
    individual growth and behavior, 83
    internal process and, 76
    solipsistic, 83
    theory and psychoanalysis, 71–83
Group Psychology and the Analysis of the Ego, 76
Group therapy, 69
    and individual therapy for children, 70
Growth, intrapsychic and interpsychic, 75
Gruenwald, Max, 52
Grunfeld, Frederic, 52
Guntrip, H., 150

Hameln, Gluckel von, 2, 15
Handbook of Innovative Therapy, 127

Harlow, 60
Hart, Moss, 47
Hartmann, H., 35, 37, 78
Hearst, Patty, 119
Hebrew Women's Organization, 16
Heine, Heinrich, 1
Herbart, J. F., 10, 11
Hermeneutics, 150n
Herzel, Theodore, 55, 56, 112
Hirschmüller, A., 13, 26
Hitchcock, Alfred, 47
Hitler, Adolf, 21, 113
Hoch, P. H., 95
Hoffman, B., 32
Hollender, M. H., 129
Holzman, Philip S., 34–41
Home for Wayward Girls and Illegitimate Children, 18, 21
Horatio Alger syndrome, 76
Horney, Karen, 12, 103, 165
Horwitz, Leonard, 164
Hospitalization, 68
Hypnosis, 3, 4, 10, 43, 45, 71, 72, 90, 161, 172
Hysteria, 2, 8, 9, 10, 44, 45, 67, 71, 72, 119, 127
    floating-uterus concept, 9
    sexual repression and, 94
Hysteria, analysis of, 158
    feminism and, 103
Hysteria neurosis conversion type, 89, 168
Hysterical childbirth; *see* Pseudocyesis
Hysterical conversion, 127, 128
Hysterical paralysis, 86
Hysterical pregnancy (pseudocyesis), 7, 9, 13, 51, 128, 133, 136, 137

Id-ego conflicts, 173
Imipramine, 94
In der Trudelbude (In the Secondhand Shop), 14, 109
Inderal, 92
Individualism, 120
Industrial Revolution, effects on family and women's roles, 120
Infantile neurosis, 48, 53

Infantile omnipotent autocratic leadership, 82
Infantile sexuality, 47
Institutionalization, 99
Integration, 158
Intelligence testing, 76
Internal vs. external realities, 74
International Congress to Fight White Slave Traffic, 18
International Council of Women, 110
International Journal of Psychoanalysis, 50
Interpretation of Dreams, The, 39
Intrapersonal dynamics and social interaction, 74–75, 76
Intrapsychic development, 74–76
Intrapsychic functioning vs. interpersonal behavior, 73, 76
Intrapsychic vs. interpersonal, 169, 170–171, 173
Intrapsychic vs. interpsychic, 79
Intrapsychic to interpsychic functioning, transition, 78
Intrapsychic vs. interpsychic growth, 75
Intrapsychic models, 72, 73
Intrasystemic conflicts, 37
Inzersdorf sanatorium, 6
Irma, 39
Isenburg, 107, 111, 113, 114

Janet, 43
Jarvik, Murray E., 169
Jensen, Ellen, 119, 121
Jerome, L., 165
Jewish community, 16, 18, 19
Jewish Orphanage for Girls, 16, 121
Jewish Problem in Galacia, The, 17, 109
Jews in Europe, 53–58
Jones, Ernest, 1, 4, 5, 11–13, 28, 53, 133, 136, 149
Judaism, 102
Judaism, custom and law, 105
Jüdischer Frauenbund, 106, 107, 110, 113
Jung, Carl, 8, 11, 12

Kant, Immanuel, 11
Kaplan, Marion A.,
Karminski, Hannah, 113
Karpe, R., 4n, 7, 16, 17, 121, 130
Katharina, case of, 54
Kernberg, O. F., 133
Khan, Musad, 158
Kimmel, E., 23n
Kinderschutz, 111
Klein, Melanie, 35
Klein, V., 120
Koch, 36, 37
Kohut, H., 37, 133
Kraeplin, 22
Krafft-Ebing, Richard von, 6
Kris, E., 78

La Ronde, 57
Lady in the Dark, 47
Landy, E., 127
Lange, Helen, 14, 103, 105, 111
Language, 148
Leader, 77, 80
Leadership, group membership and, 80, 81
  infantile omnipotent autocratic, 82
Lehrhaus, 19
Leibnitz, 10
Leonardo, 58
Lewald, Fanny, 104
Librium, 90
Lipton, S., 36, 40
Literary style, investigative tool in psychology, 31–32
Lithium, 69
Lowenstein, R. M., 37, 78
Lucy R., case of, 35, 39

Mach, 147
MacMillan, M. B., 164
Maferr (Male-Female Role Research), 121–125, 130
Maferr Inventory of Feminine Values, 124, 125
Mahler, Gustav, 52
Mahler, Margaret, 60, 78

Mahoney, P., 31
Mann, Thomas, 11
Martorano, Joseph T., 85
Marx, Karl, 120
Maslow, Abraham, 105
Masterson, James F., 42
Mayse Bukh, 113
McGee, J. P., 165
Medea, 155, 156
Medication, antianxiety, antipsychotic, antidepressant, 95
  in child therapy, 69,70
  length of use, 91
Memoirs of Gluckl von Hameln, 112
Menninger, Karl, 37
Metapsychology, 36
Methodology, 167
Meyer, Stefan, 15
Michels, R., 162
Micropsychosis, 95
Miller, 164
Minimal sufficient network, 143
Models, analytic, 78, 174
  conceptual, 75
  intrapsychic, 72, 73
Models, static, 75
Morphine, 92
Mother-child relationship, 78
Mourning and Melancholia, 76
Müller-Braunschweig, Karl, 47
Multiple modalities, in child therapy, 69-70
Muroff, Melvin, 71, 161
Mutterschutz, 111
Myths, Greek, and psychoanalysis, 132

Nagel, 161, 165, 166
Narcissism, 76
Narcissism, 169
  primary and secondary, 80, 81
Narcissistic and borderline conditions, treatment of, 42, 44-46
Narcissus, 132
National Association of Women Teachers, 105
Nazism, 20, 21, 113, 114
Neuralgia, facial, 7

Neurologisches Centralblatt, 10
Neurosis
  Freud's theory, 150
  infantile, 48
New York Psychoanalytic Society, 12
New York Times, 124, 129
New York Times Magazine, 123
Nietsche, F., 11
Nineteenth-century society, 101
Norepinephrine, 99
Noshpitz, Joseph D., 59
Nosology, 31
Nuremburg Laws, 113

Object relations, 64, 169
Oedipal attachments, 64
Oedipal father vs. preoedipal father, 43
Oedipal issues, 64-65
Oedipal phase, 78, 80, 150, 156, 173
Oedipal wishes, 77
Oedipus complex, 132
On the Condition of the Jewish Population in Galacia, 109
"On the Physical Mechanism of Hysterical Phenomena, Preliminary Communication," 10
Origin of the Species, The, 119

Pappenheim, Bertha; *see* Anna O.
Pappenheim, Flora, 1, 145, 146
Pappenheim, Henriette, 1, 145
Pappenheim, Recha Goldschmidt, 1, 2, 5, 15, 145
Pappenheim, Sigmund, 1, 2, 145
Pappenheim, Wilhelm, 1, 2, 6, 15, 17, 49, 102, 146, 147
Pappenheim, Wolf, 1
Paralysis, hysterical, 86
Paranoia, 95
Parent intervention in child therapy, 70
Parental relationships, 64
Penis-envy complex, 49
Penner, L. A., 23n
Phallic implications, 66
Phenomenological approach, 82, 83
Piaget, J., 60

Pletsch, C., 31
Polatin, P., 95
Pollack, G. H., 15, 26, 27, 30, 47, 50, 149
Postadolescence, 64–65
Preoedipal patient, 132, 135, 137, 139
Pride and Prejudice, 120
Prophets Without Honor, 52
Propranolo, 92
Pseudocyesis, 51, 86, 87, 128, 133, 136, 137
Psychoanalysis, 1
  basic assumptions, 166–167
  contradictions, 40
  criticism of, 58, 73
  and Darwinian model, 171
  development of, 118
  and Greek myths, 132
  and group process theory, 71–83
  history of, 34–41
  medical origins, 39
  methodology, 74, 167
  organizational aspects, 35
  and social psychology, 74
  status of, 174
  treatment technique, 39, 40
Psychoanalytic theory and group, social
    psychology, 76
Psychological dynamic approach, 169
Psychoneurosis, cause of, 47
Psychopathology, social learning theory, 165
Psychopharmacological approach, 86
  addictive considerations, 98
  decrease in interpersonal contact with
    physician, 98
  excessive sedation, 97
  negative aspects, 97
  practical advantages, 98–99
  side effects and toxic reactions, 98
  treatment of Anna O., 85–99
Psychopharmacological treatment
  with anxiolytic agent, antidepressants,
    antipsychotic agents, combined ap-
    proach, 96
  flow sheet, 92, 96
  with Inderal (Propranolol), 96
  time considerations, 99

Psychosexual and psychosocial develop-
    ment, 74
Psychosis, manic-depressive, 133
  toxic, 32
Psychotherapeutic approach, 67
Psychotherapy, psychoanalytic oriented,
    128
Puberty, Anna O. and, 62–63
Pumpian-Mindlin, E.,
Putnam, Emily Jane Smith, 129

Question of Lay Analysis, The, 37
Quindlen, A., 129

Rank, 165
Rapaport, David, 35, 166
Rat Man, case of, 53
Reality testing, 80, 81
Regression, 151–153, 155
  malignant, 157
Relevant family systems, 142–143
Repression, 11
  sexual and hysteria, 94
Resistance, 11
Resnikoff, P., 132
Rickels, K., 91
Ricoeur, Paul, 150n
Rogers, 165
Roles, family, 68–69
  feminine, 124: crosscultural, 125
Roosevelt, Theodore, 75
Rosenbaum, Max, 1
"Rosie the Riveter," 122
Ryan, Mary, 103

Sachs, Hanns, 12
Saidel, D. H., 165
Salomon, Alice, 105
Salpêtrière Hospital, 8, 9
Sanatorium Bellevue, 5, 7, 13, 14
Schiller, Johann von, 10
Schizoid problems, 150
Schizophrenia, 95, 133, 138
Schnitzler, Arthur, 57, 58
Schopenhauer, Arthur, 11

Scopolamine, 169
Sedative effects, anticholinergic, 94
Settlage, C. F., 78
Sex roles, 144
Sexual repression and hysteria, 11, 12
Sexuality, infantile, 47
Shelley, Mary, 14n
Shutkin, Anne Victoria, 129
Side effects, adverse, 94
   anticholinergic or cardiotoxic, 94
   ticholinergic, 99
Single-drug vs. polydrug user, 91
Sisyphus Work, 110
Skynner, Robyn, 143
Snake imagery, 66
Social behavior, 77
Social interaction, intrapersonal dynam-
   ics and, 74–75, 76
Social interaction dynamics, 76
   interpsychic, 162
Social psychology, 78
Socialization, 78
Solipsistic group process, 83
Some Reflections on Schoolboy Psychology, 76
Spellbound, 47
Spiegel, John P., 52
Spotnitz, Hyman, 132–134
Stanton, Elizabeth Cady, 104
Static model, 71
Stearns, B. C., 23n
Steiner, G. A., 164
Steinmann, Anne, 118, 124
Stekl, Wilhelm, 12
Stewart, Walter A., 47
Story of Anna O., The, 47
Stowe, Harriet Beecher, 122
Strachey, James, 29
Strategy, operational, 87
Strupp, Hans H., 162
Studies on Hysteria, 4, 6, 10, 12, 13, 19,
   26, 29, 36, 54, 141
Sublimation, 82
Sullivan, K., 165
Supportive therapy, 67–68
Symonds, Alexandria, 123
Symptomatology, 86, 89, 151
   depressive, 91

Symptoms, neurovegetative, 93
   as unconscious representations, 74
Systems, interacting static and dynamic,
   75
Szold, Henrietta, 21

Taine, H., 118
"Talking cure, the," 5, 7, 8, 10, 32, 119,
   121, 126, 128, 130, 135
Testing, 66–67
Tetracyclics, 99
Theory, analytic, 75
Therapist, family systems, 142
Therapy, expressive vs. suppressive, 67
   goals of, 67
   supportive, 67–68
Thompson, Clara, 12
Thorazine, 86
Tiresias, 132
Totem and Taboo, 76
Toxic psychosis, 32
Tragic Moments, 112
Tranquilizer
   major, 88
   minor, 90
Transference, 9, 35, 36, 40, 43–45, 47,
   67, 73, 81, 82, 87, 92, 127–130,
   132, 136, 147, 157, 162, 169
   group process approach, 81
   narcissistic, 133–135
   oedipal, 132
   positive vs. negative, 40
   preoedipal, 133, 135
Transference love, 12, 136
Transference-countertransference
   eroticized, 158
   narcissistic, 133, 134
Tranxene, 90
Treatment, analytic method, 72, 73
   anxiolytic, 90, 91, 94
   of borderline, hysterical, or schizo-
      phrenic patients, 133
   classical psychoanalytic, 151
Triavil, 97
True self–false self, 150
Twenty-four-hour therapy, 127

Uncle Tom's Cabin, 123
Unconscious, 9–11, 26, 47
Unconscious functioning, 73
Urban, H. B., 164, 165

Valium, 89
Verdrangung, 11
Victorian era, 103–105
Vienna, 52
Vienna, sexual atmosphere, 57
Vienna Medical Journal, 10
Vienna Psychoanalytic Society, 12
Viennese culture vs. present culture, 59
Viennese Jewish Princess Syndrome,
   53, 56, 57
Viennese Jewish Society, 53, 54
Vieth, V., 9
Vindication of the Rights of Women, A, 14,
   103, 109, 119, 123
Virchow, R., 37

Wachenheim, Hedwig, 104
Washington Psychoanalytic Institute,
   141
Weibliche Fürsorge, 109
Wertheimer, M., 165
White slavery, 102, 106, 109
Wiederstand, 11
Wife of Bath, 120

Winnicott, D. W., 150, 152, 153, 155,
   157–159
Wittgenstein, Ludwig, 147
Wolff, C. von, 11
Wolf-Man, 39, 54
Wollstonecraft, Mary, 2, 14, 15, 19, 30,
   103, 109, 119, 123
Wolpe, 164
Woman, The, 105
Womanhood in America, 103
Women, The, 14
Women's movement
   German, 105
   Jewish, 111
Women's Rights, 15, 16, 48, 49, 109, 123
Wordsworth, H., 10
World as Will and Representation, The, 11

Xanax, 90

Young adulthood, 65
Youth Aliyah, 21

Zander, A., 171
Ze'enah U-Ree'nah, 113
Zentralwohlfahrtstelle der Deutschen Juden,
   106
Zionism, 20, 21, 55–56, 112